IMAGINING NATIONS

MANCHESTER
UNIVERSITY PRESS

YORK STUDIES IN CULTURAL HISTORY

edited by Geoffrey Cubitt

IMAGINING NATIONS

MANCHESTER UNIVERSITY PRESS

MANCHESTER AND NEW YORK

distributed exclusively in the USA by St. Martin's Press

Published by Manchester University Press
Oxford Road, Manchester M13 9NR, UK
and Room 400, 175 Fifth Avenue, New York, NY 10010, USA

Distributed exclusively in the USA by
St. Martin's Press, Inc., 175 Fifth Avenue, New York, NY 10010, USA

Distributed exclusively in Canada by
UBC Press, University of British Columbia, 6344 Memorial Road,
Vancouver, BC, Canada V6T 1Z2

British Library Cataloguing-in-Publication Data
A catalogue record for this book is available from the British Library

Library of Congress Cataloging-in-Publication Data
Imagining nations / edited by Geoffrey Cubitt.
        p.   cm.
    Includes bibliographical references (p.   ) and index.
    ISBN 0-7190-5115-0
    1. Nationalism – Great Britain – Historiography.   2. National
characteristics, British – Historiography.   3. National
characteristics, English – Historiography.   4. National
characteristics, German – Historiography.   5. Nationalism – Germany –
Historiography.   6. Great Britain – In literature.   7. England – In
literature.   I. Cubitt, Geoffrey.
    DA1.143   1998
    320.54–dc21   97–47408

ISBN 0 7190 5115 0 *hardback*
     0 7190 5460 5 *paperback*

First published 1998

    05 04 03 02 01 00 99 98   10 9 8 7 6 5 4 3 2 1

Typeset by Servis Filmsetting Limited, Manchester
Printed in Great Britain
by Redwood Books, Trowbridge

Contents

Figures

NOTES ON CONTRIBUTORS

GEOFFREY CUBITT is Lecturer in History at the University of York. He is the author of *The Jesuit Myth: Conspiracy Theory and Politics in Nineteenth-Century France* (1993), and a number of articles on conspiracy theories and on modern French political, religious and cultural history.

STEPHEN DANIELS is Reader in Landscape and Cultural Geography at the University of Nottingham. He is the author of *Fields of Vision: Landscape Imagery and National Identity in England and the United States* (1993) and of a forthcoming book on Humphry Repton, *Landscape Gardening and the Geography of Georgian England*.

ROY FOSTER is Carroll Professor of Irish History at Oxford University. His books include biographies of Charles Stewart Parnell and Lord Randolph Churchill, *Modern Ireland 1600–1972* (1988), *Paddy and Mr Punch: Connections in Irish and English History* (1993) and the first volume of his authorised *Life* of W. B. Yeats, *The Apprentice Mage, 1865–1914* (1997).

JOANNA DE GROOT is a Lecturer in the History Department and the Centre for Women's Studies at the University of York. Her main fields of research and publication are in social and cultural history in both a European and a Middle Eastern and Indian context, and in the positioning of gender within these histories.

LUDMILLA JORDANOVA teaches cultural history at the University of East Anglia, where she is a Professor in the School of World Art Studies and Museology. Her training was in the natural sciences, history and philosophy of science, and art history, and her current research enthusiasms include eighteenth- and early nineteenth-century visual culture, portraiture, and gender. Among her publications are *Images of the Earth* (2nd edn, 1997, co-editor), *Lamarck* (1984), *Sexual Visions* (1989) and *Nature Displayed* (forthcoming).

PETER LAMBERT lectures in Modern European History at the University of Wales, Aberystwyth. He is the author of a number of articles on twentieth-century German historiography, and is currently writing a book on the historiography of the Weimar Republic.

MAIKE OERGEL is Lecturer in German at the University of Nottingham. She is the author of *The Return of King Arthur and the Nibelungen: National Myth in Nineteenth-Century English and German Literature* (1998) and of articles on the construction of national identities in Germany and England 1750–1900, on

Anglo-German intellectual and literary relations during the same period, and on Romantic literary theory.

MARCIA POINTON is Pilkington Professor of History of Art at the University of Manchester. She has written extensively on British and French art in the eighteenth and nineteenth centuries, on portraiture and on patronage and issues of gender in visual culture. Her recent published works include *Naked Authority: the Body in Western Painting 1830–1908* (1990), *The Body Imaged: the Human Form and Visual Culture since the Renaissance* (1993, edited with Kathleen Adler), *Hanging the Head: Portraiture and Social Formation in Eighteenth-Century England* (1993) and *Strategies for Showing: Women, Possession and Representation in English Visual Culture 1650–1800* (1997).

GEOFF QUILLEY is currently a lecturer in History of Art at Leicester University, and is doing research into the iconography of the sea in eighteenth-century British art.

JANE RENDALL is a Senior Lecturer in the History Department and the Centre for Women's Studies at the University of York. Her publications include *The Origins of Modern Feminism: Women in Britain, France and the United States, 1780–1860* (1985) and *Women in an Industrializing Society: England 1780–1880* (1990). She is currently working on eighteenth- and nineteenth-century British narratives of women's history, and on the early women's suffrage movement in Britain.

NICHOLAS STARGARDT is Lecturer in Modern European History at Royal Holloway College, University of London. He has written *The German Idea of Militarism: Radical and Socialist Critics, 1866–1914* (1994) and is currently working on a study of children's lives in Nazi Germany.

J. ADAM TOOZE is University Assistant Lecturer in Modern European Economic History at the University of Cambridge and a Fellow of Jesus College. He is currently completing a study of the development of German official economic statistics, 1914–45.

JAMES VERNON is author of *Politics and the People: a Study of English Political Culture 1815–1867* (1993) and has edited *Re-reading the Constitution: New Narratives in the Political History of England's Long Nineteenth Century* (1993). He is currently working on a collection of essays on the cultural history of modern Britain.

Acknowledgements

Apart from the Introduction, the essays in this volume originated as contributions to the first York Conference in Cultural History, held under the title 'Imagining Nations' at the University of York in April 1995. The organisers of that conference, besides the present editor, were Allen Warren, Chris Clark, Ludmilla Jordanova, Joanna de Groot, Jane Rendall and Bill Trythall. Thanks are due both to them and to all the other contributors to the conference for their part in making the present volume possible, and to the University of York and its Vice-Chancellor for financial assistance with the conference itself. The editor wishes to thank Oxford University Press for permission to reproduce in Chapter 3 material previously published in similar form as the text of Professor Foster's inaugural lecture to the University of Oxford, *The Story of Ireland* (OUP, 1995). He wishes finally to thank Vanessa Graham of Manchester University Press for much encouragement and forbearance during the book's preparation and production.

Geoffrey Cubitt

Introduction

We live in a nationalised world. The concept of the nation is central to the dominant understandings both of political community and of personal identity. Perceptions of politics are framed in terms of national interest and of international relations. The influence of nationalism – taking that word in its broader sense, to refer to the system of thought that takes nations to be the basic and natural units of analysis – is not, however, confined to the political arena. Notions of national distinctiveness and of international competition or comparison have become intrinsic to the ways in which we think and speak about matters as varied as economics and topography, art and climate, sport and literature, diet and human character. We are equipped, as one ethnologist has put it, with a 'nationalising eye': when we wish to describe or explain difference, we think of it in terms of nations.[1]

But if, as Eley and Suny observe, 'being national is the condition of our times',[2] it is a condition more easily evoked than defined. In common usage, the term 'nation' serves sometimes as a virtual equivalent of 'people', sometimes of 'country', sometimes of 'state'; it designates now a community, now an environment, now a component in a global political system. The nation is presented sometimes as an object requiring a passionate commitment, sometimes merely as a descriptive category permitting individuals to be conveniently located for administrative or referential purposes. In short, nations as things remain elusive. Their assumed existence and importance form an imaginative field on to which different sets of concerns may be projected, and upon which connections may be forged between different aspects of social, political and cultural experience.

It is with the analysis of some of these projections and connections that the essays in this volume are concerned. Taken together, they seek to demonstrate some of the varied possibilities of an approach to nations and nationalism that is both historical and culturally focused – one which seeks, in other words, to understand the nation as both the object and the product of complex and evolving assignations of meaning, and to make an analysis of these shifts of meaning an integral part of a broader effort to understand social change over time. Nationalism has had a global impact, but the examples considered here are drawn from a limited geographical area – essentially western Europe, with the emphasis on Britain and Germany. The purpose of the volume is not to extrapolate from the experience of this area generalisations that will necessarily hold true for other regions of the globe, but to explore from a variety of angles the mental structures and discursive strategies that have shaped images and concepts of the nation in one region where nationalist modes of thinking have been deeply influential.

The essays reflect some of the dominant tendencies in recent historical work on nations and nationalism. In particular, they are informed by the two basic understandings that have shaped the direction of much of that work, at least since the appearance of the influential general studies by Gellner, Anderson and Hobsbawm in the 1980s.[3] The first of these has been the understanding that nationalism is a phenomenon of recent historical origin.[4] Nations, as Gellner puts it, 'are a contingency, and not a universal necessity'.[5] They are products of history, not its basic raw materials, and this is true also of the style of thought that asserts their existence and importance. Despite the claim which many nations make to some kind of primordial origin, the nation as it is understood in the prevailing nationalist discourses of our day is a cultural and political form that would not have been recognisable in centuries before the eighteenth. Nationalism proposes conceptions of community and identity that are by no means simple continuations of earlier ones. It has, of course, often provided a conceptual language within which members of pre-existing ethnic, linguistic or political communities could express a sense of their collective being, but the use of this language has been part of a process of cultural transformation in the course of which earlier identities have been decisively refashioned.[6] Nationalism has developed as a way of thinking about community and identity in the context of the broader social, political and cultural evolutions that have remodelled European and American societies over the last two and a half centuries, and whose effects have also been global: the development of capitalist economies, of new forms of print technology and culture, of secular and bureaucratic state structures, of new modes of political participation, and of modern styles of imperialism and colonialism. This observation does not commit us to a functionalist understanding of nationalism premised on a reified vision of a homogeneous 'modernity'. Nationalism is not the mental lubricant of a neatly describable transition from one inherently coherent cultural system to another. It is a conceptual language whose uses have been shaped in complex ways by the conflicts and tensions which each of the 'evolutions' referred to above has generated in particular historical contexts: it has proved adaptable to the needs both of imperial aggression and of anti-imperial resistance, both of economic traditionalism and of capitalist 'progress', both of the political right and of the political left, both of the expansionist state and of its critics. It is through the imaginative labour involved in these multiple and locally variable confrontations that nations have acquired their central place in the conceptual schemes that govern political and social thinking.

The second understanding that has informed recent scholarship has been that nations are best regarded as imaginative constructs. They develop, no doubt, out of social and political experience, but they are the products of an imaginative ordering of that experience, not its revealed reality. To describe them as fictions is to draw too sharp a line between mental construction and social reality: nations (like many other social formations) exist to the extent that discourse and behaviour and institutional structures are organised around the assumption of their existence. Yet this existence is always ontologically unstable: however institutionalised they become, and however well established the symbolism that denotes them, nations remain elusive and indeterminate, perpetually open to contest, to elaboration and to imaginative reconstruction.

This view of nations as mental constructs sustained in being by imaginative labour and discursive habit has produced a number of significant shifts in the ways in which nationalism and nationhood are studied. The earlier focus on the specific histories of nationalist movements and ideologies geared to the promotion of particular national causes has tended to yield to a broader enquiry into the cultural construction of national identity. Nationalism is now envisaged less as an essentially political body of ideas, and more as a mode of sensibility, projected and elaborated across a wide range of cultural fields.[7] The analysis of this mode of sensibility has been taken to require a sensitivity not just to the more explicit statements of a nationalist world-view, but also to the various forms of what Michael Billig has called 'banal nationalism'[8] – to assumption as well as assertion, to clichéd utterance as well as heroic gesture, to stale as well as to vibrant symbolism, to 'the repertoire of the obvious'[9] in the culture under investigation as well as to its canonical texts. An important effect of these shifts of emphasis has been to open the study of nationhood and nationalism – formerly the preserve of political and intellectual historians, political sociologists and political scientists – to new kinds of interdisciplinary enquiry, drawing methods and material from fields like art history, literary studies,[10] cultural anthropology, geography,[11] museology[12] and gender studies.

This book seeks to contribute to the further development of interdisciplinary approaches capable of connecting the different cultural realms within which nationalist sensibilities develop and over which they exert an influence. The essays in it are written from a variety of disciplinary standpoints (intellectual history, art history, economic history, history of science, historical geography, literary studies), and trace the elements and implications of nationalist habits of thought across fields as varied as historiography, cartography, visual art, science and economic statistics, as well as through the thickets of some more specific cultural interactions – between, for example, gender ideology and philosophic history (Rendall), travel literature and ethnography (Vernon), art and commercial ideology (Quilley), literature and imperialism (de Groot), portraiture and monetary exchange (Pointon), cartography, rambling and citizenship (Daniels).

The value of Benedict Anderson's influential description of nations as 'imagined communities'[13] lies not only in its emphasis on imaginative construction, but in its reminder that it is in the elaboration and reinforcement of a sense of community that this imaginative labour is expended. Indispensable to the imaginative construction of a nation, in other words, is the assumed existence of a human collectivity, whose members are possessed of common interest, of the capacity for mutual recognition and sympathetic association, and – at least potentially – of joint volition. It is further assumed that, however divided the members of that collectivity may appear at any given moment, what they have in common – both actually and potentially – supplies a sufficient basis for the attribution to them of an essential common identity, which makes demands upon them as individuals, and which should command recognition – usually taken to include some kind of political recognition – from others. This assumption is, of course, seldom a piece of unmotivated social fantasy: those who imagine a nation generally imagine themselves as part of it. A nation is a device for identification, for self-invention; to imagine one is to formulate a sense of belonging.

Since nations are often institutionally embodied as nation-states, the language of nationality is often intertwined in practice with that of citizenship. The resulting more or less institutionalised conceptions of national membership reflect in their variety the diversity of the specific political and cultural histories through which these two conceptual languages have been brought into interaction. In France, for example, where notions of citizenship developed within the frameworks of a well-established territorial state, the dominant tendency has been to model the nation as a community defined by territorial residence; in Germany, where the sense of citizenship preceded the formation of a unitary national state, a more ethnocultural understanding of national belonging has prevailed.[14] It is a mistake, however, to see the notion of citizenship as fundamental to the idea of nationhood or even as one of its necessary expressions. In the first place, not all nations correspond to states. In the second, as Martin Thom has indicated, the conceptions of political community which found expression in modern nationalism arose initially in contradistinction to those which were embodied in the ideal of the classical city, as envisaged by Enlightenment thought.[15] A nation was imagined to be something more than, and different from, a transient assembly of participating citizens: it was an organic community, forged through a mixture of common descent, shared social experience, and joint relationship to territory. Nations, in short, possessed a durability and a quality of natural social existence that bodies of citizens could not automatically claim. This is still, despite changes in intellectual fashion, how nations are broadly imagined – not as creations of political rationality, but as communities naturally embedded in time and space, and established on accumulated funds of common experience.

One effect – or one sign – of this is that efforts to define what it is that members of a nation have in common – to capture that elusive quality of 'Englishness' or 'Frenchness' or 'Germanness' – are often cast not as analyses of political or social relationships, but as flights of essentialist impressionism. For Stanley Baldwin, for example, the essence of England was most accessible 'through the ear, through the eye, and through certain imperishable scents' – the tinkle of the hammer on the anvil, the sound of the corncrake on a dewy morning, the sight of the plough-team coming over the brow of the hill, and other uniformly rural impressions, right down to the smell of 'that wood smoke that our ancestors, tens of thousands of years ago, must have caught on the air when they were coming home with the result of the day's forage' – the olfactory proof of the continuities of national existence.[16] One recent Swedish writer, mixing the social and the sensory, begins the evocative catalogue with the Swedish summer, Christmas morning and high-school graduation, and ends it with having walked across a barracks square and having stood by a grave.[17]

This habit of projecting the sense of being national in terms of symbolically charged personal experiences, whose often socially restricted character is disguised by the implicit assumption of their national typicality, is one instance of the more general set of processes by which the idea of the nation is 'naturalised'. This 'naturalisation' involves the blurring of distinctions, not just between the nation as an abstraction and the life experiences of its members, but also between the nation's present and its past, and between its human organisation and its geographical setting. A sense of national identity becomes communicable and shareable to the extent that the symbolic references through which these processes of 'naturalisation' are achieved acquire the status of common currency.

The acquisition of such status means that the references become recognisable elements in the imaginative vocabularies through whose deployment the meanings and values attached to the nation are negotiated; it seldom means that they themselves acquire fixed meaning or stable value. Repertoires of national symbols do not arise painlessly from consensual reflection on a naturally homogeneous national experience; they are forged in conditions of contest between different political and social as well as cultural interests. The dominant imaginative constructions of the nation reflect the uneven distributions of power within society, and often also the active interest both of state agencies and of nationalist intellectuals in the shaping of the national image. Such constructions are asserted against three kinds of potential resistance: from other nations, from resistant elements within the body of the nation being imagined, and from rival definitions of that nation.

To imagine a nation is, first, to differentiate it from others. The imaginative developers of one national identity may, in certain circumstances, claim a kind of kinship or commonality with others (the common Germanic descent recognised by English and Germans, discussed in this volume by Maike Oergel, is an obvious example), or may seek to articulate one kind of national identity within the larger framework of another (Scottish within British, for example); in general, however, nations are assumed to be separate and distinctive – to be the possessors of separate histories, geographies, and sets of national characteristics. In practice, of course, the raw materials for constructions of nationhood are not so tidily distributed. Palestinians and Israelis map their opposing histories on the same terrain;[18] the Elgin marbles acquire a national significance both for Britain and for Greece; national identities all over the globe have been established, imaginatively as well as politically, in the teeth of initial resistance from imperial powers. The symbolic constituents of a separate national identity have, in short, often to be assembled under competitive conditions.

Second, they have to be assembled from potentially recalcitrant materials. The nationalist imagination invests a social and political field that is already covered by other imaginative forms – other kinds of imagined community, other symbolic systems, other spatial concepts or historical narratives. Nationalist politics has often involved a deliberate effort to suppress forms of political or cultural identity that are built upon these rival imaginative bases – to replace a dynastic history with a national one, to subordinate religious to national loyalties, to break down locally based systems of loyalty through national integration. But, while such suppressions may be successful in particular cases, a nation founded on the denial of all such social and cultural connections is bound to strike most people as intolerably abstract. Most imaginative constructions of nations seek selectively to incorporate affections and loyalties of a local or particular kind. This happens in two ways. First, the emotional dispositions that might sustain competing senses of identity are converted into facets of national character: the Englishman's home is his castle, attachment to *Heimat* is part of being German.[19] Second, often through the deployment of a notion of 'typicality', selected specimens or images of the local or particular are woven into the symbolic fabric of the national: the costumes and customs of Dalecarlia are presented as those of the 'typical' Swedish peasant;[20] the landscape of the southern downlands becomes the typical scenery of rural England.[21] Privileged but decontextualised, these selected fragments of a socially and regionally differentiated culture service the illusion of national homogeneity, and encourage the transfer to the imagined community of the nation of at least some of the affective capital that attaches to other, more local-ised, experiences. The cost of this, of course, is the implicit marginalisation, in national terms, of lifestyles, landscapes, cultures and traditions that do not attain this emblematic status.

Third, any imaginative description of the nation is likely to involve the exclusion of rival versions, embodying different readings of national history or different social or political or religious ideologies. The tensions between different ways of imagining the nation may, of course, be contained within capacious structures of tolerance and ambiguity – sometimes, indeed, within explicit ideologies of national diversity or plurality. Differences of vision are not always, however, reducible to allowable differences of perspective. The politics of early Third Republican France, for example, reflected a frequently explicit opposition between Republican and anti-Republican (whether nation-alist or monarchist or Catholic) conceptions of French identity and national purpose – a conflict fought out on diverse terrains (social ideology, religious politics, education, political symbolism), but rooted in incompatible readings of national history and tradition. Even where such open conflicts of imagina-tion exist, nationalist rhetoric sometimes denies them by insisting on the inte-grating quality of the national spirit. Beneath the cover of such rhetoric, however, strategies of exclusion persist: oppositions are created between the values and memories that are part of the national tradition and those that allegedly misconstrue it.

The incorporations, marginalisations and exclusions which are practised in the imaginative construction of national identity reflect the exchanges between nationalism and other discourses. Understandings of nationhood and nationality are often marked, for example, either by religious discourses, with their concepts of election and predestination, sacrifice and redemption, or by racial ones, with their notions of inbred difference and genetic descent and their powerful language of purity and pollution. Once the nation's importance as a focus of value is established, its imagined attributes are further defined and refined through its functioning as a stake in the debates that develop around notions like progress, civilisation, citizenship and democracy. Running through many of these ideological interactions, furthermore, is a persistent interplay (explored in this volume by Rendall and de Groot especially) between the imaginative categories of nationalism and those of gender.[22] Whether through the application to the nation of the gendered rhetoric of family, or through the conversion of male and female social roles into gender-specific modes of national service, or through the contrasting use of male and female emblematic figures to symbolise the nation in the public arena, or through the association of the nation with ideal images of manliness and femininity, or through the invocation of the national interest or the nation's 'health' as a justification for policies establishing or sustaining separate gender roles and uneven distributions of power between men and women, or through the expression of masculine anxieties about an insidious feminisation of the national spirit, constructions of masculinity and femininity have repeatedly been central to the functioning of nationalist discourse.

The imaginative construction of a nation involves more than the assembly of a repertoire of symbolic references; it involves the deployment of these references within imaginative frameworks of a narrative or descriptive kind, which confer upon the nation a settled existence in time and space. A concern with these temporal and spatial constructions of the nation is what links the essays in Parts II and III of this book. Space and time are not, of course, envisaged here as somehow separable realms within either of which a nation may be coherently imagined, but rather as entangled dimensions of a nation's imagined existence, which may nevertheless be imaginatively connected in different ways, and receive different degrees of formal emphasis in different kinds of literature or iconography.

First, then, nations are imagined as things enduring – endowed with origin, tradition, memory, heritage, history, destiny. They are imagined as communities not just of the living but of the living in continuity with the dead and the yet unborn, and (to use Balibar's term) as 'projects' – transmissions from generation to generation of 'an invariant substance'.[23] In a famous lecture in 1882, Ernest Renan described the nation as 'a spiritual principle', whose essence lay precisely in the connection between past and present existences: 'Two things, which in truth are but one, constitute this soul or spiritual principle. One lies in the past, one in the present. One is the possession in common of a rich legacy of memories; the other is present-day consent, the desire to live together, the will to perpetuate the value of the heritage that one has received in an undivided form.'[24] If Renan stressed the joint investment of will in the continuation of a national identity, George Orwell, seeking in 1940 to capture the elusive essence of Englishness, focused on a more inadvertent and organic kind of national durability. English culture – that culture 'somehow bound up with solid breakfasts and gloomy Sundays, smoky towns and winding roads, green fields and red pillar-boxes' – was continuous as well as distinctive: 'it stretches into the future as well as the past, there is something in it that persists, as in a living creature'.[25]

This basic theme of continuity in national life has, of course, been subject to countless variations: it has been applied to language, to institutions, to national character, to religion, to territory, to relationships to nature, as well as to genetic inheritances and lines of descent. The continuity has been conceived of sometimes in terms of mere endurance, sometimes as the survival of an original essence, sometimes as progressive evolution, sometimes as movement towards the fulfilment of destiny. In the discourses of antiquarianism, archaeology and history most obviously (but also of linguistics, historical geography and epic poetry), the production of these narratives has been presented as part of a process of national self-discovery: the movement forward across the past of an ancient legacy is matched by the backward reach of modern nationalist scholarship.

The nationalist mythologies that developed in Europe in the late eighteenth and early nineteenth centuries related modern nations to ancient tribal origins – Celtic, Germanic, Gaulish, Gothic or Sarmatian.[26] The heroic histories, poetic legacies, and elevated mores of these ancestor peoples were enlisted not just in validation of modern claims to national status, but also (as Rendall's essay illustrates) in debates over what the modern nation should be like. Such myths of origin performed significant groundwork for later nationalist historiographies, establishing points of narrative departure, suggesting narrative frameworks (hinging on the conquest and dispossession, survival and revival of the original national people), and promoting the basic notion of historically transmitted common identity that such historiographies, whether or not they clung to a predominantly racial understanding of national identity, would refashion. Nineteenth-century nationalist scholarship often continued, as Maike Oergel's essay indicates, to locate the essential strength of modern national cultures in the survivals of an aboriginal inheritance, whether linguistic (in Germany) or legal and constitutional (in England).

In nineteenth-century historiography, such primordialist themes coexisted with accounts of state formation and institutional development and with themes of national destiny.[27] The narratives that resulted combined an often powerful mythical structure with a wealth of scholarly detail and scientific pretension. Peter Lambert's essay shows how, in the case of Germany, the developing professional identity and self-image of historians was closely linked to the production of such narratives and to the development of the broader 'historicist' ideology in terms of which they were accredited. In Germany, but also elsewhere, history's claims to precedence as a discipline were founded in large measure on its ability to tell the story, and perhaps foretell the destiny, of the nation. Roy Foster's essay, which draws on the variegated historical literatures produced in the less rigidly professionalised intellectual arena of late nineteenth- and early twentieth-century Ireland, shows how the telling of this story could be shaped as much by the conventions of legend and folk-tale as by those of 'historicist' scholarship, and how the narrative structures and conventions imaginatively imposed on the national past could generate moods of prophetic expectancy with a powerful bearing on contemporary politics.

The grand and essentially linear narratives of nationalist historiography supply the most obvious framework within which the elements of a national past may be assembled: they provide the thematic strands and chronological divisions on which the notion of a distinctive national history depends. The twentieth century in particular, however, has witnessed impulses to process the national past in other ways – to organise commemorative ritual around its heroes and salient events, to conserve its material remains, to reconstruct its ways of life for public consumption. All of these shift the balance from linear narrative towards a conception of the national past that is at once more cumulative and more fragmented – a past shaped less as progression than as selectively remembered accretion, less as story than as memory and heritage.[28] When the past is thus organised, its spatial distribution – the geography of remains and sites of commemoration – becomes as important as its chronology. The nation as thing enduring merges into the nation as thing extending.

Considered in this dimension, the nation possesses shape, territory, boundaries, surface, landscape, environmental conditions. Atlases show nations as self-contained spatial entities, symbolic shapes with recognised places in the jigsaw of world political geography.[29] In doing so, of course, they disguise the often conflictual processes by which the boundaries of nations have been arrived at, and their still often contested nature. This combination of apparent fixity and latent uncertainty helps to give borders and the frontier regions that adjoin them an often remarkable symbolic importance in the defining of national identity. It is at borders that nationality is checked, and national difference most formally asserted;[30] it is in frontier regions that national belonging, being most at risk, is often most persistently invoked.[31] The boundaries that the imagination assigns to a nation are not, of course, always those which the nation-state possesses: the yearning for lost provinces and the quest for 'natural' frontiers can also be powerful expressions of an imagined national identity.[32]

Maps plot national space not merely as a shape, but also, as Stephen Daniels's essay reminds us, as a field of detailed knowledge, layered in often complex ways with topographical, geological, demographic, administrative, historical and onomastic information. Cartographic surveys have often, of course, been associated with the aspirations of governments both to extend control over their territories, and to measure resources with a view either to economic development or to fiscal exploitation.[33] In serving such governmental projects, maps facilitate the imaginative 'nationalisation' of territory, habitat and resources. By submitting the diversities of local physical and human geography to standard representational codes, they encourage the imaginative interpretation of these diversities as the internal relations and variations of a 'national' system. Other censuses and surveys – of place-names, of population, of economic statistics, of folklore, of religious practice – can perform a similar 'nationalising' function.[34]

By mapping human and physical geography together on to a space defined as national, maps prompt the understanding of that space as one within which a unique interaction between nature and human action produces a distinctive national habitat and way of life. The intimate connections between landscape, lifestyle and national character also supply a powerful theme in geographical and ethnographic writing, as well as in art and literature. For Wilhelm Heinrich Riehl, writing in 1854, the contrasts between hills and dales, fields and forests were 'contrasts so familiar as to go all but unnoticed, yet they determine many a subtle, hidden trait in the life of a nation'; many of the most striking differences between German and English national character were 'inevitably predetermined' by the fact that Germany, unlike England, still possessed genuine open forest land.[35] In France, the influential geographer Vidal de la Blache conceptualised the French nation as a harmonious compound of regional differences, shaped by the persistent interplay of natural environment and human activity.[36] In Britain, these themes were susceptible to various developments. Geoff Quilley shows how, in the eighteenth and early nineteenth centuries, both painting and poetry contributed to the development of the image of an essentially maritime nation, whose national character, commercial life and civic liberty were all bound up in a special relationship to the sea. In the early twentieth century, as Stephen Daniels shows, the dissemination and use of Ordnance Survey maps, with their associated literature and artwork, served both as a vehicle for projects of national education and as a prompt to the articulation of notions of citizenship. To be English was to know and appreciate the national geography, to relate to the nation as an environmental condition.

At least since Celia Fiennes stated her conviction that 'Journeys to visit their native Land', as well as curing people of the vapours, might add to England's 'Glory and Esteem' in their minds, and cure them of 'the evil itch of over-valueing foreign parts', notions of travel, of displacement, of circulation have been central to the ways in which ideas about nationality are articulated.[37] Descriptions of journeys, whether real, imagined or recommended, have given the narrative structure of discovery to discourses that have been moral as well as geographical. The pedagogical uses of such narratives are well illustrated by the seminal French schoolbook *Le Tour de la France par deux enfants*, in which two children (refugees from German-occupied Lorraine) glean from each province in turn the edifying histories of its great men and the details of its local economic activity, learning from their circuit of the national territory the supreme lesson of the intimate connection between social duty and national regeneration: 'Devoir et Patrie'.[38] The travel and tourist literature of the age of the bicycle and the motor car – touched on here by Vernon as well as Daniels – offered to the predominantly urban traveller or reader a kind of imaginative access not only to the celebrated diversity of the nation's heritage but also to the imagined inner recesses of national being.

Both in travel literature and in a range of other geographical or ethno-graphic discourses, this effect of national self-discovery is achieved by the establishment of spatial contrasts: it is through passages between urban and rural, or core and periphery, or metropolis and provinces, that the essence of the nation is articulated. In some cases, the highlighting of these contrasts may serve the needs of a centralising ideology: for many nineteenth-century Frenchmen, for example, the vital forces of national unity radiated from the Parisian centre, co-ordinating the diverse provinces and counteracting their backwardness.[39] In other cases – especially in Britain – the rhetoric has been ruralist, contrasting the traditional values of the countryside with the spiritual deficiencies of urban life. A somewhat different reading of the polarities has come into play when – as with the Celtic fringes of Britain and France – the rural population could also be construed as ethnically 'other'. In such cases, as James Vernon's essay illustrates in the Cornish case, spatial differences have often been imaginatively converted into temporal ones, the rural Cornishman serving as representative of a 'primitive' kind of natural existence, to be treasured from the standpoint of a confident English or British moder-nity. As Vernon also shows, however, modified versions of these images of the primitive have then been incorporated into the discourses both of an English anti-urban or anti-centralist reaction and of a separatist Cornish national-ism.[40] Different constructions of nationhood have fed on the same kinds of material.

If the imaginative handling of contrasts and movements within the space of the European nation-state provided one way of articulating particular conceptions of national identity, the European experience of empire overseas introduced further horizons of difference and new sensations of displacement. As well as contributing to the eventual development of nationalist sentiments both among indigenous peoples and among colonial settlers, the imperial experience, as Joanna de Groot's essay reminds us, had a profound imagina-tive impact on the imagining of national identities within Europe.[41] It gener-ated new ideologies both of national glory and of national destiny (sometimes expressed as religious or civilising mission), new conceptions of service and sacrifice, new breeds of national hero. Assumptions about national character and civilisation were given new kinds of definition through contacts – both real and imaginary – with an exotic (and generally politically and militarily subordinated) 'other'. Empire also, as de Groot's study of Kipling's first novel illustrates, created fresh standpoints – again both real and imagined – from which the present forms of national life could be evaluated, and generated new and more globalised conceptions of the space over which a quality like

'Englishness' might properly be projected. Anxieties about the social and political health of the mother nation could be expressed through a cult of the higher ideals and more natural modes of action preserved in the (essentially masculine) realms of colonial enterprise and overseas adventure.

Spatial and temporal projections of the nation interconnect in ways which vary according to historical circumstances. The USA and Britain provide contrasting examples. In the USA, where the political establishment of nationhood involved an explicit historical rupture with the Old World, geographical and topographical references – the natural majesty of the American wilderness, the beckoning spaciousness of the frontier – were initially central to the imaginative establishment of ideas of national identity and national destiny. Only later, in response to the social tensions of the later nineteenth and early twentieth centuries, were the elements of an essentialist historical culture – the cult of the Founding Fathers, for example – firmly established.[42] Even then, dominant understandings of American history were often moulded by geographical assumptions: in Frederick Jackson Turner's influential vision, for example, national history, national character and national destiny were all bound up with the central dynamic of westward expansion.[43] In Britain, by contrast, a broadly 'Whiggish' narrative of national history as a record of continuous and progressive constitutional development provided the essential underpinning of dominant constructions of national identity well into the twentieth century.[44] The multifaceted explorations of national space that were a feature of late nineteenth- and early twentieth-century British culture were not efforts to escape from history into geography; they related the latter persistently to the former. The celebration of rural England was a vehicle for the assertion of the fundamental continuity of English history, an invocation of the real presence of the past. For many of its admirers, the English landscape was no mere reservoir of accidental natural beauty, but a kind of scenic analogue of the British constitution, the product of many generations of responsible labour by the English working in harmony with natural forces.[45] Others, like Kipling, celebrated a mnemonic topography, whose features were reminders of a past elsewhere recorded as national epic:

> See you the dimpled track that runs,
> All hollow through the wheat?
> O that was where they hauled the guns
> That smote King Philip's fleet.[46]

Here, history ran through geography, not vice versa.

Embedded in space and time, each nation appears irreducibly unique. To imagine a nation is, however, to imagine something that is generic as well as distinctive. To claim separate national status for a people or community is to demand recognition of its particularity; it is also, however, to invoke a broader set of assumptions about the kinds of qualities and properties that nations possess. As the habit of thinking of community and identity in terms of national belonging has become more and more universally established, standard understandings of nationhood have, on the whole, become increasingly densely textured. Instead of being seen as communities definable in terms of one or two basic characteristics – language and territory, for example – nations came in the course of the period from the late eighteenth to the early twentieth century to be regarded as the possessors of a far wider range of standard properties. Orvar Löfgren describes the composition of this 'inventory':

> The experiences and strategies of creating national languages, heritages and symbolic estates, etc., are circulated among intellectual activists in different corners of the world and the eventual result is a kind of check-list: every nation should have not only a common language, a common past and destiny, but also a national folk culture, a national character or mentality, national values, perhaps even some national tastes and a national landscape . . . , a gallery of national myths and heroes (and villains), a set of symbols, including flag and anthem, sacred texts and images, etc.[47]

The effect of this inventorisation of national identity has been to set nations up as units for comparison, and as natural competitors, in a wide range of cultural fields. The essays in Part IV of this book explore some of the aspects or implications of this process.

It is a process that may be considered on two levels. The first has seen the imposition of the conceptual grid of nationality on exchanges and interactions in the global arena. The concepts of international relations and international competition have been extended from fields like war and diplomacy into areas like sport and literature. Patterns of trade and economic production, as Adam Tooze reminds us, have come to be understood in terms of competition between national economies, which are reified by being treated as statistically measurable. The iconography of banknotes, studied in this volume by Marcia Pointon, is also instrumental in imposing a nationalist frame of consciousness on economic exchange, both at a global and at a local level: the currency issued within each state appears as the symbolic bearer of a distinctive national history and fund of national achievement.

Second, at the level of individual nationalities, the period since the eighteenth century has seen the endowing of an increasing range of activities and cultural fields with national significance – their construction, in other words, as fields within which national character is made manifest, national interests served, national resources augmented, or rivalry with other nations sustained. The regulation of language, for example, became a matter of national importance. 'As an independent nation', Noah Webster told his American audience, 'our honor requires us to have a system of our own, in language as well as government'; a national language was 'a bond of national union'.[48] Nations came to be seen as the possessors of national canons of literature, national schools or traditions of art or music.[49] Individual achievement in these fields was viewed as a contribution to the nation's cultural welfare, and to its standing vis-à-vis other nations. Even in a field as ostensibly cosmopolitan as science, as Ludmilla Jordanova shows, the claim to be of service to the nation and to be contributing to the fund of national achievement was an important element in the development of professional self-images and claims to public notice. Scientific heroes like Davy and Watt could take their place in the increasingly variegated pantheon of the nation's famous sons; their status as benefactors of humanity reinforced rather than undercut their national significance.

Increasingly during the period from the eighteenth to the twentieth century, this idea of national achievement in fields like art, music, literature and science came to be seen not only in terms of competitive excellence, but also in terms of the development of distinctive national styles. Such styles were increasingly assumed, furthermore, to be expressions of something fundamental to the nation – of 'national character', or of some native genius of the national folk. Music affords interesting examples of this. When Addison wrote that Italian artists could not agree with English musicians in appreciating Purcell 'because both Nations do not always express the same passions by the same sounds',[50] he referred to a difference in musical language. In the course of the nineteenth and early twentieth centuries, however, such perceptions of difference gave way to far more comprehensive theories of the relationship between musical achievement and national self-expression. Not only was a healthy musical culture seen as something to which a self-respecting nation must aspire; it was seen as something that could be achieved only through the recognition and cultivation of indigenous resources and national qualities. For Zoltán Kodály, there was a fundamental connection between individual genius and national culture: 'the characteristic features of his or her nation can be found in every great performing artist'.[51] For Ralph Vaughan Williams, lecturing on 'National music' in 1932, the evocative power of music was dependent on its ability to draw on and appeal to a fund of common experience and shared forms of expression. Great music must spring from and resonate within the soul of a people bonded together by language, environment, customs and history. Its most natural source of inspiration was therefore, in Vaughan Williams's view, the nation's traditional folk music.[52] What is striking in this idea is the composer's readiness to assume that 'folk-song is, by nature, necessarily national',[53] rather than primarily regional, local or occupational, and that musical creativity is likewise essentially national (rather than merely not cosmopolitan) in spirit. The nation is established as the basic unit for cultural comparison, the primary focus for attributions of cultural value.

Taken together with the imaginative constructions of the nation in time and space considered earlier, this imaginative conversion of cultural fields into facets of national culture and spheres of development of national character tends to produce a sense of the nation as a kind of compound of community, environment and mentality. Sir Ernest Barker's lectures on 'National character and the factors in its formation', delivered in 1925–26, elaborated the hypothesis that 'a nation is a material basis with a spiritual superstructure'. The former was composed of the elements of race, physical environment, economics and demography. The latter was 'a mental organization connecting the minds of all the members of a national community by ties and connections as fine as silk and as firm as steel'; its main elements in the English case, according to Barker, had to do with law and government, religion, language and literature, and education.[54] Elsewhere, Barker wrote of the life of a nation as like an iceberg, the unseen part of which (again in the English case) consisted of 'a mass of individual skills, which find a harmony by their own gift of adaptability, and find it in a temper of equanimity and phlegm'.[55]

To imagine a nation in such terms is to imagine it as something which pervades and draws on the whole existence of its members. Nations become inescapable; they become the natural forms through which history, geography and culture are experienced. National belonging becomes a total condition of being. The scientific study of nations becomes the study of the component parts of humanity. This is a view of nations that has been gradually established over three centuries, and one that is hard to shake off. To study some of the processes that have contributed to its formation is to explore a highly significant area of modern cultural history. Nicholas Stargardt's essay, which follows, reminds us that efforts to explore this area themselves have an intellectual and indeed a political history.

Notes

1 A. Linde-Laursen, 'Small differences – large issues: the making and remaking of a national border', *South Atlantic Quarterly*, 94:4 (1995), 1133.
2 G. Eley and R. G. Suny, 'Introduction: from the moment of social history to the work of cultural representation', in G. Eley and R. G. Suny (eds), *Becoming National: a Reader* (New York and Oxford, 1996), p. 32.
3 E. Gellner, *Nations and Nationalism* (Oxford, 1983); B. Anderson, *Imagined Communities: Reflections on the Origins and Spread of Nationalism* (London, 1983; rev. edn, London, 1991); E. J. Hobsbawm, *Nations and Nationalism since 1780: Programme, Myth, Reality* (Cambridge, 1990). Hobsbawm's book was based on lectures originally given in 1985. For another important discussion, emanating from a different intellectual tradition, see E. Balibar, 'The nation form: history and ideology', in E. Balibar and I. Wallerstein (eds), *Race, Nation, Class: Ambiguous Identities* (London, 1991). An important selection of readings indicating recent developments in the field is provided by Eley and Suny, *Becoming National*.
4 'The basic characteristic of the modern nation and everything connected with it is its modernity', writes Hobsbawm, *Nations and Nationalism*, p. 14. For a rather differently

conceptualised understanding of nationalism as 'the constitutive element of modernity', see L. Greenfeld, *Nationalism: Five Roads to Modernity* (Cambridge, Mass., 1992), p. 18.

5 Gellner, *Nations and Nationalism*, p. 6.

6 For a balanced discussion of relationships between national and ethnic identity, avoiding the extremes of both 'primordialist' and 'constructionist' views of nationhood, see A. D. Smith, *National Identity* (Harmondsworth, 1991); his 'Gastronomy or geology? The role of nationalism in the reconstruction of nations', *Nations and Nationalism*, 1:1 (1995), is also relevant.

7 Eley and Suny, 'Introduction', p. 22, describe this sensibility as 'something transmitted from the past and secured as a collective belonging, something reproduced in myriad imperceptible ways, grounded in everydayness and mundane experience'.

8 M. Billig, *Banal Nationalism* (London, 1995). Also relevant here is Lauren Berlant's use of the term 'National Symbolic', to refer to 'the order of discursive practices whose reign within a national space produces, and also refers to, the "law" in which the accident of birth within a geographic/political boundary transforms individuals into subjects of a collectively-held history': L. Berlant, *The Anatomy of National Fantasy: Hawthorne, Utopia and Everyday Life* (Chicago, 1991), p. 20.

9 The term is borrowed from F. Spufford, *I May Be Some Time: Ice and the English Imagination* (London, 1996), p. 7.

10 See, for example, D. Sommer, *Foundational Fictions: the National Romances of Latin America* (Berkeley, 1991); Berlant, *The Anatomy of National Fantasy*; K. Trumpener, *Bardic Nationalism: the Romantic Novel and the British Empire* (Princeton, 1997).

11 See D. Hooson (ed.), *Geography and National Identity* (Oxford, 1994); Daniels's essay in this book (ch. 7) supplies further references.

12 See, for example, F. Kaplan (ed.), *Museums and the Making of 'Ourselves': the Role of Objects in National Identity* (London, 1994).

13 Anderson, *Imagined Communities* (1991 edn), p. 6.

14 R. Brubaker, *Citizenship and Nationhood in France and Germany* (Cambridge, Mass., 1992).

15 M. Thom, *Republics, Nations and Tribes* (London, 1995).

16 S. Baldwin, 'England' (1924), in his *On England and Other Addresses* (London, 1926), pp. 6–7.

17 F. J. Nordstedt, quoted in O. Löfgren, 'The nationalization of culture', *Ethnologia Europaea*, 19:1 (1989), 14. Löfgren discusses such catalogues of 'imponderabilia' in the context of his effort to deconstruct the over-amorphous concept of 'national culture' (pp. 13–16).

18 See R. Khalidi, *Palestinian Identity: the Construction of Modern National Consciousness* (New York, 1997), pp. 13–18. For a recent discussion of some of the sites invested by Israeli historical consciousness, see Y. Zerubavel, *Recovered Roots: Collective Memory and the Making of Israeli National Tradition* (Chicago, 1994).

19 On the significance of the notion of *Heimat* in German national consciousness, see C. Applegate, *A Nation of Provincials: the German Idea of Heimat* (Berkeley and Los Angeles, 1990), esp. pp. 1–19. Applegate writes (p. 15) of 'a persistent belief that the abstraction of the nation must be experienced through one's common appreciation of a locality, a *Heimat*'.

20 Löfgren, 'The nationalization of culture', p. 10.

21 See A. Howkins, 'The discovery of rural England', in R. Colls and P. Dodd (eds), *Englishness: Politics and Culture 1880–1920* (London, 1986), pp. 62–4, 74–5.

22 For discussion of some of these interactions, see N. Yuval-Davis, *Gender and Nation* (London, 1997); the 'Gender, nationalism and national identities' special issue of *Gender & History*, 5:2 (1993); G. Mosse, *Nationalism and Sexuality: Middle-Class Morality and Sexual Norms in Modern Europe* (Madison, 1985).

23 Balibar, 'The nation form', p. 86. Balibar points out that this idea of 'project' is gener-
    ally coupled with the idea of 'destiny'.
24 E. Renan, 'What is a nation?' (English translation by M. Thom), in H. Bhabha (ed.),
    Nation and Narration (London and New York, 1990), p. 19; also in Eley and Suny (eds),
    Becoming National, p. 52. The French text is in E. Renan, *Discours et conférences*
    (Paris, 1887), pp. 277–310.
25 G. Orwell, *The Lion and the Unicorn* [1941] (Harmondsworth, 1982), p. 37.
26 On these mythologies, see the references cited by Rendall below, p. 70, n. 11; also K.
    Pomian, 'Francs et gaulois', in P. Nora (ed.), *Les Lieux de mémoire*, 6 vols in 3 sections
    (Paris, 1984–92), III:1; E. Weber, 'Gauls versus Franks: conflict and nationalism', in R.
    Tombs (ed.), *Nationhood and Nationalism in France, from Boulangism to the Great War,
    1889–1918* (London, 1991).
27 See, for example, J. W. Burrow, *A Liberal Descent: Victorian Historians and the English
    Past* (Cambridge, 1981); M. Gauchet, 'Les *Lettres sur l'histoire de France* d'Augustin
    Thierry', in Nora (ed.), *Les Lieux de mémoire*, II:1.
28 There are now substantial relevant literatures on commemoration, on 'public memory'
    and on the 'heritage industry': see, among many others, J. Bodnar, *Remaking America:
    Public Memory, Commemoration, and Patriotism in the Twentieth Century* (Princeton,
    1992); J. Gillis (ed.), *Commemorations: the Politics of National Identity* (Princeton, 1994);
    Zerubavel, *Recovered Roots*; D. Lowenthal, *The Heritage Crusade and the Spoils of
    History* (Harmondsworth, 1996); R. Samuel (ed.), *Patriotism: the Making and Unmaking
    of British National Identity*, 3 vols (London, 1989); Nora (ed.), *Les Lieux de mémoire*.
29 See Anderson, *Imagined Communities* (1991 edn), p. 175, for the significance of these
    national shapes; also E. Weber, 'In search of the hexagon', in his *My France: Politics,
    Culture, Myth* (Cambridge, Mass., 1991).
30 See Khalidi, *Palestinian Identity*, pp. 1–6, for an interesting account of the significance
    of border checking for those – like Palestinians – whose national identity is repeatedly
    denied or called in question. For some further conceptual remarks on borders and
    frontiers, see G. Bennington, 'Postal politics and the institution of the nation', in
    Bhabha (ed.), *Nation and Narration*, pp. 121–2.
31 See P. Sahlins, *Boundaries: the Making of France and Spain in the Pyrenees* (Berkeley
    and Los Angeles, 1989), and Applegate, *A Nation of Provincials*, for discussions of this
    forging of national identity in frontier regions; also J.-M. Mayeur, 'Une mémoire-
    frontière: l'Alsace', in Nora (ed.), *Les Lieux de mémoire*, II:2, and P. Schöttler, 'The
    Rhine in Franco-German historiography, 1918–1939', *History Workshop Journal*, 39
    (1995).
32 See D. Golan, 'Between universalism and particularism: the "border" in Israeli dis-
    course', *South Atlantic Quarterly*, 94:4 (1995), 1058–9, for an example of this gap
    between official and imagined boundaries; the article also discusses other issues raised
    by the question of borders in disputed territory.
33 See, for example, J. W. Konvitz, *Cartography in France 1660–1848: Science,
    Engineering, and Statecraft* (Chicago, 1987); J. H. Andrews, *A Paper Landscape: the
    Ordnance Survey in Nineteenth-Century Ireland* (Oxford, 1975).
34 See, for example, Anderson, *Imagined Communities* (1991 edn), pp. 164–70; M.-N.
    Bourguet, *Déchiffrer la France: la statistique départementale à l'époque napoléonienne*
    (Paris, 1988); S. Rycroft and D. Cosgrove, 'Mapping the modern nation: Dudley Stamp
    and the Land Utilization Survey', *History Workshop Journal*, 40 (1995).
35 W. H. Riehl, *The Natural History of the German People*, trans. and ed. D. J. Diephouse
    (Lewiston, 1990), p. 47. The passage is taken from *Land and People*, first published
    separately in 1854.
36 P. Vidal de la Blache, 'Tableau de la géographie de la France' (1903), originally forming
    vol. I:1 of E. Lavisse, *Histoire de France depuis les origines jusqu'à la Révolution*, 9 vols

(Paris, 1903–11). The first part of Vidal's text is translated as *The Personality of France* (London, 1928). See P. Claval, 'From Michelet to Braudel: personality, identity and organization of France', and M.-C. Robic, 'National identity in Vidal's *Tableau de la géographie de la France*: from political geography to human geography', both in Hooson (ed.), *Geography and National Identity* (Oxford, 1994).

37 *The Journeys of Celia Fiennes*, ed. C. Morris (London, 1949), pp. 1–2. On travel literature, see, for example, E. Moir, *The Discovery of Britain: the English Tourists 1540–1840* (London, 1964); S. Gerson, 'Parisian littérateurs, provincial journeys and the construction of national unity in post-Revolutionary France', *Past and Present*, 151 (1996).

38 G. Bruno, *Le Tour de la France par deux enfants* (Paris, 1885). See J. and M. Ozouf, '"Le Tour de la France par deux enfants"', in Nora (ed.), *Les Lieux de mémoire*, I.

39 See, for example, the concluding section of J. Michelet, *Tableau de la France*, ed. L. Refort (Paris, 1949), pp. 89–95 (originally published in 1833 as part of Michelet's *Histoire de France*). See Gerson, 'Parisian littérateurs', pp. 156–7, for the coexistence of pro- and anti-Parisian (or anti- and pro-provincial) visions of France during the early nineteenth century. See also A. Corbin, 'Paris-province', and M. Agulhon, 'Le centre et la périphérie', in Nora (ed.), *Les Lieux de mémoire*, III:1.

40 See, for comparison, Bourguet, *Déchiffrer la France*, pp. 288–90, on the way in which the Celtic periphery became the focus for an ethnographic vision of French national identity, established in opposition to the statist conception of the French nation as a product of centralising royal power.

41 The relevant literature is now considerable: see, for example, E. Said, *Culture and Imperialism* (London, 1993); E. Said, *Orientalism* (London, 1978); J. M. Mackenzie (ed.), *Imperialism and Popular Culture* (Manchester, 1986); R. H. MacDonald, *The Language of Empire: Myths and Metaphors of Popular Imperialism, 1880–1918* (Manchester, 1994); A. McClintock, *Imperial Leather: Race, Gender and Textuality in the Colonial Context* (London, 1995); S. Gikandi, *Maps of Englishness: Writing Identity in the Culture of Colonialism* (New York, 1996).

42 D. Lowenthal, 'The place of the past in the American landscape', in D. Lowenthal and M. J. Bowden (eds), *Geographies of the Mind: Essays in Historical Geography in Honor of John Kirtland Wright* (Oxford, 1976). See also S. Daniels, *Fields of Vision: Landscape Imagery and National Identity in England and the United States* (Cambridge, 1993), chs 5, 6.

43 F. J. Turner, 'The significance of the frontier in American history' (1893), in his *The Frontier in American History* (New York, 1921).

44 On this historical discourse, see H. Butterfield, *The Englishman and his History* (Cambridge, 1944), esp. pp. 1–2; Burrow, *A Liberal Descent*; R. Samuel, 'Continuous national history', in Samuel (ed.), *Patriotism*, I. The term 'Whiggish' refers here to the general belief in continuous progressive development; as Samuel points out (pp. 12–13), this basic myth was available in both 'Whig' and 'Tory' versions.

45 See, for example, the editor's introduction to H. J. Massingham (ed.), *The English Countryside: a Survey of its Chief Features* (London, 1946), p. 2: 'He [the countryman] became his theme; he got rid of the encumbrances that were in the way of its due and right expression. He remade England by fitting himself into its manifold parts, so that in the long run it can hardly be decided whether he made the country or the country made him.'

46 R. Kipling, 'Puck's song', in his *Puck of Pook's Hill* (1906, new edn Harmondsworth, 1987), p. 41.

47 Löfgren, 'The nationalization of culture', pp. 8–9.

48 N. Webster, *Dissertations on the English Language* (Boston, 1789, repr. Menston, 1967), pp. 20, 397. See R. Rollins, 'Words as social control: Noah Webster and the creation of the American dictionary', in L. Zenderland (ed.), *Recycling the Past: Popular Uses of American History* (Philadelphia, 1978).

49 See, for examples in an English context, J. Barrell, 'Sir Joshua Reynolds and the Englishness of English art', and F. Mulhern, 'English reading', both in Bhabha (ed.), *Nation and Narration*; and the essays by B. Doyle ('The invention of English'), P. Brooker and P. Widdowson ('A literature for England'), and J. Crump ('The identity of English music: the reception of Elgar 1898–1935'), all in Colls and Dodd (eds), *Englishness*.

50 *The Spectator*, 29 (3 April 1711), in *The Spectator*, ed. D. F. Bond, 5 vols (Oxford, 1965), I: 121.

51 Z. Kodály, 'Hungarian musical education' (1945 lecture), in *The Selected Writings of Zoltán Kodály* (London, 1974), p. 152.

52 R. Vaughan Williams, *National Music and Other Essays* (London, 1963), esp. pp. 1–11, 39–41 (lectures originally given in 1932).

53 *Ibid.*, p. 62.

54 E. Barker, *National Character and the Factors in its Formation* (London, 1927), pp. 2–4.

55 E. Barker, 'An attempt at perspective', in E. Barker (ed.), *The Character of England* (Oxford, 1947), p. 554.

PART I

CONCEPTUALISING NATIONALITY

Beyond the liberal idea of the nation

The nation, Max Weber told the second conference of German Sociologists in 1912, is a 'community of sentiment, which could find its adequate expression only in a state of its own, and which thus normally strives to create one'.[1] In 1983, Ernest Gellner unwittingly echoed Weber's words in his opening statement on the subject. 'Nationalism', he wrote, 'is primarily a political principle, which holds that the political and the national unit should be congruent. Nationalism as a sentiment, or as a movement, can best be defined in terms of this principle.'[2] The resonances of defining the nation politically carry across the seventy years separating these two definitions and alert us to an important tradition of thinking about nationalism and the nation-state, whose origins are to be found in the restless optimism of those who wanted to transform the Austro-Hungarian Empire in its final decades. This is a tradition of thought which has had to assert itself more than once against what appeared to both Weber and Gellner to be the dominant ways of talking about national identity in their own day, national naturalism. In contrast to the norm of treating nations as objective facts, Gellner and Weber quite deliberately laid the emphasis on nations' tenuous dependence on subjective belief, on the nation as social and political construct. In so doing they moved beyond classical nineteenth-century liberal ideas about the nation, whilst – tantalisingly – still advocating a liberal politics.

In shaping those views of the world in which nations serve axiomatically as the bedrock of social structures, historians have played a leading part. The establishment of modern history as a full academic discipline in the nineteenth century was intimately connected with writing political and even social history within national frameworks. Assumptions about the inherently national character of, especially, modern history as practised in western Europe and the English-reading world have remained safely ensconced in their dominance well into the post-1945 era. Even today, as real border controls are being removed, at least within the European Community, national boundaries discretely impede traffic across its narrative landscape. Separate histories and tacitly national methodologies survive. Even the deconstruction-ist wave of scholarship which has sought in the 1980s and 1990s to demystify the nationalist imagination has, despite the intentions of its leading advocates, been applied largely within the national frame. Both Benedict Anderson and Eric Hobsbawm set out to study nationalism comparatively as a way of getting out of nationalist paradigms; yet most scholars who have taken up ideas such as the 'invention of tradition' or 'imagined communities' have done so within discrete national units, thereby subtly reinstating at the centre what they claim to be so keen to displace.[3]

This essay seeks to provide what has hitherto been lacking – an account of the intellectual origins of this new critical social theory and constructivist historiography of the nation. The provision of such an account is important for two reasons. First, this theory was first shaped, before 1914, at a moment of intellectual openness and doubt to the like of which we have only recently returned: the seventy years separating Gellner from Weber were dominated by the certainties of inter-war nationalism, Soviet Marxism and cold-war liberal-ism. Second, however positive the early critiques of the 'naturalness' of nation-alism may have been, they were not themselves entirely immune to nationalist commitments, albeit in a veiled form. These commitments are almost always more obvious in retrospect. In traversing a subject where the recourse to polit-ical violence has been so unrestrained in the twentieth century, it clearly pays to probe even the least nationalistically tinged and most humane theories carefully.

The resemblance between Weber's and Gellner's ideas goes beyond the coincidence of the quotations with which this essay began. Their common emphases on the role of sentiment and belief in defining national identity act to block off and to delegitimate the claims of ethnic or cultural nationalists. There is no room in either theorist's account for the concept of an unmedi-ated or a primordial nation. There is no primary, umbilical belonging, and so the nation cannot be said to 'cause' anything either. The history of national identities replaces the history of nations. Perhaps surprisingly, neither Weber nor Gellner was particularly intellectually curious about the identities and sentiments themselves. The 'precise doctrines', Gellner noted dismissively, 'are hardly worth analysing. . . . Generally speaking, nationalist ideology suffers from pervasive false consciousness. . . . It claims to protect an old folk society while in fact helping to build up an anonymous mass society,'[4] Weber, despite his own well-advertised German nationalism, did not attempt to enquire into the substance of nationalist belief.

Instead, both men passed on swiftly to elucidating the political and social ramifications of such sentiments. Each, in his different way, was slightly reluc-tant to explain the causal process which led to the establishment of nation-states. Weber, faced with other attempts to sketch out a constructivist theory

of the nation, argued that the heterogeneity of possible sources of identity –
common language, common religion, common cultural practices, common
territory – precluded any monocausal model. At the 1912 meeting with which
this essay began, Weber insisted to his fellow sociologists that they could only
find the unifying principle in the nation's political future and not in its social
past: 'The meaning of "nation" and "national" is absolutely not clear-cut. We
cannot uncover it in terms of a shared quality which generates community,
but only from the side of its goal, what it is that it strives for, what we refer to
under the heading of nationality: independent statehood.'[5] Gellner, too, dwelt
less on the causes of nationalism than on the causes it served. Here his argument, centring on the interlocking cultural and political requirements of the
economy, had a distinctly functionalist tinge:

> So the economy needs both the new type of cultural centre and the central
> state; the culture needs the state; and the state probably needs the homogene-
> ous cultural branding of its flock, in a situation in which it cannot rely on
> largely eroded sub-groups either to police its citizens, or to inspire them with
> that minimum of moral zeal and social identification without which social life
> becomes very difficult.[6]

The 'requirements' which have to be met, in this formulation, are those of
a 'modern economy', or more precisely of a new kind of horizontal, regionally
mobile, division of labour allegedly engendered by industrialisation. From a
historical point of view this notion is only useful either as an ideal type against
which to measure the actual achievements of nation-states or as a window on
the possible motives of would-be nation builders. It does not tell us directly
why nations are 'made' or 'invented'. On this question, Gellner turned back to
the work of E. H. Carr and enlisted a variety of contingent political factors,
ranging from the introduction of mass education and military conscription to
the activities of elites. Faced with the same problem, Max Weber – fore-
shadowing Benedict Anderson – included newsprint in an otherwise similar
list.[7] All of these factors – elite politics, mass conscription, mass education
and the mass press – had already been widely canvassed in imperial Germany
for their allegedly positive nation-building functions. In Wilhelmine Germany
the army had been much touted as the 'school of the nation'. After Prussia's
victories over Austria in 1866 and France in 1870, no less a figure than
Bismarck had publicly thanked the primary-school teachers for their contribution to inculcating national consciousness and asked them to continue to
school the nation.[8] For any theorist, these were explanatory causes waiting to
be plucked out of the political common sense of the times.

In this period of self-conscious national engineering Weber was not alone
in seeking to understand the phenomenon. Nor was he alone in regarding it
as a matter of social engineering. In fact, liberal-minded constructivists were

in the majority at the 1912 conference of German Sociologists. For once, primordialists, like Paul Barth from Leipzig, were in the minority. Only one voice was raised in favour of the new-fangled racial doctrine of the nation. Whatever credence such opinions might hold in the world of popular politics outside, inside the academic conference the dominant voices – those of Ferdinand Tönnies, Robert Michels, Eduard Bernstein, Ludo Moritz Hartmann and Max Weber's brother Alfred – were all sceptically historicist in their approach to national identity . There was also one major participant in the 1912 discussions who was not present in person. He was the Austro-Marxist theorist Otto Bauer.

Five years previously, and three years before Weber penned the key pas-sages on the nation in *Economy and Society*, Bauer had written a large and cel-ebrated tome, *The Nationalities Question and Social Democracy*, in which he set out in comparative historical terms a constructivist theory of the nation.[9] In his view there were three distinct stages to the emergence of nations. The first focused on what Bauer described as the 'community of language' (*Sprachgemeinschaft*). In Bauer's theory, as in Gellner's, the creation of this community was primarily a matter of economic unification. Regional labour and product markets supposedly broke down the narrow isolation of rural communities. The second stage brought the 'cultural community' (*Kulturgemeinschaft*) into being. Bauer's account also centred on the work of elites in creating and dispersing a 'high' culture. From his Viennese per-spective, it may have seemed obvious that these high cultures started as aris-tocratic creations, and only in the nineteenth century were emulated by the rising bourgeoisie, the cultural 'trickling-down' percolating at the start of the twentieth century to the working class. It was on these cultural foundations, Bauer argued, that the final and vital stage had to be built: the creation of political sentiment, of belief in the nation as a 'community of fate' (*Schicksalsgemeinschaft*). Redeploying Hegel's unfortunate phrase about peoples 'with' and 'without' history to new effect, Bauer sought to explain here how the historical *memory* of past struggles and former statehood could be invoked to legitimate a sense of national entitlement in communities like the Poles and the Czechs who, living under imperial rule, had no immediate institutions which they could invest with nationalistic symbolic significance. In making this move he opened up a fruitful vein of investigation for future historians and pointed the way towards Hobsbawm's notion of the 'invention of tradition'.[10]

It fell to the least well-known of the theorists present at the 1912 confer-ence, Hartmann, a Viennese economic historian of medieval Italy, to ensure that Bauer's views were heard and discussed. Weber did not yet in 1912 support the Austrian Social Democratic position; when he made up his mind in the middle of the First World War that it offered the 'only solution ever possible', it would be to Hartmann that he would turn as his confidant and political intermediary in dealing with Otto Bauer.[11] Hartmann had begun his political career by noting that Austrian Social Democracy was uniquely qualified to resolve the nationality conflicts in the Habsburg lands because of its supranational status. He would end it under Bauer as the first ambassador of the new Austrian Republic to Weimar Germany.[12]

The essential context for understanding these intellectual and polemical exchanges was the one which had alarmed Hartmann in the first place, namely the dramatic eruption of nationality conflict in the Austrian half of the Dual Monarchy in 1897. The forms which this conflict took were inseparable from the development of mass politics and the 'public sphere'. The Social Democrats therefore had an interest in finding a solution to them which would allow their supranational, class-based agenda once more to take centre stage. In late November 1897 crowds blocked the Ringstrasse in Vienna for several days while inside the parliament building German, Czech and Polish members came to blows and had to be dragged out by police. This tumult was triggered by the question of the *Amtssprache*, the official language for internal bureaucratic communication. With a centralised and quasi-absolutist form of government, appointments to the civil service were the focus of university students' ambitions. The question of the language in which it conducted its own internal affairs therefore aroused passions among educated Czechs comparable with current debates about the correct language for education and the civil service in contemporary India. The demonstrators of 1897 objected in particular to having German as the official medium for internal government decisions in Bohemia.

The Prime Minister, Count Badeni, a Polish aristocrat with a devastating penchant for combining authoritarian decrees with reforming tendencies, had tried to meet long-standing Czech calls for equality. The previous administration had already accepted, in 1880, that the government should communicate with the public in both Czech and German. But Badeni's decision in 1897 to recognise Czech and German as languages of equal status in the Crown Lands of Bohemia and Moravia stipulated further that all officials would have had to learn both languages by 1901. This immediately raised the prospect that the German stranglehold on official appointments would be broken. The Pan-Germans of the *Deutschnationale Verein* and German Liberals mobilised against such tangible concessions to Czech nationalism and embarked on a six-month mass campaign in the German parts of Bohemia, promptly sparking off a counter-campaign by the Young Czech movement. Demonstrations and counter-demonstrations were held in Prague. Meanwhile, Badeni's reliance on the political support of Conservative large agrarian interests and his blatant disregard for parliamentary procedure finally alienated the other major German Austrian parties, the Christian Socials (a Catholic pro-peasant and small business party similar to but considerably more conservative than the German Centre Party) and the Social Democrats (also modelled on its German namesake). In the face of such an array of popular forces, the Emperor dismissed Badeni. He was succeeded by a series of weak ministries who also tried – especially in 1900 and 1903 under Körber and in 1909 under Bienerth – to carry through some sort of language reform. Like Badeni's, their proposals were blocked in parliament and the reforms failed. Also like Badeni, they resorted to administrative fiat to continue the daily running of government.[13] By the time universal suffrage was introduced in 1907, the Social Democrats had become not only the largest and most popular party – alongside the Christian Socials – but also the only party which bridged the national divisions between Czechs and Germans. (The movement had, after all, been founded on a merger of Czech and German labour associations in 1888–89.) Crucial to preserving this position was the party's adoption of a programme which promised democracy and equal rights to the different nationalities within the Empire and a decentralised, federalist organisational structure to their own party.[14] In effect, they proposed a multinational democracy.

With their territorially mixed communities of language and culture, the Habsburg lands provided a classical instance of the difficulty of creating nation-states in eastern Europe which would accord in any obvious way with the *risorgimento* liberal principle of a correspondence between unitary nation and unitary state. Despite the gathering symbolic violence with which Czech and German conflicts about national rights were waged from 1897 onwards, there was widespread consensus on the liberal left that political solutions based on forced assimilation or expulsion, let alone on murder, were unthinkable. Even the young Czech nationalist Edvard Beneš accepted in 1905 that an independent Czechoslovakia was not to be thought of. The point was not, or not only, that the Habsburg monarchy would crush any such attempt, but that the social preconditions were themselves absent. 'One cannot seriously think about establishing a Czech state', Beneš conceded, 'if one third of the population of the country [i.e. the Germans in Bohemia] is ready to fight against it with all means.'[15] It was this reluctance to override social consent or to force society to fit the bed of nationalist doctrine that encouraged the political project of democratic multinationalism.[16]

The consensual and democratic solution to the problem of 'mixed' population areas which the Social Democrats proposed was one which sought to reduce nationalist claims to their principal elements alone. Since nationalist claims in central Europe drew their inspiration from German romanticism and posited the cultural particularism of language, the Social Democratic response was to treat the 'nationality question' as primarily a cultural and linguistic one. The chief hallmark of the programme was what its architect, Karl Renner, called the 'personality principle'.[17] This meant delivering all the major public services in those languages which citizens would register for on an individual basis by signing up to voluntary associations. It would make cultural identity portable within the country as a whole. Renner clearly also hoped that wider conflicts over cultural difference could be avoided by fostering economic interests on the basis of multicultural regions such as the Danube, and by creating new federal and democratic structures of government which would also cut across the old and, in some cases, proto-national boundaries of the traditional 'Crown Lands'. Just as Ernest Gellner later expected consumer culture to mitigate nationalism, so at the beginning of the twentieth century Renner believed that greater economic growth could be delivered by maintaining the integrity of a large multinational territory such as the Habsburg customs union, and that this economic success in its turn would create other interest groups to cut across and counterbalance nationalist ones. As Renner wrote in one of his many writings on the subject, 'We must draw a double network on the map . . . . We must cut across the functions of the state. We must separate national and political affairs . . . . We must organise the population twice: once along the lines of nationality, the second time in relation to the state.'[18]

This sort of thinking cogently expresses the starting point of an open democratic politics, where national belonging is expressed – and indeed acquired – through citizenship and individual entitlement rather than ethnicity and group rights. This was probably the sort of politics which Otto Bauer, as a leading member of the Social Democratic left, wanted to pursue for its own sake and from traditional socialist motives. For him, as for the founder of Austrian Social Democracy, Victor Adler, the increasing nationality conflicts of the 1890s and 1900s represented a major obstacle thwarting any strong and unified labour movement: nation cut across class.[19] Adler and Bauer drew the obvious conclusion that the nationality question had to be solved in Austria *before* any real pressure could be brought to bear for meaningful social reform, let alone for revolution. In their multinational empire, they drew the opposite conclusions from the ones later reached by the Bolsheviks in theirs. Not only were the Austro-Marxists more moderate in separating the problems of nationalism from those of socialism, which is precisely what made their theoretical ideas more rigorous, but they also took diametrically different views from the Bolsheviks about the relation between political party and nationalism. The Leninist line would combine the promise that the revolution would deliver national independence to the peoples conquered by tsarist expansion with the maintenance, in practice, of a centralised party cutting across the national divides of the Romanov empire. This party in due course became the nucleus of a renewed centralism under the aegis of the new party-state which emerged out of the revolution and the civil war. The Austrian Social Democrats, whilst preaching multinationalism, nonetheless accepted federalism within their own party. In doing so, they guaranteed the Czech Social Democrats an independent organisational base which would stand them in good stead when, after 1918, they had to organise themselves within an independent Czechoslovak state.

Renner and Weber, for their part, were guided by rather different motives from Bauer. Renner quite simply regarded the possible break-up of the Habsburg Empire with horror and wanted to perpetuate German dominion. He found himself as opposed to the cessionism of the Pan-Germans, who wanted German-speaking Austrians to join the Reich, as to that of Slav nationalists. 'Whatever the cost,' Renner had insisted in 1903, German Austria had a historic mission to keep the 'South and East Slavs' with the west 'and not to drive these peoples into the arms of all-devouring Russia'.[20] Renner did not discard this vision lightly: in the autumn of 1918, in the midst of Austria's defeat and break-up, he put the finishing touches to his final version of the multinational constitution.[21]

Weber's priorities were yet more aggressively imperialist. He may have been a democratically-minded liberal, but he was still a Wilhelmine Liberal. As Wolfgang Mommsen has cogently argued, Weber's concern for the primacy of the state in building the nation was matched by a view of politics in which the geopolitical competition between states took pride of place. Weber was an unembarrassed champion of expanding the German sphere of influence in eastern and south-eastern Europe. Like Renner, he rejected Pan-German projects. Even after the collapse of the Habsburg Empire in December 1918 – and at a time when even German and Austrian Social Democrats were attempting to unify the German-speaking remnant of Austria with Germany – Weber maintained that Bismarck had been right to preserve the Habsburg Empire for higher geopolitical reasons. He had been right to save 'an institution which sacrificed the participation of ten million Germans in the Reich in order to neutralise thirty million non-Germans politically'.[22]

Weber and possibly even Renner may have been attracted to Austrian Social Democracy because they saw it as a possible vehicle for perpetuating German influence by introducing measures of formal equality. Both had been much influenced intellectually by the neo-Kantian revival of the 1880s and 1890s, and were well able to distinguish between the formal application of universal principles of equal and reciprocal rights of the kind which underpinned their nationality programme, on the one hand, and real power, on the other. Bauer did not subscribe to such nationalistic goals. Nor did he conceive of the role of the state in such externally aggressive terms. Yet all three observers applied an intellectual model of the nation as defined through politics and 'cultural work'. What they did not agree about was what kind of 'cultural work' the state was meant to perform. Whereas Weber saw this principally in terms of great power politics, envisaging the creation of a Machtstaat, Bauer put the emphasis mainly on domestic social and economic policy. In this sense, Ernest Gellner's idea of the state's nation-building functions had more in common with Otto Bauer than with Max Weber.

Weber's 'open' liberal belief that the nation was shaped by its aspiration for a state found its corollary in an acute anxiety that the nation would cease to exist if the state failed. This gave a particular edge to his 'all or nothing' prognoses about the fate awaiting the German nation before and during the First World War. Part of the intellectual difficulty here was that Weber's theorising was extremely ambiguous. He refused to define the content of 'culture', leaving a potential void at the heart of his theory of the relation between nation and state. There were theoretical as well as political reasons for his difficulty. The obvious escape from the circularity of identifying nation with state and state with nation was to construct a historical and causal explanation of the formation of both. This, after all, had been the whole point of Otto Bauer's three-stage model. But whereas Bauer was willing to offer a model which assumed the historicity of cultural nationalism without believing in it very strongly himself, Weber believed in it vehemently but was too intellectually self-critical to reduce all nationalisms to a central European linguistic and cultural model.[23]

The major strength and central innovation of both Bauer and Weber lay in their identification of the nation with 'modernity' and their denial to it of any mystical primordiality. Their concept of 'modernity' was – and still remains – very problematic. In defining nationalism as part of the modern world, Bauer and Weber (like Gellner later) both drew heavily and explicitly on Ferdinand Tönnies's celebrated dichotomy between *Gemeinschaft* and *Gesellschaft*.[24] Tönnies had used the word *Gemeinschaft* to conjure up the image of an 'organic' medieval community in which trust and solidarity were natural and immediate, in order to criticise the abstract, individualist and rational world of modernity.[25] Both Bauer and Weber applied this dichotomy to modernity itself, as a means to distinguish between those social identities which were spontaneous and pre-rational, like nations, and those which individuals could choose to join or withdraw from, like the institutions of state and civil society (parties, trade unions and co-operatives). For both theorists the central theoretical problem was to show by what contingent means a *Gesellschaft* could aspire to the non-contingent status of a *Gemeinschaft*. National identity became the secular religion which performed this sorcery. Again, both theorists turned to the same explanatory mechanisms: politics and the 'cultural work' of the ruling classes and state institutions provided the means for transmitting common values and language. Both also – in marked contrast to the internationalism proposed by most Marxist theorists of their generation – considered, in Weber's words, that 'with the democratisation of culture belief in the exclusiveness of their language community seizes the masses as well'.[26]

The dichotomy between *Gemeinschaft* and *Gesellschaft* depends on drawing a caesura between the medieval and early modern, on the one hand, and the modern, on the other. It is here that the social teleology set out by Weber, Bauer and Gellner has aged badly. Economic historians have discarded the thesis of an abrupt rupture in favour of more evolutionary explanations of industrialisation. Social historians have rethought the longer-term continuities of cultural norms and gender relations linking the early modern and the modern. Theories of 'modernisation' and 'capitalist development' have been widely criticised as functionalist and unhistorical. These developments tend to break down the large theoretical building-blocks of class and nation. Weber and Bauer, of course, thought that national identity always did require more explanation than did social class. This partly protects their insights from such critiques; only partly, however, for all the component categories which they invoked to explain the formation of nations then themselves become the targets of a similar deconstruction.

This brings us back to the alleged rupture between 'traditional' and 'modern' society. Tönnies mourned the disappearance of the romantic communities of medieval and early modern Europe, which had never existed in the form he imagined. Weber, Bauer and Gellner did not. Yet, in lifting his key notion of *Gemeinschaft* and placing it in the contemporary 'impersonal' world of 'modernity', Weber and Bauer, and later, Gellner, set the modern state a task it could never achieve in a world in which the identities of large social groups were, as they saw only too clearly, malleable. Their formulation of the problem creates a conceptual imbalance between the early modern and the modern which obstructs historical enquiry. Early modern community was not a romantic 'golden age'; it was the site of murderous conflicts between near neighbours, of infanticide and witch-hunting.[27] The alleged break between the 'traditional' and the 'modern' also suggests that historians of 'modernity' do not need to study the earlier period. Yet it may be precisely in elements of cultural continuity that historians will find the primary social cement which is used in a changing social and political context to fashion national identities.

The Austro-Marxist programme was never implemented in Habsburg Austria. By the time the monarchy fell it was too late anyway. It is tempting to ask whether it ever could have worked. The question is interesting because it helps to throw the key factor into sharp relief. The programme would only have been practicable if there had been a strong and internally unified state willing to enact it. Thanks to the work of Hobsbawm and Gellner, Anderson, Weber and Bauer, we are all familiar with the thesis that integral national identities depended in large measure on the active efforts of states to cultivate such sentiments. Cavour's famous dictum that 'We have made Italy; now we have to make the Italians' aptly sums up this view. What has been less noticed is that this same thesis holds true of the multinational or multicultural polity. Here, however, the stakes are potentially higher: Cavour had to face only indifference and regional particularism; multinationalism in Habsburg Austria or the former Yugoslavia were programmes to re-educate a population which had already been exposed to a mass media steeped in nationalism. The multinational state would have had to *un*make the nationalism of many of its citizens.

That this was never attempted in Austria may have been a historical accident attributable to the unwillingness of the Habsburgs to reform until far too late, and to the effect of their aggressive foreign and intransigent domestic policies on inflaming national division, perhaps as part of an intentional strategy of divide and rule. Types of multiculturalist politics, similar in principle to the Austrian Social Democratic idea, have after all emerged more recently in countries of official immigration, such as Canada, Australia and, less straightforwardly, the USA. These were, however, not policies embraced in the face of a fundamental challenge to the very survival of those states. Indeed, all of the states in question had been established through the ruthless application of genocidal cultural intolerance, a cultural monism which the colonists did not necessarily find at odds with their own formulation of classical liberal principles. In this light, it may not seem so inherently self-contradictory that Renner and Weber could advocate both multinational democracy and German great power politics. This was at least a more inclusive liberalism than that which John Locke proposed for the Amerindians.[28]

What is involved here, as a matter of theory and ethics as well as a matter of the historical record, is a basic problem of democracy. If the state stands as the educator of its citizens, what happens to the classical definition of political legitimacy as resting on popular sovereignty? What happens when the citizens refuse to respond with the required 'sentiments'? Can the state go on acting as a pedagogue? If it were to try, then it could scarcely do so by liberal and democratic means. In principle, this dilemma is as relevant to a state pursuing tolerant multinational politics against the wishes of its citizens as to one pursuing intolerant nationalist politics. In practice, most states have been founded on the intolerant cultural values of relatively narrow social groupings. The semi-moribund Habsburg monarchy, as Victor Adler put it, proved too slovenly an autocracy to be capable either of effective reform or of effective repression.[29] But those states which have most effectively introduced multicultural politics in the contemporary world were not established on multicultural premises. From this perspective the very failure of the Habsburg state to carry through such a reform in its last decades points not just to the lack of political will at the top but to the lack of social consensus below. The sad irony must be that the pursuit of multinational consensus politics depends on conditions at least as special as does integralist nationalism.

From this exploration of connections between the ideas of the 1980s and those of the 1900s, two points stand out in sharp relief. The first is the very durability of 'constructivist' ideas of nationhood, or rather their capacity to re-emerge from partial oblivion. On both occasions, in the 1900s and in the 1980s, the leading theorists were seeking to explain national identity in eastern and south-eastern Europe almost a decade ahead of the most militant displays of integralist nationalism. The fact that the political outcome still had to be settled endows their writing with a particularly open yet strongly engaged quality. The second point of comparison is the intellectual consensus between liberal proponents of 'modernisation theory', like Weber and Gellner, and Marxist adherents to a notion of 'capitalist development', such as Bauer or, more recently, Hobsbawm. The differences in their terminology are far out-weighed by the shared assumption that it is in socio-economic structures and state formation that the key elements of any explanation of nationalism are to be found. During the long years of intellectual cold war between the Soviet Union and the west, the complex shared legacies between varieties of Marxism and liberalism went unrecognised. In the late 1950s, at the height of the cold war, Wolfgang Mommsen wrote the classic account of Weber's politics, bril-liantly elucidating his German nationalism. His twin brother Hans, mean-while, wrote a major study of the Habsburg Social Democrats and the nationalities issue. It seems not to have occurred to either brother that the two subjects might overlap.[30]

In accounting for this degree of intellectual openness on both sides of the liberal–Marxist divide, political timing holds the key. What united Weber and Bauer across the liberal–socialist divide in the 1900s was the same issue which, in the uncertainties of a post-cold war world, united the two erstwhile cold-war foes, Gellner and Hobsbawm: a fear of the destructiveness of resurgent nationalism and with it an intellectual hostility to interpretations of national-ism which rest on inflated claims of primordial community, common ancestry or ancient statehood.

At the turn of the nineteenth century, this intellectual stance meant step-ping outside the mainstream, including the liberal mainstream. Its current ran precisely towards 'naturalising' the nation and making the parvenu appear eternal. As Bauer put it, in words Weber echoed later, 'for us, history no longer represents the struggle of nations; instead the nation itself appears as the reflection of historical struggles'.[31] It meant taking up arms against old nation-alist historians like Treitschke, whose lectures Weber had attended in Berlin as a student in the 1880s. And it also meant treating the new social sciences with discrimination. Karl Renner singled out the new 'social sciences' of anthropology and ethnology particularly as culpable because, by making an academic discipline out of ancient cultural hatreds, not to mention tribal and racial belonging, they offered 'indispensable scientific props to the nationalist politician'. Max Weber inveighed against what he dubbed the 'racial mythol-ogy' of claims to a community of blood.[32] But this tradition of thought, for all its liberalism and radical antecedents, carries a heritage of cultural intolerance. And some of that freight is still with us. By defining cultural difference as a matter of individual preference and relegating cultural rights to the private sphere, Renner offered a way out of the cul-de-sac of integralist nationalism. He also implied that the basic structures of economy, society and state could be free of cultural values, whilst – virtually in the next breath – demanding that German domination be preserved. It is this slippage in the definition of the relationship between culture and power which should make us wary of subscribing to the current vogue for distinguishing tritely between 'good' models of national identity defined by citizenship, on French and American lines, and 'bad' models based on culture and ethnicity along the lines of German romanticism.[33] It may be easier to join the *citoyens* than the *Volk*, but both have historically required that recruits assimilate to the dominant culture. These dilemmas may paradoxically have provided the point of origin for an acknowledgement of the fragility of claims to national belonging and the starting point for a multicultural politics, but at the close of the twentieth century we would do well to accept that this is also a deeply flawed origin.

Notes

I have been particularly grateful to Ernest Gellner, Emma Rothschild, Gareth Stedman Jones and Lyndal Roper for their comments.

1 *Verhandlungen des zweiten deutschen Soziologentages vom 20.–22. Oktober 1912 in Berlin* (Tübingen, 1913), p. 50. Unless otherwise indicated, all translations from the German are by the present author.

2 E. Gellner, *Nations and Nationalism* (Oxford, 1983), p. 1. For more on Gellner's theory of nationalism, see N. Stargardt, 'Gellner's nationalism: the spirit of modernisation?', in J. Hall and I. Jarvie (eds), *The Social Philosophy of Ernest Gellner* (Amsterdam, 1996), pp. 171–89; and E. Gellner, 'Reply to critics', *ibid.*, p. 639.

3 B. Anderson, *Imagined Communities* (London, 1983); E. J. Hobsbawm and T. Ranger (eds), *The Invention of Tradition* (Cambridge, 1983); E. J. Hobsbawm, *Nations and Nationalism since 1780* (Cambridge, 1990). Eugen Weber's classic account of nation-building in *fin-de-siècle* France pioneered this kind of argument in a regional and national context: E. Weber, *Peasants into Frenchmen: the Modernisation of Rural France, 1870–1914* (London, 1979); see also R. Samuel (ed.), *Patriotism: the Making and Unmaking of British National Identity*, 3 vols (London, 1989).

4 Gellner, *Nations and Nationalism*, p. 124.

5 *Verhandlungen des zweiten deutschen Soziologentages*, p. 74.

6 Gellner, *Nations and Nationalism*, p. 140.

7 E. Gellner, 'Nationalism and the international order', in his *Encounters with Nationalism* (Oxford, 1994), pp. 20–33; E. H. Carr, *Nationalism and After* (London, 1945), pp. 1–37; Weber, in *Verhandlungen des zweiten deutschen Soziologentages*, p. 51.

8 On Bismarck's greeting to the primary-school teachers in 1871, see K. A. Schleunes, *Schooling and Society: the Politics of Education in Prussia and Bavaria, 1750–1900* (Oxford, 1989), p. 160; on the military, see N. Stargardt, *The German Idea of Militarism: Radical and Socialist Critics, 1866–1914* (Cambridge, 1994), part 1.

9 O. Bauer, *Die Nationalitätenfrage und die Sozialdemokratie* (Vienna, 1907; 2nd enlarged edn, Vienna, 1924), cited here from O. Bauer, *Werkausgabe*, I (Vienna, 1975): 49–622 (see esp. pp. 69–221); M. Weber, *Economy and Society*, ed. G. Roth and C. Wittich, 2 vols (Berkeley, 1978), pp. 395–8, 921–6.

10 There is a direct lineage from this work to the writing of Eric Hobsbawm. As a critical Marxist, Hobsbawm also generously acknowledges the work of the Czech theorist Miroslav Hroch when it comes to schematising the stages by which nineteenth-century European nationalism was propagated from a preserve of intellectual elites until it became a mass phenomenon. Hobsbawm, *Nations and Nationalism since 1780*, esp. pp. 7–12, and M. Hroch, *Social Preconditions of National Revival in Europe* (Cambridge, 1985).

11 M. Weber, *Gesammelte politische Schriften* (Tübingen, 1971), p. 175.

12 L. Hartmann [pseud. Verus], 'Die Nationalitäten in Österreich und die Sozialdemokratie', *Die neue Zeit*, 15:2 (1896–97), 688ff. For his 1912 lecture, see *Verhandlungen des zweiten deutschen Soziologentages*, pp. 80–97. Hartmann was also one of the founders of the *Zeitschrift für Sozial- und Wirtschaftsgeschichte* in 1893 with Carl Grünberg and Stephan Bauer; *Neue deutsche Biographie*, VII (Berlin, 1965): 737; *Österreichisches biographisches Lexikon*, II (Graz, 1959): 195–6. For references to the Weber–Hartmann correspondence, see W. J. Mommsen, *Max Weber and German Politics* (Chicago, 1984), especially the notes to chs 7 and 9.

13 R. A. Kann, *The Multinational Empire: Nationalism and National Reform in the Habsburg Monarchy, 1848–1918*, 2 vols (New York, 1950), I: 200–6; L. Brügel, *Geschichte der österreichischen Sozialdemokratie*, 5 vols (Vienna, 1922–25), IV: 318–43; H. Mommsen, *Die Sozialdemokratie und die Nationalitätenfrage im habsburgischen Vielvölkerstaat, 1. Das Ringen um die supranationale Integration der zisleithanischen Arbeiterbewegung (1867–1907)* (Vienna, 1963), pp. 266–94. Unfortunately Mommsen never published the promised second volume of his work, which was meant to deal expressly with the ideas of Karl Renner and Otto Bauer and cover the period 1907–18.

14 H. Mommsen, *Die Sozialdemokratie und die Nationalitätenfrage*, pp. 155–80.

15 E. Beneš, *Le Problème autrichien et la question tchèque* (Paris, 1908), p. 258; cited also in Kann, *The Multinational Empire*, I: 212.

16 P. Crabitès, *Beneš: Statesman of Central Europe* (London, 1935). It is this premise of consensus that makes these pre-1914 multinational programmes interesting once more today; the intervening years have witnessed all the violent, forced-fit solutions which Bauer and Beneš at this stage rejected as unthinkable, but to which, as the respective Czechoslovak and Austrian foreign ministers lobbying the Entente powers about the Austrian–Czech border in the summer of 1919, they would themselves contribute.

17 As a civil servant, Renner felt obliged to publish all his early writings under pseudonyms: Synopticus, *Staat und Nation: Staatsrechtliche Untersuchungen über die möglichen Principien einer Lösung und die juristischen Voraussetzungen eines Nationalitätengesetzes* (Vienna, 1899); Rudolf Springer, *Der Kampf der österreichischen Nationen um den Staat, 1. Theil, Das nationale Problem als Verfassungs- und Verwaltungsfrage* (Vienna, 1902); Rudolf Springer, *Die Krise des Dualismus und das Ende der Deakistischen Episode in der Geschichte der habsburgischen Monarchie* (Vienna, 1904); and his last work published under the name Rudolf Springer, *Grundlagen und Entwicklungsziele der österreichisch-ungarischen Monarchie* (Vienna, 1906).

18 Springer, *Grundlagen*, p. 208.

19 Victor Adler, the founding leader of Austrian Social Democracy, put it to his party's 1904 conference with characteristic irony: 'We cannot fight against a class state which does not show any signs of life . . . A strange situation arises in which we are calling for a state, a living modern state, while at the same time we are perfectly aware that this will

not be our state. We differ from all other countries of Europe by fighting merely for a basis on which to carry on our struggle.' V. Adler, *Aufsätze, Reden und Briefe*, 11 vols (Vienna, 1922–29), VIII: 240.

20 Springer, *Der Kampf der Nationen*, p. 170; see also Springer, *Grundlagen*, p. 248.

21 K. Renner, *Das Selbstbestimmungsrecht der Nationen in besonderer Anwendung auf Österreich, 1. Teil, Nation und Staat* (Vienna, 1918).

22 Weber, *Gesammelte politische Schriften*, p. 449; W. J. Mommsen, *Max Weber and German Politics*, esp. ch. 3.

23 Weber, *Economy and Society*, pp. 395–6, and even more explicitly, *Verhandlungen des zweiten deutschen Soziologentages*, p. 51.

24 O. Bauer, 'Bemerkungen zur Nationalitätenfrage', *Die neue Zeit*, 26:1 (1907–8); on Weber on this point see D. Beetham, *Max Weber and the Theory of Modern Politics* (Cambridge, 1985), pp. 28ff. Gellner, 'Nationalism reconsidered and E. H. Carr', *Review of International Studies*, 18 (1992), 289.

25 F. Tönnies, *Gemeinschaft und Gesellschaft: Abhandlung des Communismus und des Socialismus als empirische Kulturformen* (Leipzig, 1887).

26 Weber, *Gesammelte politische Schriften*, p. 234; Beetham, *Max Weber*, p. 123.

27 See R. Briggs, *Witches and Neighbours: the Social and Cultural Context of European Witchcraft* (London, 1996); L. Roper, *Oedipus and the Devil: Witchcraft, Sexuality and Religion in Early Modern Europe* (London, 1994).

28 J. Tully, *An Approach to Political Philosophy: Locke in Contexts* (Cambridge, 1993).

29 *Protokoll des internationalen Arbeiter-Congresses zu Paris* (Nuremberg, 1890), p. 43; J. Braunthal, *History of the International, 1864–1914* (London, 1966), p. 215.

30 W J. Mommsen, *Max Weber and German Politics*, and H. Mommsen, *Die Sozialdemokratie und die Nationalitätenfrage*.

31 Bauer, *Werkausgabe*, I: 196.

32 *Verhandlungen des zweiten deutschen Soziologentages*, p. 74; Springer, *Der Kampf der Nationen*, pp. 6, 21.

33 For an ambitious attempt to argue this case, which descends into Germanophobic assertions and French chauvinism, see A. Finkielkraut, *The Undoing of Thought* (London, 1988).

Part II

THE NATION IN TIME

Storylines: narratives and nationality in nineteenth-century Ireland

In 1992 a document was issued by the Irish Tourist Board, called *Heritage Attractions Development: a strategy to interpret Ireland's history and culture for tourism*:

> Irish history, due to the influence of many peoples, cultures and conflicts, is not easily understood by visitors . . . . Visitors' time is also limited . . . so it is important to help increase visitors' understanding by creating interpretative 'gateways' into our heritage. This will heighten their experience, increase satisfaction levels, and help in awareness and appreciation of individual sites, the end result will be more repeat business, better word of mouth publicity and the creation of a strong brand image of Ireland as quality heritage destination, with unique heritage attractions.[1]

The argument goes on to emphasise 'storylines' in Irish history, epitomised in heritage centres. 'It is proposed that all storylines be clustered around five key themes' (landscapes, work, religion, nation building, the spirit of Ireland); the consultants' report thoughtfully suggested thirty storylines to be tapped into, adding that 'new storylines are possible under all of the themes'. Thus an accessible narrative is located in a trouble-free (or thought-free) way. It is the kind of process which leads Fintan O'Toole to conclude that Ireland has moved from archaism to postmodernism without ever becoming modern (much as America allegedly moved straight from barbarism to decadence without experiencing civilisation).[2] And it highlights the way narrative has been used as an actual component of nation building, to such an extent that the structure of the narrative conditions the nature of the nation.

The idea of nationality as a narrative is becoming a cliché: but it is not a cliché of recent creation, fashionable as it has become in the work of various postmodern critics. It has been mobilised with striking explicitness since the Romantic period. One classic example is Poland: historical epic in the work of Mickiewicz and his contemporaries provides a wealth of enduring examples. Another is Ireland. Just as we begin to analyse this, ironically, the presentation of history itself in narrative form has come back into a certain vogue. But so has the study of the assumptions and exclusions represented by the narra-tive form itself.[3] What does this mean for the way Irish history is told? For the last thirty years the questioning of accepted versions of Irish history has taken a firmer and firmer hold, and advanced from academic orthodoxy into public debate. Irish historians, working in many areas, have tried to break up the seamless construction of narrative incident which was presented as the story of Ireland, and to analyse the moment, rather than simply follow the flow. At the same time, however, the compelling power of the old sequence has held its mesmeric force. (I found this myself, when I set out to write a general treat-ment of Irish history intended to break out of the genre, and ended by adher-ing much more closely than I had realised to the story form.) And the morality of the tale is still mobilised for political purposes.

In the Irish story, personal experience and national history remain woven into an apparently logical and self-referencing construction.[4] The story of an exemplary life often carries a powerful national metaphor, of sacrifice to redeem the national soul. Life stories, as Paul Ricoeur has remarked, are only made intelligible through the borrowing of plots from history and fiction. This process can lie even behind autobiography: to take an Irish example, the classic memoirs by Tómas Ó Crohán and Muirís Ó Súilleabháin are often taken as narratives embodying the pure experience of prelapsarian western island life; it turns out, however, that they were written under the direct inspiration of reading Maxim Gorky's *My Childhood,* lent by a visiting intel-lectual.

This makes such evidence all the more interesting, but more compli-cated. And when one thinks about the shape of Irish history, or argues about the accuracy and significance of certain generally accepted themes, one is struck again and again by the importance of the narrative mode: the idea that Irish history *is* a 'story', and the implications that this carries about a begin-ning, a middle, and the sense of an ending. The formal modes of *Bildungsroman*, ghost story, deliverance-tale, family romance, have all lent motifs to the ways Irish history has been told.[5] Like all storytelling, this has to do with reassurance, which lay, according to Isaiah Berlin, at the heart of populist nationalism in the Romantic period, in countries dominated by pow-erful neighbours.

Thus we might approach nineteenth-century storytellers of Ireland who subordinated history to narrative mode. They may have intended to present diametrically different political views, but they all helped to validate the way that the national story was conceived in the age of independence. To intro-duce the very concept of 'The Story of Ireland' is to evoke a proliferation of books written under this heavily loaded title. From the early nineteenth until the mid-twentieth century, it was chosen by novelists, journalists, polemi-cists, prophets and educators. In fact, the compelling notion of a Story of

Ireland, with all the implications of plot, narrative logic and desired outcome, reached its apogee in the later nineteenth century; the historiography thus created was intimately connected with the discovery of folk-tale, myth and saga as indices of the national experience. The development of Irish national-ism was strongly influenced by the transference of these forms into the nar-rative of nationality;[6] this lay behind the rise of exclusivist cultural nationalism, à la Sinn Féin, and the decline of the inclusive idea of a politic-ised collectivity of citizens argued for by Isaac Butt (and, on occasion, Daniel O'Connell). Instead of developing into a broad church, the Irish nation became a revealed religion. By 1900, the Gaelic League was preaching pure Herder, though it probably did not know it and had certainly simplified his message. Herder argued that organic nations were manifestations of the divine plan, evolving uniquely by a complex process enshrined in the language of the common people. The Gaelic League agreed, but put it thus: '[God] wished us to be by ourselves out in the ocean, with our own particular lan-guage, music, religion, customs and other things. In addition, he made the ancient Romans afraid to come near us, so that we are not like any other nation in Europe.'[7]

More obliquely, the process of defining a national story is intimately con-nected with the peculiarities of Irish literature, and specifically with the Irish approach to narrative. Anyone familiar with the structure of Irish folk-tales, or saga poetry, or still more with the idiosyncratic range of nineteenth-century Irish fiction in English, will note a characteristic approach to telling stories. The probable reasons are many: a powerful oral culture, a half-lost language, the necessary stratagems of irony, collusion and misdirection which accom-pany a colonised culture. A recurring theme is the deliberate gap in the nar-rative: the significant elision, the leap in the story. One of the most significant Irish novels, Maria Edgeworth's Castle Rackrent, was originally to be about a family called the 'Stopgaps'. Given that they carry Irish history, so to speak, on their backs, this is an important conceit. The other characteristic Irish mode is the story within the story – a key to Sterne, Maturin, LeFanu, Flann O'Brien, and most of all, Joyce. The assertion that Irish literary culture is defi-cient in great novels, or does not possess a Balzacian tradition of novels as 'the private history of the nation', may simply indicate that Irish writers had neither time nor inclination for the novel as formally conceived in the great age of English or French fiction. And the thesis that asserts a close connection between the emergence of the novel and the growth of a sense of national identity needs to be sharply interrogated for the Irish case. Homi Bhabha's useful collection of writings on nation and narration oddly glides over the Irish question;[8] this may be at least in part because in Ireland history – or histori-ography – is our true novel.[9] Certainly at the point in the eighteenth century when the English novel was allegedly emerging as a contributing factor to the sense of nation, discourse in Ireland was obsessed by history-writing – a competitive genre of national storytelling, in which the ownership of the narrative,[10] and the moral authority conferred by a story with a known or expected ending (that secret known to all Marxists) were vital issues.

Romanticism in early nineteenth-century Ireland – as elsewhere – sustained the idea of national history as a transfiguring wonder-tale: this was a period when fiction was preoccupied with historical subjects, but also when history-writing was obsessed with constructing a compelling fiction.[11] It provided the seedbed for the work of inspirational storytellers of Ireland, whose names will recur. One was Samuel Ferguson, producer from the 1830s of stories, poems and reconstituted bardic epics, which interrogated the disputed question of an Irish identity which could be both Protestant and nationally minded.[12] Ferguson came from a tradition deeply interested in continental literature. One of his circle was the translator of *Faust*, and works of Mickiewicz like *Pan Tadeusz* may also have been known to them. The other major Irish Romantic narrativist was the Young Ireland revolutionary John Mitchel, equally a product of those un-Irish figures Carlyle and Herder, but one who argued the nationalist morality-tale with all the zeal of a Presbyterian convert. Mitchel is today remembered for his *Jail Journal*, but his other narratives of Irish history compel attention. His history both responded to and helped to create the Irish emigrant consciousness of a national story from which England, cruel stepmother, had written them out.[13]

By the time of Mitchel's death in 1875, the story of Ireland had emerged from myriad retellings in its accepted narrative form. I have used the phrase 'cruel stepmother', as well as 'wonder-tale'; discussing Irish nationalist myths evokes that great organiser of narrative themes, the Russian structuralist Vladimir Propp. In *The Morphology of the Folk-tale* Propp argued his way through to certain basic conclusions about the function of fairy tales, stressing the limitation and the repetitive form of their functions. Literary critics like Frederic Jameson have applied Propp's ideas to classic fictions,[14] but the classic tales of Irish history also uncannily conform to the functions which he rigidly spelt out. One can do a Jameson with the Norman invasion, with the story of Parnell or with Hugh O'Neill's resistance to the Elizabethan state. Here is the latter example, mapped against Propp's first nine functions:

1: *'One of the members of a family absents himself from home'*: O'Neill is sent from Ulster to be brought up at the English court.
2: *'An interdiction is addressed to the hero'*: O'Neill is made to swear fealty to the Queen.
3: *'The interdiction is violated'*: O'Neill makes a bid for overlordship in Ulster.
4: *'The villain makes an attempt at reconnaissance'*: Sir Henry Bagenal is repulsed at the battle of the Yellow Ford.

5:    'The villain recieves information about his victim': Bagenal suborns local
      chieftains.
6:    'The villain attempts to deceive his victim in order to take possession of him
      or of his belongings': the news of the Queen's death is withheld from
      O'Neill.
7:    'The victim submits to deception and thereby unwittingly helps his enemy':
      O'Neill signs the Treaty of Mellifont.
8:    'The villain causes harm or injury to a member of the family': Red Hugh
      O'Donnell is poisoned by English agents.
9:    'Misfortune or lack is made known; the hero is allowed to go or he is
      despatched; the hero leaves home': the Flight of the Earls.

One could go on, but this kind of thing is addictive: Propp's narrative modes
and functions lend themselves neatly to the ur-stories of the Irish national
history. In the fairy-tale form, of course, the hero reaches Function 15 ('led to
the whereabouts of an object or search') or even Function 19 ('The hero
returns'), whereas in the Stories of Ireland these last happy stages did not
happen to O'Neill, or O'Connell, or Parnell, or Hibernia herself. Still less did
they ever attain Function 31, 'The hero is married and ascends the throne'.
(Parnell's Home Rule story, alas, was the only one that ended with a wedding,
at Steyning Registry Office, and that was shortly followed by a funeral.) The
point of the Story of Ireland as retailed in classic form was, in fact, that though
all the elements were there (villains, heroes, helpers, donors), it had not yet
reached its ending. But through omission of elements that did not suit the
fairy tale, and adherence to established narrative forms, the right ending could
be inferred.[15]

This may be illustrated by looking at the most famous book written under
the title *The Story of Ireland*, first published by A. M. Sullivan in 1867. Sullivan,
a journalist and politician from Cork, helped to create the popular Irish
concept of nationalism through his newspaper *The Nation* and his oft-
reprinted *Speeches from the Dock*. The *Speeches*, which had a constantly self-
renewing and expanding publishing history, are themselves a narrative of Irish
history described purely from the vantage of high-souled rebels, all of independent means (something Sullivan heavily emphasises, presumably to indicate their altruism rather than to establish their *couche sociale*). In *The Story
of Ireland*, written (he said) 'hand to mouth . . . with printers like wolves at my
heels for copy',[16] Sullivan produced one of the great best-sellers of all (Irish)
time, rapidly shifting 50,000 copies and going into twenty-five editions within
twenty years. It is worth dwelling on this text, not only because of its huge
influence, but because it best encapsulates the formalities, motifs, elisions,
parallelism and – of course – gaps that characterise the story. Sullivan
defended his decision to present a narrative based on 'chief events', 'easily

comprehended and remembered', just as the Tourist Board strategy document cited earlier excluded minor incidents or qualifications which might 'confuse and bewilder'.[17] He addressed himself to the young, the 'Irish Nation of the Future', telling them Ireland's story 'after the manner of simple storytellers'. But the sequence and emphasis were really aimed at a far wider target. The central theme was established from the beginning – Ireland as the Isle of Destiny, invaded from Spain by Milesians (and thus implicitly linked from its origins to Catholic Europe). Archaeology was used to buttress claims of rule by accomplished sovereigns from about 1500 BC – 'liberal patrons of art, science and commerce', who instituted orders of chivalry and 'regularly convened parliaments'.[18] From the beginning of her history, in other words, Ireland had known legitimate independence, equal status with other European nations, the capacity for self-government: Home Rule 3,000 years *avant la lettre*. Sullivan's mercilessly present-minded preoccupation drives on through Christianity, accomplished peacefully in Ireland alone: Catholicism had remained unchanged since St Patrick; enforced emigration originated with St Columba (conforming to Propp's first Function).

On the story rolls, through centuries of bondage: native kings are beset by false friends, magical donors, renegade relations; 'national unity' is forever dangled as the object of the quest, and as often, cruelly removed; justice, of a sort, is searched for in every narrative twist. Despite 'the innate virtue and morality of the Irish national character',[19] the Irish kings *deserved* the Norman invasion because of their factiousness; however, the Irish nation retains moral advantage even in adversity. 'It is a singular fact – one which no historian can avoid noting – that every one of the principal actors on the English side in the eventful episode of the first Anglo-Norman Invasion ended life violently, or under most painful circumstances.'[20] Nevertheless, the English won dominion because for all their faults they were nationally minded: even the villain of the story, Cromwell, 'a despot, a bigot and a canting hypocrite, was a thorough nationalist as an Englishman'. And where an Irish hero nearly won – as with Hugh O'Neill – it was as reward for demonstrating his patriotism and commitment to 'national independence and freedom', which is the point of the story. Thus in the seventeenth century Irish exiles organised revolutionary cells 'in the design of returning and liberating their native land' (Propp's twentieth Function). The evidence adduced was garnered from the early nineteenth-century treasure-house of Irish Romanticism: Tom Moore's historical ballads, Samuel Ferguson's bardic fantasies, and the writings of John Mitchel.

There are high points in Sullivan's narrative: in 1641, the Irish unite at last in a bloodless rising against the oppressor and the Ulster Protestant plantation vanishes 'like the baseless fabric of a vision' (perhaps the most fantastical element of all in this fairy-tale). However, with the advent of James II, the Irish fall foul of Propp's twenty-fourth Function – 'A false hero presents unfounded

claims'. Loyalty to the Stuarts condemns them to suffer through the eighteenth century 'an agony the most awful, the most prolonged, of any recorded
on the blotted page of human suffering'.[21] Grattan's Parliament, another false
dawn, precedes the betrayal of the Union and the selling into bondage. 'In cru-
elties of oppression endured, Ireland is like no other country in the world.'[22]

Mickiewicz would have disagreed, and in fact thirty years earlier had used
exactly the same language to equate the story of Poland with the story of the
crucifixion and resurrection. With Sullivan too, nation becomes religion. 'It
could be no human faith that, after such a crucifixion and burial, could thus
arise glorious and immortal! This triumph, the greatest, has been Ireland's;
and God, in His own good time, will assuredly give her the token of victory!'
The Story ends for the moment in the year of publication, 1867, with the failed
Fenian Rising, a hopeless skirmish in a snowy wood.[23] Sacrifice, we are explicitly told a half-century before Patrick Pearse, will redeem the nation's soul.[24]
Moreover, Ireland's historical destiny was to export virtue back to England,
where family life, Sullivan airily remarked, was 'one black catalogue of mur-
dering, wife-beating and infant-choking'. Most importantly, the Story of
Ireland must not be absorbed into England's corrupt narrative, substituting
'her history of falsehood, rapine and cruelty for ours of faithfulness, noble
endurance and morality – giving us the bloodstained memoirs of her land and
sea robbers in place of the glorious biographies of our patriots and our
saints'.[25]

Sullivan's book constructed (often by careful exclusion) the accepted Irish
national memory, and it was the kind of memory which, in Michel de Certeau's
phrase, 'is linked to the expectation that something alien to the present will or
must occur'.[26] In so doing it supplied the canon for Irish history as taught for
generations by the Christian Brothers, and it was followed by a rash of
volumes under variations of the title *The Story of Ireland*, a title which must
have been thought to guarantee financial success. Emily Lawless's and Justin
MacCarthy's *Stories*, as well as countless others under less barefacedly imita-
tive titles, used Sullivan's structure though often – significantly – fitting the
tale into a series of 'stories of the nations' which carried a distinctly imperial
message. Overall, though, the story conformed: it began with Mediterranean
origin-myths and proceeded to the advent of Home Rule via Christianity and
suffering, asserting moral authority over debased England. Determinism was
explicit: thus Justin MacCarthy, in his Story of Ireland, often links the narrative with remarks such as: 'Then there came about an event so common in the
history of nationalities that any intelligent reader might be able to anticipate
it.'[27] (Any reader of Propp, at least.) The formula brilliantly popularised by
Sullivan from 1867 created the terms learned by the succeeding generation.
And this was not only the generation which lived through the rise of Home
Rule, and the assertion of a popular nationalist culture in Catholic Ireland. It

was also the generation when the foundations were laid for an Irish cultural revival using the sources of ancient Irish history and literature, which carried their own highly charged narrative forms.

This development was facilitated by educational developments still not fully analysed and too often generalised about, especially if we believe, with Ernest Gellner, that socialised education lies at the heart of nationalism. Certainly in the fifty years following the publication of Sullivan's *Story of Ireland* an intermediate education system was introduced which subsidised Catholic education; the Irish language entered the primary and secondary curriculum; the Royal University became the National University, with a specifically Catholic stamp; and the personnel of the Irish civil service increased tenfold.[28]

Though the preoccupation with the ancient Irish past went back to the end of the eighteenth century,[29] the popularisation of it began in the 1860s, often through the agency of the generation which succeeded the circle round Ferguson on the Unionist side, and Mitchel's Young Irelanders on the other. Though their politics may have been different, the logic of their narrative was curiously similar. Ferguson's wife, for instance, wrote *The Story of the Irish Since the Conquest* to point a Unionist moral, but the narrative form she used, and the poetic inspirations which she built into the story, helped to create a powerful sense of national destiny and nationalist *amour-propre*.[30] It is at this intersection that we encounter the apprentice littérateurs of the mid-1880s, George Russell (who would re-christen himself by the Gnostic symbol, Æ), and his friend William Butler Yeats.

Æ wrote:

> Every Irishman forms some vague ideal of his country born from his reading of history, and from contemporary politics, or from an imaginative intuition; and this Ireland in the mind is not the actual Ireland which kindles his enthusiasm. For this he works and makes sacrifices; but . . . the ideal remains vague . . . . To reveal Ireland in clear or beautiful light, to create the Ireland in the heart is the province of national literature.[31]

In this self-conscious process of actually realising Ireland, writers like Æ and Yeats would help create a school of reinvented national literature, drawing heavily on the myths and beliefs of ancient Ireland. Their prophet was Standish James O'Grady.

O'Grady's work got off to a rocky start in the late 1870s, but for the literary avant-garde of the next decade it became canonical. Æ and Yeats knew, and said, that legends as symbols were more potent than historical truths (which from their point of view was just as well). In fact O'Grady – Unionist, Carlylean, anti-democratic, at once scourge and champion of the landlord classes – was equally aware of the transforming power of the imagination, being obsessed by what he called (100 years before Homi Bhabha) 'the national narrative'. In his bardic histories of early Ireland, published in 1878 and 1880, he put it into the most arresting and imaginative shape he could: actually confronting the question of narrative modes and national consciousness, discussing the different strategies (annalistic, anecdotal, all-inclusive) and rejecting them for his own poetic version. In his first volume, the *Heroic Period*, he attempted to recreate a bardic history from the material reassembled by scholars earlier in the century, and to do this by using archaeological insights and poetic vision. The point was to recreate the heroic age, recognising (like Propp) that 'all the great permanent relations of life are the same'. The influence of that unrecognised founding-father of Irish national rhetoric, Thomas Carlyle, is stamped upon this epiphanic history as on Mitchel's, twenty years before.[32]

Early Irish history, O'Grady maintained, was bardic invention and should be appreciated as the imaginative and psychological record of a nation – its wished-for history, made magically coherent. A brutal Irish friend remarked that O'Grady 'did very well considering that all the materials in his history were lost in the Flood'.[33] But the salvaged elements were familiar from the *Transactions of the Ossianic Society*, or even from Lady Ferguson, though their composition dates were assumed to be much earlier than is now thought to be the case.[34] O'Grady assembled them into a series of visionary epiphanies, Pre-Raphaelite in clarity and detail, depicting 'life' through exact, tiny details about buildings, decorations, dress, stressing a common culture in the pre-materialist age, and giving the bard a status which late nineteenth-century intellectuals must bitterly have envied.

As usual there was a present-minded note as well: pre-Christian Ulster (Ulla) was described as 'the black country . . . a people altogether given up to the making of weapons and armour, where the sound of the hammer and the husky voice of the bellows were for ever heard',[35] which must owe more to Harland and Wolff than the *Tain* saga. This also bears out a feature of other, more obviously nationalist, writing: the Story of Ulster does not quite fit, yet it does not have a narrative myth of its own. It illustrates the point made by Hugh Seton-Watson, Norman Davies and many others about nationalism in eastern Europe: that states and nations need not neatly overlap. Ulster remained awkward. It was in the generation just after O'Grady, starting with the Home Rule crises of the 1880s and 1890s, that the idea of an 'Ulsterman' and 'Ulsterwoman' began to be marketed, using elements of the nationalist conception to argue against the assumptions of separatist, Catholic nationalism. For Ulster the myth was regional and historical (looking back to Pictish origins as well as the Walls of Derry). But in the process Ulster also claimed a distinctive Irishness, Protestant, industrious and imperial-minded as it was.[36] This would be soldered into imperial Britishness by anti-Home Rule rhetoric, and by the bonding process of war; but even before then, it could not be assimilated into the Irish Story as created by Sullivan and company (hence Sullivan's belief that the plantation somehow vanished in 1641).

O'Grady, in fact, thought his kind of history could make the imperial, anti-Home Rule case too. But also, like a true Romantic, he believed that the essence of history was revealed in epic poetry; the development of the critical spirit, demanding formal perfection and consistency, had smoothed away the reality of history. He would restore the colour and the vehemence.[37] He would also (willingly or not) present a self-validating dynamic of decline, renewal and regeneration. The present-minded argument is there throughout (Cuchulain visits Dublin, looks in shop windows, and rails against the cash nexus);[38] but essentially O'Grady tried to restore to the Irish their mythological pedigree.[39] The story he told, therefore, presented – just as Sullivan had done – the riches of an Irish narrative posited against the poverty of an English narrative. Nationalists would use this to present the Irish Unionist world-view as impoverished and restricted, whereas unionists would see their nation as a broader identification, not a narrower one, based on a grander imperial narrative, and a story of defence of hearth, home and sea-coasts against marauding Catholics, at home and abroad.

O'Grady really wanted to revive the leadership classes of Irish life, who had lost their spirit, and whom he attacked in savage polemic at this very time. His enemy was Gladstonian democracy and its allies, the Catholic Church triumphant and the Home Rule Party; he wanted to head off modern nationalism and revive feudal values (including fealty to a king of England). But these were not the priorities of the literary generation who (like Æ) explored Ireland's holy places with O'Grady's volumes as their vade mecum, who put themselves (as Maud Gonne did) under the occult protection of gods like Lugh, or who assembled at Tara to prevent the local farmer from allowing the British Israelites to excavate it in search of the Ark of the Covenant.[40] From the mid-1880s (not, as Yeats would later have it, after the fall of Parnell in 1891) literary societies were meeting in Dublin and invoking O'Grady, but they were distinctly advanced-nationalist in their politics. In Yeats's memoirs, written as a heroic frieze, O'Grady is immobilised as a spiritual father-figure,[41] calling the Irish to their past and releasing those buried warriors. The side of O'Grady that warned (in 1882) that Irish nationalist politics would end in 'anarchy and civil war . . . [and] a shabby sordid Irish republic, ruled by corrupt politicians and the ignoble rich' was left aside. His preoccupation with Parnell helped iconise that lost leader as sacrificial redeemer. His followers used material from O'Grady's Story, but filtered it through the ideology of A. M. Sullivan's.

Meanwhile in 1893, the year the second Home Rule Bill passed the Commons (but was thrown out by the Lords), O'Grady retaliated with a book called . . . The Story of Ireland.[42] The familiar title is not accidental. Like

O'Sullivan's, the book was addressed to youth; like O'Sullivan's, it was a work of passion and colour. But it was written directly against O'Sullivan and the whole school of nationalism then apparently coming into its own. It begins, traditionally, with the Milesian invasions, and ends more idiosyncratically with O'Grady's memories of the recently deceased Parnell: gods, heroes and saints succeed each other in the early chapters. But there is a subversive undertow. Modern sectarian or political divisions are read backwards: Catholic and Protestant cultures are interpreted as Christian saints versus ancient pagans. The saints represent 'a lack of straightforward, bold and honest dealing, which afterwards became a national vice, so that many of our great saints were also great liars, and fell under the just scorn and contempt of those who had no religion at all but simply preserved the old instinctive Pagan abhorrence of falsehood and doubledealing'.

O'Grady's scheme could hardly have been clearer; it is unsurprising to read on and discover that the Irish deserved all they got in the Viking invasions. Indeed 'Ireland, as distinguished from the monks, rather welcomed than withstood the Norsemen' – reliable, fair-minded (and fair-haired), honest and sincere.[43] The Norman Conquest 'ought to have been a great blessing [to the Irish] as it had been to the Saxons';[44] King John *was* a good king; Norman barons and Irish chieftains were brothers under the skin, affectionately sharing beds with each other after signing peace treaties; 'Ireland' liked the Tudors. Sullivan's villain, Oliver Cromwell, appears here as merry, animated, decisive, charismatic, like the best kind of pagan – 'a most sagacious ruler and a most valiant fighter', disciplining his soldiers, preventing looting, trying to discuss religion with the Dublin Catholics who

> for one reason or another, probably bad reasons, frequented his rude and simple court . . . . Bold as the prophecy may be, I predict the coming of a day when his memory will be dearer to Ireland than that of the greatest Irish worthy that we can furnish down to date. He was, to go no further, the first fighting man who waged war in Ireland with any approximation to civilised methods.[45]

It is hard to exaggerate the offensiveness of this revisionist view, but O'Grady airily ploughed on with his narrative *tour de force*: providing *inter alia* a memorably surreal description of James II's flight across Ireland,[46] and a brilliant image of *nouveau* landowners in the eighteenth century occasionally entering a tenant's cabin and 'seeing a ghost' – the supplanted former owner, or his heir, being deferentially entertained. The picture of the nineteenth century is largely predictable – the Anglo-Irish 'dropping out of our historical saga', displaced by the 'fraudulent and theatrical' O'Connell. But the O'Grady view of Parnell anticipates that of Paul Bew: 'I think he had planned out ways and means of preserving the Irish gentry, not at the cost of the Irish peasant but at the cost of the imperial Treasury, also that he intended to manoeuvre so as to have Ulster on his side not at his flank.'[47] In this, as in much else, O'Grady's *Story of Ireland* not only reflected the conditions of the early 1890s – the second Home Rule Bill and the era of constructive unionism – but also completed his own expiation for the unintended encouragement which his early work had given to nationalism.[48] It tried – belatedly – to build Ulster into the story of Irish lost leadership. Thus it changed the characters in the story in order to suggest a different moral and even a different ending, and to conform to Herder's notion of the nation as spiritual entity.

Despite the spectacular political incorrectness of O'Grady's real opinions, the influence of his impressionist and prophetic history lay behind the ideas of Yeats, Æ and others as they rediscovered their national 'story' in the 1890s. Moreover, his apocalyptic vision and his rediscovery of heroic myth interacted potently with the currents of occultism and mysticism which also characterised their circle (and the age). As the millennium approached, Yeats and his circle became preoccupied by a seductive thought: if Irish history was a 'story', and its beginnings and middle were – as they thought – well established: what about its end? By the late 1890s, they had become convinced that a millennial 'ending' was just round the corner. Horoscopes, the French illuminati tradition, Theosophy, the Order of the Golden Dawn and the Celtic propaganda of Fiona MacLeod had much to do with this; but so, in the Irish context, had the notion of history as a story.

The people thus affected were an identifiable group, who had usually graduated from Protestant bourgeois backgrounds via the avant-garde mill to claiming Celtic identity through occult affinities: they required a visionary answer to the confusion left by Parnell's collapsed enterprise. (Again, there are close parallels with Polish nationalists, who were often from mixed or recently assimilated backgrounds and needed a certain kind of story for self-realisation.) Particularly in Æ's personal religion, figures from the Irish past created by O'Grady were built into a structure of promised revelations and a promised liberation. In his writings and painting, Æ peopled the Irish landscape with prophetic avatars, with Gonne, Yeats and Fiona MacLeod, he frantically worked on organising an Order of Celtic Mysteries, as midwife to the new age. Scots Celticists like MacLeod and English Celtic-wannabes like Lionel Johnson added a flavour of romantic Jacobitism, which chimed perfectly with the Sullivan *Story of Ireland*.

In this millennial surge towards the end of history, two further inputs need to be noted. One was the highly selective approach to Irish folk-tales and their deconstruction,[49] pioneered by Yeats; through his eyes, many of these tales could be read as exemplary narratives of Irish history. A good example is 'Kidnapped' in *The Celtic Twilight*, supposedly a folk-tale about a boy whose mother is taken by the fairies (in a nice Oedipal reversal) and who goes in search of her. He finds her in a cellar in Glasgow, working hard and well fed. She offers him a reunion dinner, but he refuses, knowing it is fairy food designed to entrap him; and he returns, hungry but free, to Sligo. It does not take Vladimir Propp to read this as a metaphor for rejecting British materialism in favour of austere commitment to one's native place. The other input was the millennial influence of advanced Irish nationalism in the 1890s, epitomised by the Irish Republican Brotherhood (IRB) or Fenian movement. For in the late 1890s the IRB, and its offshoot the Irish National Alliance (INA) to which Yeats and Gonne were affiliated, were also expecting the millennium, their attention centred on their commemoration of the 1798 Rising and their hopes of international unrest in South Africa. The cleansing war which Yeats divined in Irish folk prophecy, his poetic visions of the stars being blown about the sky, were reinforced by the discussions with Irish nationalist cabals in rooms off Chancery Lane. The arguments were underpinned by the belief held, in different ways, by A. M. Sullivan and Standish O'Grady, and reiterated in their *Stories* – that Ireland's special idealism would show the rest of the world the way. The story was reaching its end.[50]

As it happened, when the actual millennium came in 1900, apocalypse stayed away. The 'Story' as laid down by both Sullivan and O'Grady, and the uniquely influential generation of literary power-brokers reared by them, presumed an ending round about 1900, but the millennial year came and went without writing the final page. Even the Boer War, important in many other ways for Irish history, failed to provide the expected final severance. And Yeats, whose poetry and polemic in the 1880s and 1890s had done so much to popularise the idea of an individual national culture, was beginning to run into trouble with the guardians of nationalist probity. In the 1890s he had written of Ireland as a holy land, with an identity married to rock and hill, preserved in the stories and beliefs of the people. But just as the act of prophecy failed him, his own art began to run counter to the suppositions both of middle-class morality and of nationalist piety.

In the theatre movement which preoccupied him for ten years from the turn of the century, Yeats expressed his developing view of Irish culture. Initially he was aided and abetted by the scandalous novelist George Moore, and Moore wrote an account of these years (*Hail and Farewell*), which provides another version of the Story of Ireland. This was written to reverse the St Patrick story: the hero is sent back to Ireland to *rescue* it from Christianity. Yeats, too, was becoming bent on subversion. Significantly, the subject matter of his theatre involved all the characters reinvented by Lady Mary Ferguson, Standish O'Grady and others – Cuchulain, Deirdre, Senchan, King Guaire, and Diarmuid and Grania – interpreted in a manner that infuriated O'Grady beyond reason. But the stories of Ireland which Yeats's theatre told were more and more at odds with the received version; as time went by he used the theatre to wage war on nationalist pieties. Finally, in 1907, as the audience rioted against the presentation of Ireland in Synge's *Playboy of the Western World*, he wrote: 'I stood there watching, knowing well that I was seeing the dissolution of a school of patriotism that had held sway over my youth.'

The end of the story was not what had been expected. After 1900 it seemed that the old Home Rule version, back on the agenda, was going to provide a diminuendo closure.[51] In fact, *that* future evaporated too; in the next decade new storytellers appeared, like James Connolly, a Marxist who wanted to turn the clock back to pre-capitalism, believing (O'Grady-style) that ancient Ireland had pioneered communism. Much more influentially, Patrick Pearse would bring A. M. Sullivan's story of the Christ among nations to its own preordained ending, proving – like his Polish predecessor Cieszkowski – that Catholic messianism could coincide with insurrectionary nationalism, and even provide it with a self-fulfilling narrative. (As in Poland, it could also embrace anti-Semitism as a cohering element.) The First World War provided the opportunity for a Fenian insurrection, as it would also reinforce Ulster's myth of imperial blood-brotherhood. In Catholic Ireland, after the Rising of 1916, the Sullivan Story would predominate: Sinn Féin tracts of 1917 refer to the establishment of Ireland as the Kingdom of God, the image of perfection upon earth.[52] If the nation thus defined reflected the culture epitomised by the Story of Ireland, its boundary had to stop at the six-county border. And it did.

Both the expected future of all-Ireland Home Rule, achieved constitutionally, and the wilder alternatives would be forgotten – especially those dreamt up by a subversive intelligentsia of *déclassé* Protestants. As it turned out, the story was not ended by the cultural revivalists' New Age; nor by the Home Rulers' old one; nor even – though the unexpected class reversals of the revolutionary period deserve more attention than they have received – by the Sinn Féin Republic. It remains no less important to recapture what the future looked like to the opinion-makers up to about 1912 – even though, if Anthony Smith is right in seeing nationalism as a strategy for solving the crisis of an intelligentsia, that strategy signally failed to solve the various crises of the *fin-de-siècle* generation. As for the accepted story, in a partly independent Ireland, determinism ruled – the wonder-tale shadowed out by Sullivan, in which a virtuous Ireland finally reached the desired destination, thus fulfilling the final function delineated by Vladimir Propp. As late as the 1930s de Valera was reiterating that 'the Irish, stressing spiritual values rather than material values, have been fitted in a special manner for helping to save western civilization'.[53]

Much of this rhetoric was an unconscious attempt to explain dilemmas which might have been approached from other directions – as Irish historians have recently tried to do. Still, from unexpected quarters, we sometimes hear the old insistence on the seamlessness of the web of national narrative: some unlikely fellow-travellers have turned to a venerable form of Irish nationalism as a refuge from their ideological disorientations (or an emotional investment which may pay career dividends). This can lead to an attack upon the concepts of liberalism and pluralism as un-national, indeed un-Irish; the words 'Irish community' and 'Irish culture' are sometimes used to refer to one tradition alone. Political correctness demands chronological elision.[54] This often posits a highly questionable version of the order in which things happened.[55] It can also impose a strangely limited notion of state, nation, allegiance and identity. It is often asserted that modern cultural limitations have made us forget our history; with Irish history, the problem may be that we remember too limited a version. Renan pointed out long ago that creating a nation involves getting one's history wrong;[56] but those who have subsequently tried to rearrange the narrative are – interestingly – attacked in terms that are sometimes both religious and racial.[57]

However, history shows that Irish people can reinterpret their experience away from supposedly preordained patterns and endings; and I think sub-versive history-writing has played its part in this. Irish historical interpretation has too often been cramped into a strict literary mode; the narrative drive has ruthlessly eroded awkward elisions. There *are* ascertainable facts and progres-sions, often unexpected; there are other models, tales within tales, which might allow more room for alternative truths and uncomfortable specula-tions.[58] There is a need for a historical strategy that recaptures uncertainties and thereby unlocks contemporary mentalities; for instance, group biography, or local history, can recreate realities that are not forced into episodes in the preordained national narrative. One can do it, I think, by looking at the condi-tioning and expectations of those writers and readers of the Story of Ireland surveyed here. Not least A. M. Sullivan, author of the ur-Story, who finally came to England (home of wife-murderers and infant-chokers) as a Home Rule MP. He found he rather liked it, surprised his colleagues by expatiating on the virtues of the British character, and finally admitted that he 'looked back with intense regret upon the unreasoning hatred in which I have grown up'.[59] So he wrote another book, called *New Ireland*, which preached the national story in terms which Polish nationalists would call 'Conciliationist'. But it was too late; nobody read it.

Notes

Another version of this essay has been published by Oxford University Press as *The Story of Ireland* (1995).

1 Quoted in Fintan O'Toole, *Black Hole, Green Card: the Disappearance of Ireland* (Dublin, 1994), p. 33.
2 'Tourists in our own land', in O'Toole, *Black Hole, Green Card*.
3 For example, P. Ricoeur, *Time and Narrative,* trans. K. Mclaughlin and D. Pellamer (London, 1984–88); H. White, *Metahistory: the Historical Imagination in Nineteenth-Century Europe* (Baltimore, 1973); H. White, 'The historical text as literary artefact', in

R. H. Canary and H. Kozicki (eds), *The Writing of History: Literary Form and Historical Understanding* (Milwaukee, 1978); F. Jameson, *The Political Unconscious: Narrative as a Socially Symbolic Act* (London, 1981); N. Frye, *The Secular Scripture* (Cambridge, Mass., 1976); M. de Certeau, *The Practice of Everyday Life*, trans. S. Randall (London, 1984), esp. ch. 6, 'Storytime'.

4 Cf. P. Ricoeur, 'Personal identity and narrative identity', in *Oneself as Another,* trans. K. Blaney (London, 1992), p. 114n.: 'Do we not consider human lives to be more readable when they have been interpreted in terms of the stories that people tell about them? And are not these life stories in turn made more intelligible when the narrative models of plots – borrowed from history or from fiction (drama or novel) – are applied to them? It therefore seems plausible to take the following chain of assertions as valid: self-understanding is an interpretation; interpretation of the self, in turn, finds in the narrative, among other signs and symbols, a privileged form of mediation; the latter borrows from history as well as from fiction, making a life story a fictional history, or, if one prefers, a historical fiction, interweaving the historiographic style of biographies with the novelistic style of imaginary autobiographies.' Also see Jameson, *The Political Unconscious*, p. 30, on how collective history is iconised into an individual life by a strategy of 'repressive simplification'.

5 Cf. Jameson, *The Political Unconscious*, p. 35. 'History is not a text, not a narrative, master or otherwise, but . . . as an absent cause it is inaccessible to us except in textual form and . . . our approach to it and to the real itself necessarily passes through its prior textualisation, its narrativisation in the political unconscious.' Also see Lynn Hunt's comments on how the historical events of the French Revolution conformed (at least in the telling) to the narrative conventions of comedy, romance and tragedy in succession: *Politics, Culture and Class in the French Revolution* (Berkeley, 1984).

6 For another aspect of this see C. Brennan Harvey, *Contemporary Irish Traditional Narrative: the English Language Tradition* (Oxford, 1992).

7 R. Mac Searraigh Gordon, *Fainne an Lae*, 24 September 1898.

8 H. K. Bhabha (ed.), *Nation and Narration* (London, 1990).

9 Cf. C. Toibin, 'Martyrs and metaphors', in D. Bolger (ed.), *Letters from the New Island* (Dublin, 1991), where Irish history is visualised as a series of short stories.

10 A process surveyed in C. O'Halloran, 'Golden ages and barbarous nations: antiquarian debate on the Celtic past in Ireland and Scotland in the eighteenth century', unpublished Ph.D. thesis (Cambridge, 1991).

11 See my 'History and the Irish Question', in *Paddy and Mr Punch: Connections in Irish and English History* (London, 1993).

12 See J. A. Spence, 'The philosophy of Irish toryism, 1813–52: a study of reactions to liberal reformism in the generation between the First Reform Act and the Famine, with especial reference to expressions of national feeling among the Protestant Ascendancy', unpublished Ph.D. thesis (London, 1991).

13 Other influential Mitchel titles include *The Last Conquest of Ireland (Perhaps)* (New York, 1860) and a two-volume *History of Ireland from the Treaty of Limerick to the Present Time* (Dublin, 1869).

14 See Jameson's application of Propp to Stendhal's *La Chartreuse de Parme* in *The Political Unconscious*, pp. 119–21. Also see his discussion of Lévi-Strauss's critique of Propp on the grounds of 'empiricism' and his own criticism that the Propp approach is not sufficiently 'historicised'.

15 Cf. V. Propp, *The Morphology of the Folk-tale*, trans. L. Scott (Bloomington, 1958), 'The Functions of Dramatis Personae, XXXI': 'Just as cloth can be measured with a yardstick to determine its length, tales may be measured by [my] scheme and thereby defined . . . the problem of kinship of tales, the problem of themes and variants, thanks to this, may receive a new solution.'

16 Quoted in R. Moran, 'Alexander Martin Sullivan (1829–1884) and Irish cultural nation-
     alism', unpublished MA thesis (University of Cork, 1993), p. 31.
17 A. M. Sullivan, *The Story of Ireland*, 25th edn (London, 1888), p. 229.
18 *Ibid.*, p. 22.
19 *Ibid.*, p. 107.
20 *Ibid.*, p. 134.
21 *Ibid.*, p. 477.
22 *Ibid.*, p. 565.
23 Deliberately paralleled with the death of Brian Boru at Clontarf, or the Earl of
     Desmond's last resistance in Munster, in the manner of Sullivan's telling.
24 Sullivan's last paragraph runs as follows: 'Victory must be with her. Already it is with
     her. Other nations have bowed to the yoke of conquest, and been wiped out from
     history. Other people have given up the faith of their fathers for a mess of pottage: as
     if there were nothing nobler in man's destiny than to feed, and sleep, and die. But
     Ireland, after centuries of suffering and sacrifice such as have tried no other nation in
     the world, has successfully, proudly, gloriously, defended and retained her life, her
     faith, her nationality. Well may her children, proclaiming aloud that "there is a God in
     Israel", look forward to a serene and happy future, beyond the tearful clouds of this
     troubled present. Assuredly a people who have survived so much, resisted so much,
     retained so much, are destined to receive the rich reward of such devotion, such con-
     stancy, such heroism' (Sullivan, *The Story of Ireland*, p. 582).
25 See *The Nation*, 27 April 1872 and 24 March 1868. T. D. Sullivan's *Story of England*
     (Dublin, 1872) enshrined this view. The Christian Brothers adopted this version of Irish
     history, explored by Barry Coldrey in *Faith and Fatherland: the Christian Brothers and
     the Development of Irish Nationalism 1838–1921* (Dublin, 1988) and brilliantly used by
     Conor Cruise O'Brien in *Ancestral Voices: Religion and Nationalism in Ireland* (Dublin,
     1994).
26 De Certeau, *The Practice of Everyday Life*, pp. 86–7: 'Far from being the reliquary or
     trash-can of the past it sustains itself by *believing* in the existence of possibilities and
     by vigilantly awaiting them, constantly on the watch for their appearance.'
27 J. MacCarthy, *Ireland and her Story* (London, 1903).
28 M. Goldring, *Pleasant the Scholar's Life: Irish Intellectuals and the Construction of the
     Nation State* (London, 1993), p. 172.
29 See 'The rediscovery of the Irish past', in V. Mercier, *Modern Irish Literature: Sources
     and Founders* (Oxford, 1994). The *Revue Celtique* was founded in 1870. However,
     stories such as 'Deirdre' were in circulation, through Theophilus O'Flanagan in the
     Transactions of the Gaelic Society, as early as 1808. This was much used by Douglas
     Hyde in his *Literary History of Ireland* (London, 1899), which was more accessible to
     many of the popularists of the Revival.
30 At this point of self-education, if not at many others, Irish nationalism fits easily into
     the 'Ruritanian' model proposed by Gellner in *Nations and Nationalism* (Oxford, 1983),
     p. 57.
31 Goldring, *Pleasant the Scholar's Life*, p. 27.
32 Right down to explosive one-word chapter titles, and Old-Testament excoriations.
33 Lord Morris, quoted in H. A. O'Grady, *Standish James O'Grady: the Man and the Writer*
     (Dublin, 1929), p. 36.
34 See D. Ó Corráin, 'Early Ireland: directions and re-directions', in *Bullán*, 1:2 (Autumn
     1994). Thurneysen thinks the *Tain* was composed in the eighth century and written
     down in the ninth; Ó Corráin thinks it originated in the ninth.
35 S. J. O'Grady, *History of Ireland: Heroic Period* (Dublin), 1878, p. 110.
36 See I. McBride, 'Ulster and the British Problem', in R. English and G. Walker (eds),
     Unionism in Modern Ireland: New Perspectives on Politics and Culture (London, 1996).

37   See S. J. O'Grady, *Cuculain and his Contemporaries* (London, 1880), p. 65. O'Grady
     even tried to construct a chronology, starting in 2379 BC, based on the 'mythological
     record of the bards', using Keating, and ending with Cuchulain's death in AD 9.

38   The hero becomes 'dejected when he looked upon the people, so small were they, and
     so pale and ignoble, both in appearance and behaviour; and also when he saw the
     extreme poverty of the poor and the hungry eager crowds seeking what he knew not'.
     Ibid., pp. 290–1.

39   'The account which a nation renders of itself must, and always does, stand at the head
     of every history.' *Ibid.*, p. 119.

40   For a contemporary version of this imbroglio see 'The British Israelites at Tara', in
     H. Butler, *The Sub-Prefect Should Have Held His Tongue*, ed. R. F. Foster (London,
     1990), pp. 68–72.

41   See also 'A general introduction to my work', in E. Callan, *Yeats on Yeats: the Last
     Introductions and the 'Dublin' Edition* (Dublin, 1981), and 'How I became a writer', in
     The Listener, 4 August 1938, and in J. P. Frayne (ed.), *Uncollected Prose by W. B. Yeats*,
     2 vols (London, 1970–75). The emphasis is even stronger in these late writings, after
     O'Grady's death.

42   It was dated 1894, but copies were in circulation in December 1893.

43   S. J. O'Grady, *The Story of Ireland* (London, 1894), p. 78. They were probably well
     thonged, too. 'A young, handsome Norseman, dressed in his gala attire for an assem-
     bly, and bearing the splendid weapons which they made in those lands, was as beauti-
     ful a spectacle as Europe anywhere produced at this time' (p. 81).

44   *Ibid.*, p. 98.

45   *Ibid.*, pp. 132–3. O'Grady claimed that the victims at Drogheda were combatants, given
     due warning; the Protector was ruthless but fair, and his soldiers (like good Protestants)
     'paid for provisions and everything they got at market rates' (p. 138). Cromwell is com-
     pared vitriolically to the Papal nuncio Rinnuccini, a 'jocose forger and ecclesiastical
     liar' (p. 140).

46   In the style of a Carlylean wonder-tale, with an Irish twist. 'He ran past Dublin. Lady
     Tyrconnel, from the Castle battlements, cried out to him: "Is that you, James? Where
     is your army from you? Wouldn't you turn in, James, and have some lunch?' But James
     only waved the back of his royal hand, as much as to say, "No more now, dear lady, I'll
     tell you about it at Versailles, if I ever get there", and never stopped running . . . By day
     and by night, under the sun and under the moon and stars, without closing an eye or
     taking an honest meal, breaking the bridges behind him, placing guards at every defen-
     sible point along the way, through all Meath, through all Leinster, ran the last of the
     Stuarts. "I am going to France for succours", he said. "No, I am going to France to make
     a plunge for England now that this dreadful Prince of Orange is out of it." Farewell for
     ever to King James' (*ibid.*, pp. 158–9).

47   *Ibid.*, p. 211. A similar analysis is given in P. Bew, *C. S. Parnell* (Dublin, 1980).

48   W. E. H. Lecky, at more or less the same time, had to execute a parallel manoeuvre;
     see D. McCartney, *W. E. H. Lecky, Historian and Politician 1838–1903* (Dublin, 1994),
     ch. 7.

49   See J. W. Foster, *Fictions of the Irish Literary Revival: a Changeling Art* (Syracuse, 1987),
     pp. 226–7, 239–40. *The Celtic Twilight* is a key text here, and should be related to Yeats's
     occult fiction of the period.

50   R. J. Finneran, G. M. Harper and W. M. Murphy (eds), *Letters to W. B. Yeats*, I (London,
     1977): 32; also A. Denson (ed.), *Letters from Æ* (London, 1961), pp. 17–18. The process
     is discussed in my *W. B. Yeats, A Life. I: The Apprentice Mage, 1865–1914* (Oxford, 1997),
     chs. 7, 8.

51   See P. Bew, *Ideology and the Irish Question: Unionism and Irish Nationalism 1912–1916*
     (Oxford, 1994).

52 Goldring, *Pleasant the Scholar's Life*, p. 44.

53 *Ibid.*, p. 13.

54 Thus Dr Alf O'Brien at the Desmond Greaves Summer School 1994, as quoted in the *Irish Times*, 29 August 1994: 'The central theme in modern Irish history was the fact of the conquest . . . Whatever the complexity of Anglo-Irish relations in the nineteenth century (a century particularly favoured by the "revisionist" school), or the problems of Irish landlords in that period, the fact of conquest still remained. He went on to examine the basic forces which brought about that conquest and its effects on both Ireland and England.'

55 For instance, the relationship of the Treaty to Partition; or of land-tenure reform to the eclipse of constitutional nationalism.

56 E. Renan, 'What is a nation?', reprinted in Bhabha (ed.), *Nation and Narration*, p. 11.

57 Some modern critics of 'revisionism', for instance, have resurrected D. P. Moran's self-revealing assertion that those who present a contingent, pluralist version are representing the Irish as 'mongrel'. (See his attacks on the cultural agenda of Yeats and Rolleston in *The Leader*, 5 January 1901.)

58 See Foster, *Fictions*, p. 283, for Padraic Colum's *The King of Ireland's Son* as a model of national narrative.

59 Speech in House of Commons, 30 June 1876, quoted in Moran, 'Alexander Martin Sullivan'. By then, he was preaching 'free and friendly communication' between Britain and Ireland, 'leagued for purposes of mutual protection and prosperity'. These are the views he put into his late and less influential publication, *New Ireland*.

Tacitus engendered: 'Gothic feminism' and British histories, *c.* 1750–1800

Those 'imagined communities', called nations, the emergence of which Benedict Anderson traced from the late eighteenth century, were united not only by territory and political organisation, but by affinities imagined with a common past as with a present community.[1] That common past was not necessarily conceived in entirely masculine terms. Recent work on revolutionary France, on nineteenth- and twentieth-century India, and elsewhere, has illustrated ways in which conflicting definitions of national identity might focus upon representations of womanhood.[2] And Jitka Malečková has illustrated how in nineteenth- and twentieth-century eastern European societies and in Turkey, the condition of women became an index of comparison for societies contrasting their situation unfavourably with more 'developed' or 'advanced' states, and, at the same time, a means of defining a future associated either with 'tradition' or with 'progress'.[3] This essay suggests that something similar occurred in late eighteenth-century Britain. Here the continuing inequality in the partnership between England and Scotland stimulated contrasting interpretations of the history of the British nation within an elite, scholarly and masculine Scottish culture.

David McCrone, writing of Scotland, has noted the two elements within nationalist movements, 'one oriented to the past and one to the future; their task is to unite the two'.[4] Those looking to the past in this debate had to choose their 'golden age' for women from the bewildering array of national myths of origin in European historical writing, as the search for a model of political community shifted, as Martin Thom has argued, from the classical republic to the tribe.[5] Here, the choice lay between Celtic clan and Germanic tribe, between Ossian and Tacitus. Those looking to the future looked primarily to England, for the form of 'civil society', that newly coined term, most appropriate to a united and British nation, and at the place of women within such a developing and commercial nation. It was an important element in this argument that within a modernising civil society such as the British nation, the roots of moral and political community would no longer be in republic, clan or tribe, but within the private circle of the family, linking even while separating private and public worlds.[6] By 1800 both backward- and forward-looking elements were to some degree united, in a new, Whiggish, and 'Anglo-British' synthesis of a history for British women.[7]

In this essay I focus on the meanings which sections of a single text – the *Germania*, written around AD 98 by the Roman writer Tacitus – came to bear in Britain between 1760 and 1790.[8] Tacitus's description of a warlike, yet liberty-loving, free and equal people, whose young men were initiated to manhood with the gift of shield and spear, was a major source for constitutionalist myth and national history. He had also written of German women, who followed men to battle, treated their wounds, supplied them with food, and rallied their armies when in desperate straits (chs 7–8). He alluded briefly to the belief 'that there resides in women an element of holiness and a gift of prophecy', and that for that reason men 'do not scorn to ask their advice, or lightly disregard their replies' (ch. 8). He described women's responsibility for the care of house and fields, with much detail on everyday life, dress, food and housing (chs 16, 17, 22, 23). And in three short sections (chs 18–20), he analysed the structures and expectations of marriage, 'the most sacred bond of union, sanctified by mystic rites under the favour of the presiding deities of wedlock', among the early German tribes.

The appeal to Anglo-Saxon, originally Germanic, liberties from the seventeenth to the late nineteenth century has long been familiar to historians of radical politics.[9] It was central also to nineteenth-century Whig historiography.[10] It has never, however, been suggested that Tacitus's writing on Germanic women had any relevance in this context, although Samuel Kliger in his pioneering study *The Goths in England* (1952), which traced the complex history of the use of the term 'Gothic' for the history of the 'northern nations', as well as for the Anglo-Saxons, coined the term 'Gothic feminism' in recognition of the interest which many later commentators showed in 'the Germanic veneration of women' recorded by Tacitus.[11] The relationship of 'Gothic feminism' to the political and national histories of that period has hardly been explored.

This is perhaps because the sources for identifying that relationship are not familiar ones to historians of English politics. The sections of the *Germania* dealing with German women were briefly noted by a few English historians, antiquarians and polemicists who engaged in the construction of a new 'Gothic' ancestry for English liberties from the sixteenth century onwards. However, such topics aroused little interest or comment either among writers of the political opposition of the late seventeenth and early eighteenth centuries or – despite their increasing appeals to Anglo-Saxon liberties with roots in a Gothic past – among English radicals of the 1770s.[12]

In European scholarship from the sixteenth to the mid-eighteenth century, however, alternative approaches to the *Germania* could be found. To the humanist and Protestant scholars of Renaissance Germany seeking to forge a national and northern identity, the *Germania* had offered images of the purity and chastity of Germanic womanhood, and of monogamous marriage.[13] The influential German geographer Philip Clüver followed their lead. In his *Germaniae Antiquae* (1616), a commentary on the *Germania*, he identified the common roots of the Gothic and Celtic peoples as far back as Gomer, son of Japheth, one of Noah's three sons. In this account, Celts, Gauls and Germans were all one, distinct only from the Sarmatian peoples, ancestors of the Slavs. The evidence provided by Tacitus, and by many other classical commentators, could be used for all three peoples, and Clüver particularly noted Tacitus's treatment of the women of ancient Germany.[14] So too did Johann Georg Keysler, writing in Hanover in 1720.[15] Both were used by Simon Pelloutier in his widely cited *Histoire des Celtes* (1750), which identified the Celts as the original ancestors of north-west European societies. Pelloutier also made indiscriminate use of Tacitus's *Agricola* and *Germania,* and Caesar's *De Bello Gallico*, mentioning specifically the devotion of Celtic women to liberty.[16] This confusion, between Celts, Goths, Germans and Sarmatians, lasted from the early seventeenth to the late eighteenth century, with significant results for those seeking to disentangle the origins of British peoples.

In 1755, the Genevan Paul-Henri Mallet, a disciple of Montesquieu and tutor to the future King Christian VII of Denmark, published in Copenhagen his *Introduction à l'histoire de Dannemarc*, drawing extensively on this scholarship.[17] He used the *Germania*, together with a wide range of Scandinavian sources, indiscriminately for the history of the loosely defined 'northern nations' of Scandinavians, Teutons, Celts and Germans, all here given a common Gothic inheritance.[18] In his chapter on the manners of these nations, Mallet followed the *Germania* very closely on their women. He translated Tacitus's portrait of female inspiration to men at war into a system of chivalry which had its origins in the north, which was to be carried from there to the other nations of Europe, and from which derived that polite gallantry which ultimately contributed to the shaping of the modern sensibility, known in northern Europe even during the Roman empire.[19]

But if Mallet told his Gothic history partly in the polite language of an enlightened elite, his account was also contradictory. Women were, for him, channels of divine inspiration, whose supernatural powers could also become demonic. He transformed Tacitus's hints on occasional polygamy among the German tribes into the suggestion that it was not uncommon at that time for men of the northern nations to marry two or more wives. And he also introduced to a much wider public the existence of the great literature of the Norse sagas, of the death songs of Norse heroes, and the mythology of the Valkyrie, the goddesses of Valhalla. He wrote of Norse funeral ceremonies, and the burning of wives on the funeral pyres of their husbands.[20] Mallet wrote not of

a Gothic 'golden age', but of a past within which he identified both the seeds
of a future northern European pattern of modern social, political and gender
relations, and the survivals of a former barbarity. The *Introduction* was widely
known among scholars, initiating a new interest in Scandinavian literature in
Britain, and a new phase in the recovery of the medieval past by
Enlightenment historians.[21]

The debates discussed below drew upon this European tradition. They
took place among the literati of the Scottish Enlightenment, including
academics, ministers, lawyers, doctors and intellectuals from Edinburgh,
Glasgow and Aberdeen. It was an intelligentsia which had ambivalent feelings
towards the dominance of England within the Union, seeking both to identify
a Scottish role within that partnership, and to benefit from the advantages of
Anglicisation. In the late 1750s the English refusal to permit a Scottish militia
was followed by active agitation for a militia inspired by Scottish national
feeling; that agitation was, however, rapidly followed by the accession of
George III in 1760, and the coming to power of Lord Bute, with hopes for a
regime which might recognise Scottish participation.[22]

In this context a small group of the Edinburgh literati, inspired by national
sentiment and the hope of a Scottish epic, had encouraged the young
Highlander James Macpherson to publish his *Fragments of Ancient Poetry*
(1760), *Fingal* (1761) and *Temora* (1763) as the alleged works of the ancient
Celtic bard, Ossian. Modern scholarship has suggested that the Ossian phenomenon, with its European-wide cultural effects, should be understood not
as a crude forgery, but as an intervention in a continuing debate about the literature of primitive peoples, which drew on original Gaelic fragments.[23] But,
if read together with Hugh Blair's *Critical Dissertation on the Poems of Ossian*
(1763) and Macpherson's own *Introduction to the History of Great Britain and
Ireland* (1771), the poetry of Ossian can also be seen as part of an attempt to
restate the Celtic contribution to the history of British liberties and manners,
relying partly on oral history, partly on 'the only authentic literary accounts of
Scottish history . . . those of Roman authors'.[24] Following Pelloutier,
Macpherson saw the Celts as populating much of western Germany, France,
Spain and ancient Britain during the Roman Empire, and used the *Germania*
and much other classical literature as a guide to the manners not of the
Germanic or Anglo-Saxon, but of the Celtic peoples. Macpherson argued
against Mallet that the peoples of northern Germany, including Angles and
Saxons, were of mixed Celto-Sarmatian origin, and the Scandinavians dis-
tinctively Sarmatian.[25] The Scandinavian sagas illustrated the barbarism of
Anglo-Saxon ancestors, as in their treatment of women, excluded from
Valhalla in the afterlife.[26]

Like Mallet, Macpherson for the most part recreated his heroic past in
the language of the eighteenth century. Contemporaries immediately noted

the refinement of the manners and the extraordinary delicacy of sentiment that appeared in the relationships between the women and men of ancient Scotland.[27] Hugh Blair stressed that the poetry of Ossian clearly established both 'the superior excellence of the Celtic bard' and the direct contrast between Celtic and Scandinavian (or Gothic) manners:

> when we open the works of Ossian, a very different scene presents itself. There we find the fire and the enthusiasm of the most early times combined with an amazing degree of regularity and art. We find tenderness, and even delicacy of sentiment, greatly predominant over fierceness and barbarity. Our hearts are melted with the softest feelings, and at the same time elevated with the highest ideas of magnanimity, generosity and true heroism. When we turn from the poetry of Lodbrog to that of Ossian, it is like passing from a savage desert, into a fertile and cultivated country.[28]

The case against the Celtic appropriation of sensibility was stated forcefully by Thomas Percy, in 1770, in the preface to his translation of Mallet's work as *Northern Antiquities*. Percy strongly criticised Mallet and all his predecessors since Clüver for confusing Celts and Goths.[29] He amended Mallet's interpretations of Tacitus, in this context stressing that among the Germans, unlike the Celts, it was the husband who gave a dowry to his wife, and denying that polygamy had ever been common among the Germans.[30] The confusion between the manners of Celts and Goths was greatly reduced by John Pinkerton's *Dissertation on the Origin and Progress of the Scythians or Goths* (1787), which argued in the language of racial pride against an inflated Celtic legacy, and for the Gothic origins of the Picts. Contemporary doubts of the genuineness of Ossianic poetry further limited the force of the Scottish case. The notion of the unique delicacy of ancient Scottish manners was, however, to have a much longer appeal, and to contribute far more generally to the debate on the condition of women in the early stages of society.

The appeal to a 'golden age' for women in the distant European past did not in any case depend simply on Macpherson's representations of the Celtic past. Other Scottish historians indiscriminately cited Tacitus's evidence for the early peoples of the northern nations, including ancient Britons, Scots and Germans. In 1771–74 Robert Henry, an Edinburgh minister, published the first and second volumes of his *History of Great Britain*, covering the period up to 1066. It was an ambitious project, aiming at a comprehensive history of Britain as a whole, rather than of its component parts. It also incorporated thematic treatment of seven major themes, the seventh 'the history of the manners, virtues, vices, remarkable customs, language, dress, diet and diversions' of the British people. Henry paid particular attention to the condition of women in ancient Britain and Anglo-Saxon England, using Tacitus, Clüver, Pelloutier and Mallet extensively, among other sources.[31]

The historian who did most, however, to rewrite Tacitus's vision of the women of early Germany for his own age was the Edinburgh historian, journalist, and admirer of Tacitus, Gilbert Stuart.[32] Stuart, who founded the *Edinburgh Magazine and Review* in 1773, reviewed Henry's work in 1774 harshly, criticising his failure to investigate those Anglo-Saxon laws favourable to the condition of women.[33] In Stuart's own later work, *A View of Society in Europe* (1778), the condition especially of Germanic women, sometimes extended to Celtic women, lay at the heart of the argument.

It was a major theme of the book that the earliest stages of society were most favourable to women. The best guide of all to such early stages, Stuart suggested, was the *Germania*. He stressed, first, that marriage among the Germans meant that a wife enjoyed 'her equality with her husband', as 'the partner and the companion of his toils and his cares', a partnership marked by her fidelity and chastity, as by her contribution in war.[34] Secondly, he wrote of German women acquiring rights to property, as communal landholding developed into allodial and then into early feudal forms. Interpreting Tacitus's use of the Latin term *dos*, he saw the custom of giving dower to women – as in the eighteenth-century jointure – as already present in the early German tribes.[35] Thirdly, far more than Mallet, Stuart stressed the attention paid by women to business and affairs, to the public councils of the community:

> what evinces their consideration beyond the possibility of a doubt, is the attention they bestowed on business and affairs. They felt, as well as the noble and the warrior, the cares of the community . . . . They went to the public councils or assemblies of their nations, heard the debates of the statesmen, and were called upon to deliver their sentiments.[36]

Stuart stressed the honourable nature of the domestic cares and labours undertaken by women, yet wrote critically of the superstitions which cast them as goddesses. He also noted continuities between the power of women in Germanic tribes, the appearance of queens in Gothic parliaments, and the later rights to attend parliament, or send a deputy, held by fiefholding women in late medieval England.[37]

Stuart described not only an age of equality and power for women, but also the decline of that happy condition, as the original qualities of those tribes described by Tacitus were corrupted, not in the early stages of feudalism but in the later growth of an increasingly venal, money-oriented and debauched society, a process which he regarded as under way by the thirteenth century. The final chapter has as its subheading: 'The dissolute conduct of the women amidst the decline and oppressions of fiefs'.

The strength of this vision of the power of women in the remoteness of the medieval past, which soon found sympathisers, requires explanation. Almost 300 pages of endnotes, entitled 'Authorities, Controversy and

Remarks', supplementing his 130-page text, make it clear that Stuart was actively participating in a contemporary debate among Scottish historians on the status of women in early societies. The debate lay between those who looked to the 'golden ages' of the past, Celtic or Germanic, and those who looked towards the modern civil society of the future. The latter included leading Scottish historians like William Robertson, Principal of Edinburgh University, leader of the Moderate Church of Scotland and Historiographer Royal, Lord Kames, a Lord of the Court of Session, and John Millar, Professor of Roman Law at the University of Glasgow.[38] They were writing national histories, which were at the same time histories of the progress of civil society, of the attainment of modern commercial 'civilisation'.[39] To them, the brutalised condition of 'savage' women marked the distance that had to be travelled in the achievement of a desirable civil society.

To view this debate as one between 'philosophical' historians and scholarly antiquarians would be far too simple. Writers on both sides wrote in the spirit of 'comparative' history, with an interest in the relationship between material structures and social, political and cultural life. Stuart, as an early friend of John Millar, had in 1771 edited his *Observations concerning Ranks* for the publisher John Murray. In dismissing 'that propensity for unimportant research, which is generally characteristic of inquirers into antiquity', he had called for a history of Saxon and Norman England which united philosophy with history.[40] Lord Kames had begun his publishing career with his *Essays on British Antiquities* (1747). All, in one way or another, identified themselves politically as Whigs, and had a shared interest in the history of the English constitution as well as in the Scottish past. The bitterness of the argument derived partly from Stuart's personal hostility to the historical establishment of Scotland, and in particular to William Robertson, whom he believed had twice excluded him from that most desirable of jobs, a chair at the University of Edinburgh.[41] Robertson, Kames and Millar were in a position of cultural and political dominance in Scotland, associated with the cause of improvement, commerce and politeness represented by English culture and prosperity. To some degree those, like Stuart, at a distance from the centres of cultural and political power in Scotland, tended to look backwards to a 'golden age' in the past rather than to the modern civil society of the future.

Enlightened medievalism could serve many purposes.[42] Conflicting interpretations of the key sections of the *Germania* focused on women's labour, and their public roles. Such conflicts signified, at the same time, contrasting views of the future of Scotland within Great Britain, and transition from the collective imperatives of civic humanism towards the significance of the private and domestic within the modern commercial nation, as the boundaries of public and private worlds were renegotiated. Scottish historians like Kames, Robertson and Millar were writing a history of progress, a history which had strong roots in the material growth of European societies, although it was never simply a materialist history but also one of manners. Their work tended to assume 'a natural progress from ignorance to knowledge and from rude to civilized manners', most frequently described through four stages of material development: the savagery of hunting tribes, the pastoralism of the 'barbarian', settled agriculture, and finally, commercial western civilisation.[43] The extent of European and, especially, British progress could therefore be measured through direct contrast with different versions of the 'savage' or the 'barbarian' past. As comparative historians, they sought to classify and order a variety of different cultures, both those familiar in European historical writing since antiquity, and those described in the huge range of travel literature available to them. Particularly influential were two comparative accounts of American Indian peoples, by the French Jesuits Joseph François Lafitau and Pierre Charlevoix.[44]

The *Germania* was central to the historical agenda of these Scottish writers, yet often went unsignalled in the main body of their texts. In Robertson's work it lay concealed in his ample and scholarly 'Proofs and Illustrations'. In 1769, in a ten-page note to his 'View of the Progress of Society in Europe', which paid tribute to the works of Caesar and more especially of Tacitus, Robertson noted that the similarity between the ancient Germans and the American tribes 'is greater, perhaps, than any that history affords an opportunity of observing between any two races of uncivilized people'.[45] As a portrait of European tribalism, Tacitus's *Germania* could be sharply contrasted with the achievements of eighteenth-century British modernity, just as it could be used to demonstrate the superiority of such modernity to contemporary savage or barbarian societies.

The condition of the savage woman – labouring, enslaved, and without the blessings of marriage – was a key indicator of that contrast. By the second half of the eighteenth century it was a familiar trope of European commentary on other peoples of the world. Lord Kames wrote in his *Sketches of the History of Man*:

> After traversing a great part of the globe with painful industry, would not one be apt to conclude, that originally females were everywhere despised, as they are at present among the savages of America; that wives, like slaves, were procured by barter; that polygamy was universal; and that divorce depended on the will of the husband.[46]

Millar drew a similar picture for the early Germanic nations. He translated the Latin *dos* not as dower, but as 'bride-price', denoting sale of the wife into servitude and slavery, in which Germanic practice followed the universal pattern of marriage among 'savage' nations, in which wives were 'bought and sold, like any other species of property'.[47] Millar's contrast was with the modern and domesticated family, divided by labour and united not by the exercise of authority but by 'esteem and affection', and a measure of equality.[48]

It was specifically against these unremitting representations of women in early societies as degraded drudges, slaves and servants, that Stuart wrote of a 'golden age' for women in early medieval Europe. In his 1774 review of Kames's *Sketches*, he cited Tacitus to disprove the suggestion that wives were purchased among the ancient Germanic tribes.[49] His *View of Society in Europe* of 1778 went further. The original title of the work was to have been 'An Introduction to the History of Europe; or A New Version of the treatise of Tacitus, concerning the situation of Germany, its Inhabitants and their manners'.[50] The final title deliberately echoed and challenged Robertson's 'View of the Progress of Society in Europe'. Stuart intended to correct what he regarded as the many weaknesses of Robertson's account of medieval Europe. He placed the history of women at the centre of his onslaught, and asserted that, just as liberty was ancient, so 'The state of society which precedes the knowledge of an extensive property and the meannesses which flow from refinement and commerce, is in a high degree propitious to women.' He directly criticised those like Millar and Kames who misinterpreted the *dos* as bride-price, commenting that Kames, Millar and Robertson all followed the opinions of Charlevoix on the exchange of goods among Native Americans too closely as general evidence for the situation of women in early societies.[51]

The participation by women in the public affairs of the tribe was another area of contention. Late eighteenth-century historians viewed the evidence of Tacitus in the light of Lafitau's portrait of female power and matrilineality among the Hurons and the Iroquois. Millar nowhere acknowledged the fundamental analysis of Lafitau, although the framework of his chapter on 'the influence acquired by the mother of a family, before marriage is completely established' was clearly shaped by the American paradigm, and by Lafitau's comparisons with antiquity. Where marriage as an institution had not been established, matrilocal residence, matrilineal succession and agnatic inheritance might, Millar conceded, signify the power of mothers and the maternal bond. Though Charlevoix's evidence might confirm the power of women in North American tribes in public councils, and matrilineal succession to chiefdoms, Millar noted his observation that a public role was not reached before a certain age, and concluded that nevertheless 'there is no country in the world where the female sex is in general more neglected and despised'. Similarly, he noted the evidence for women voting in public assemblies in ancient Britain as indicating a stage of society so early that marriage was not clearly established.[52]

Gilbert Stuart had translated the humanist and republican vision of a commonwealth into the remoteness of the Germanic past, heightening its effect by representing women too as having an active public role, participating in the collective bonds of the community. As a 'country' radical or commonwealthsman, he saw these earlier stages of society as characterised by 'the idea of a public', in opposition to the luxury, refinement and sexual licence to be associated with modern civil society.[53] To Millar, however, it was only the later stages of material development, and particularly the acquisition of property, which brought, with inequalities of property and rank, a higher status for women. Notions of honour, the jealousy of families and the constraints upon women of higher rank allowed romantic and imaginative attachments to develop. Not until the emergence of commercial society did 'women become, neither the slaves, nor the idols of the other sex, but the friends and companions'; though with wealth and luxury came also the danger of the corruption of sexual relations.[54]

It was to be the modernising and 'Anglo-British' version of the nation's history which dominated by the end of the eighteenth century. Nevertheless that version did incorporate elements of that 'golden age' for women rooted in the *Germania*, as it did also elements of the exceptional history of British liberties. The Ossianic debate was not without its legacy. The exceptional nature of the evidence drawn from the Scottish past had been acknowledged with some puzzlement by Millar as by all these historians of civil society: 'in the compositions of Ossian, which describe the manners of a people acquainted with pasturage, there is often a degree of tenderness and delicacy of sentiment which can hardly be equalled in the most refined productions of a civilized age'.[55] Lord Kames took up the theme of 'this one extraordinary exception' at much greater length in his *Sketches*. Citing Tacitus, Mallet and Macpherson, Kames urged the coincidence of ancient Caledonian and ancient Scandinavian manners as evidence for the distinctive history of the women of the northern nations.[56]

The new synthesis emerged most clearly through rereadings of the coming of chivalry. The impact of chivalric ideals on the situation of women was stressed by all these historians, influenced by the pioneering medievalist of the Enlightenment, Jean-Baptiste de La Curne de Sainte-Palaye.[57] Mallet had located the origins of chivalry within the Germanic forests, for all Gothic peoples. Hugh Blair had identified the same 'imaginary refinement of heroic manners' in Ossianic Scotland.[58] Stuart, like Mallet, firmly located the origin of chivalric institutions in the rites of knightly initiation and the love of warfare described by Tacitus: 'to the forests of Germany, we must trace those romantic institutions, which filled Europe with renown and with splendour'. The devotion of the knight to the female sex improved a 'natural sensibility and tenderness', as 'politeness became a knightly virtue', extended not only to the battlefield but to all the affairs of civil life, and reinforced by Christianity.[59] He traced the history of chivalric manners from the origin of the nation in the

German woods through to the ultimate decay of feudalism, manifested in the introduction of knight service, and its increasingly self-interested and commercial nature. So, too, 'the women were to lose their value and their pride' in corruption, gallantry and intrigue.[60]

The historians of the progress of civil society initially rejected this interpretation of the origins of chivalry. To Robertson, chivalry was inherited neither from the Germanic tribes nor from the institutions of early medieval Europe. Consciously disavowing 'strict chronological accuracy', Robertson had written in 1769 of chivalry as one of the many signs of a new dawn in later medieval European society, placed, in his account, somewhere between the revival of Roman law and the progress of science and of commerce.[61] Chivalry and its consequences for the relations between the sexes became in this version part of a liberal Whig perspective on late medieval Europe, one of the key elements in the transition to modernity.[62] Still, when Hugh Blair in 1774 urged Lord Kames to pay more attention to chivalric manners as the foundation of that respect paid to 'the sex' in modern times, while continuing to find the origins of such manners 'in a wild and barbarous state of society', in ancient Scotland as in ancient Germany and Scandinavia, he found a receptive correspondent. Lord Kames followed that advice in the second edition of the *Sketches*.[63]

Once James Macpherson's claims for the authenticity of Ossian were widely doubted, the *Germania* could be cited as evidence that the one significant exception in the history of women in the early stages of society was not the Celtic, but the Anglo-Saxon. In John Millar's *Historical View of the English Government* (1787), a Whig compromise was reached. In his significant chapter on the differences between the Germanic invaders and 'every other people, ancient or modern', he noted not only the gradual 'civilising' processes at work in Anglo-Saxon England, but the existence of early notions of honour, which, once settled forms of property were acquired, could bring new notions of romantic love and respect for women, with more developed institutions of chivalry. For Millar, the particular material circumstances of early medieval Europe and, especially, Anglo-Saxon England accidentally created a situation which, uniquely, favoured English women.[64]

The emergence of such a synthesis could nevertheless, in its stress on chivalry and romance, trouble late eighteenth-century Scottish historians. Chivalric reverence for women was admired, and where restrained, could come to coincide with respect for women's useful arts and domestic industry in the ages of economic improvement. But there was little sympathy for the fantastic extravagances, the pleasurable gallantries, the potential corruptions that might accompany it.[65] Such ambivalent responses, slipping between ideals of domestic companionship and mutuality and an emphasis on sexual difference and distance, indicate the complexity of this 'progressive' history.

By the 1790s the debate on national identity had moved into a new phase, one dominated by the 'Anglo-British' paradigm. Arthur Murphy's translation of the complete works of Tacitus, the first since that of Thomas Gordon in 1728, was published in 1793, and was to remain in widespread use throughout and beyond the nineteenth century.[66] It was dedicated to Edmund Burke, in the spirit of the war against revolutionary France, and may be read, as Weinbrot suggests, as a contribution to the emerging identity of a northern and commercial nation with its roots in an ancient Britain, and an ancient Germany.[67] The annotations to the key sections of the *Germania* included Mallet's Scandinavian evidence, as well as Robertson's *History of Charles V* and *History of America*. Murphy commented on the distinctiveness of marriage among the early Germans, translating *dos* as 'dowry', and cited the strength of their domestic affections as evidence of the superiority of 'the natural reason, the instinct, it may be said, of the German tribes, to the boasted philosophy of Greece and Rome!'[68]

The beginning of the nineteenth century was to see a new synthesis of Anglo-Saxon scholarship, in Sharon Turner's pioneering *History of the Anglo-Saxons* (1805), which finally dispelled all confusion between Celts, Britons and Anglo-Saxons. Though Turner tartly pointed out the failings of Tacitus's *Germania* as a source, he still drew heavily upon it. His history was one of enlightened progress, aiming 'to display the savage pirate slowly ameliorating into the civilized, moral and scientific man'. The study of Anglo-Saxon woman-hood was not a central theme, yet his treatment signals the extent to which its exceptional status had been incorporated:

> It is well known that the female sex were much more highly valued and more respectfully treated by the barbarous Gothic nations than by the more pol-ished states of the East. Among the Anglo-Saxons they occupied the same important and independent rank in society which they now enjoy. They were allowed to possess, to inherit, and to transmit landed property; they shared in all the social festivities; they were present at the Witena Gemot and the Shire Gemot; they were permitted to sue and be sued in the courts of justice; their persons, their safety, their liberty, and their property, were protected by express laws, and they possessed all that sweet influence which, while the human heart is responsive to the touch of love, they will ever retain in those countries which have the wisdom and the urbanity to treat them as equal, intelligent and independent beings.[69]

By the beginning of the nineteenth century, these issues were not merely a matter of masculine and scholarly controversy. They were well embedded within a broader cultural context, one in which the ambiguities suggested above could be turned to different purposes, in works addressed to a female as well as a male audience.[70] In such a rewriting of national identity women writers, too, might have some sense of participation in the nation's history and

its origins. Two women writers, from within the Whig traditions of the enlightened Scottish literati and English dissenters, recognised this historiography
and tried to harness it during the Napoleonic Wars. The Scotswoman
Elizabeth Hamilton, a successful novelist and educational writer, wrote of her
Memoirs of Agrippina (1803): 'It was the perusal of Tacitus, in Murphy's translation, which first excited the idea in my mind.'[71] The *Memoirs* were a commentary upon the failure of republican womanhood, on the model of German
strength in domestic fidelity, and upon the potential of that model for
Christian transformation. The Unitarian Lucy Aikin – the daughter of John
Aikin, the Edinburgh-educated translator of the *Germania* – published in 1810
her lengthy poem *Epistles on Women*, calling upon 'the impartial voice of
history' to testify that women might be 'the worthy associates of the best of
men'. The Germanic peoples, 'progenitors of the noblest nations of modern
Europe', could not be classified with nameless savages or 'wandering hordes'.
In Aikin's poem, the merits of the Germanic 'Western Genius', signalling the
doom of Rome, were located in 'the chaste virtues of his frugal home'. Aikin's
history was both patriotic and Whig, tracing from its origins a history of
English progress identified with an understanding of 'woman's feeling heart',
yet looking also to the future of a northern, commercially prosperous and maritime nation.[72]

There were to be other, more popular interpreters. Walter Scott was
steeped in the literature described above. Ulrica and Rowena in *Ivanhoe* (1819)
can be taken to reflect the contrasting faces of Saxon womanhood to be found
in the work of Paul-Henri Mallet. Many uses were to be found for the themes
indicated here in the nineteenth century, by John Stuart Mill as by Friedrich
Engels, by the historians and anthropologists of Victorian Britain, by feminists
and anti-feminists.[73] The image of the women of Anglo-Saxon England as
'more nearly the equal companions of their fathers and brothers than at any
other period before the modern age' has continued to influence scholarly
debate until the present.[74]

Through readings of Tacitus's *Germania*, the past history of British
women became a site of debate in late eighteenth-century Britain, as some
nation-states of the west acquired the characteristics of the imagined community traced by Anderson. This history was framed not as a response to any
external threat, but through the unequal partnership, the uneven development, of England and Scotland within Great Britain. An emerging Whig
women's history united the exceptional inheritance of a Germanic and Anglo-
Saxon past with an initially Scottish but ultimately 'Anglo-British' history of
civil society. In its initial appearance it had very little relevance to the social,
political or cultural lives of women in late eighteenth-century Scotland or
England. Yet at the same time it drew upon, and itself also shaped, the many
discourses of gendered behaviour through which men and women sought to

interpret and to influence their relations with each other. It united the history of the nation with the history of those private bonds intrinsic to the civil society of the future.

Notes

I should like especially to thank the editor of this volume for his advice and skilful editing, and, for their careful reading at an earlier stage, Joanna de Groot, Catherine Hall and Keith McClelland.

1 B. Anderson, *Imagined Communities: Reflections on the Origin and Spread of Nationalism* (London, 1983).

2 L. Hunt, *Politics, Culture and Class in the French Revolution* (Berkeley, 1984), chs 2–3; U. Chakravarti, 'Whatever happened to the Vedic *Dasi*? Orientalism, nationalism and a script for the past', in K. Sangari and S. Vaid (eds), *Recasting Women: Essays in Indian Colonial History* (New Brunswick, 1990); *Gender & History*, special issue on 'Gender, Nationalisms and National Identities', 5:2 (1993).

3 J. Malečková, 'Women in perceptions of uneven development', in M. Hroch and L. Klusáková (eds), *Criteria and Indicators of Backwardness: Essays on Uneven Development in European History* (Prague, 1996).

4 D. McCrone, *Understanding Scotland: The Sociology of a Stateless Nation* (London and New York, 1992), p. 30.

5 M. Thom, *Republics, Nations and Tribes* (London and New York, 1995), Introduction.

6 J. Keane, 'Despotism and democracy: the origins and development of the distinction between civil society and the state', in J. Keane (ed.), *Civil Society and the State: New European Perspectives* (London, 1988); McCrone, *Understanding Scotland*, pp. 20–6; M. Ignatieff, 'John Millar and individualism', in I. Hont and M. Ignatieff (eds), *Wealth and Virtue* (Cambridge, 1983); J. Dwyer, *Virtuous Discourse: Sensibility and Community in Late Eighteenth-Century Scotland* (Edinburgh, 1987), *passim*, esp. ch. 5.

7 In the use of the term 'Anglo-British' I follow Colin Kidd, in *Subverting Scotland's Past: Scottish Whig Historians and the Creation of an Anglo-British Identity, 1689–c.1830* (Cambridge, 1993).

8 *The Agricola and the Germania*, trans. and intro. H. Mattingly, revised by S. A. Handford (Harmondsworth, 1970); for a brief discussion of Tacitus's sources and purpose in this work, see R. Mellor, *Tacitus* (New York, 1993), pp. 14–16. On the importance of the *Germania* for the shaping of European national identities in the late eighteenth and early nineteenth centuries, see Thom, *Republics, Nations and Tribes*, pp. 213–21.

9 C. Hill, 'The Norman yoke', first published in J. Saville (ed.), *Democracy and the Labour Movement* (London, 1954); see also J. G. A. Pocock, *The Ancient Constitution and the Feudal Law: A Study of English Historical Thought in the Seventeenth Century* (Cambridge, 1957; 2nd edn, 1987).

10 J. W. Burrow, *A Liberal Descent: Victorian Historians and the English Past* (Cambridge, 1981).

11 S. Kliger, *The Goths in England: A Study in Seventeenth and Eighteenth Century Thought* (Cambridge, Mass., 1952); see also H. A. MacDougall, *Racial Myth in English History: Trojans, Teutons and Anglo-Saxons* (Montreal, 1982); J. W. Johnson, 'The Scythian: his rise and fall', *Journal of the History of Ideas*, 20 (1959), 250–7.

12 The comments in this paragraph are speculative and require more research. I have briefly surveyed key texts in seventeenth-century and eighteenth-century political writing identified by Christopher Hill and others. See H. Weinbrot, 'Politics, taste and national identity: some uses of Tacitism in eighteenth-century Britain', in T. J. Luce

and A. J. Woodman (eds), *Tacitus and the Tacitean Tradition* (Princeton, 1993); P. Burke, 'Tacitism', in T. A. Dorey (ed.), *Tacitus* (London, 1969); Hill, 'The Norman yoke', pp. 87–99; G. Newman, *The Rise of English Nationalism: A Cultural History* (London, 1987), pp. 183–200.

13 J. Ridé, *L'Image du Germain dans la pensée et la littérature allemandes de la redécouverte de Tacite à la fin du XVIème siècle* . . . (thèse présentée devant l'Université de Paris IV, 1976), 3 vols (Lille, 1977), II: 1183–6; F. Borchardt, *German Antiquity in Renaissance Myth* (Baltimore, 1971), ch. 3; D. R. Kelley, '*Tacitus Noster*: the *Germania* in the Renaissance and Reformation', in Luce and Woodman (eds), *Tacitus and the Tacitean Tradition*.

14 P. Clüver, *Germaniae Antiquae. Libri Tres* (Leiden, 1616), pp. 167–88. On Clüver's influence in Britain, see H. Weinbrot, *Britannia's Issue: The Rise of British Literature from Dryden to Ossian* (Cambridge, 1993), p. 517; H. Weinbrot, 'Celts, Greeks and Germans: Macpherson's Ossian and the Celtic epic', *1650–1850: Ideas, Aesthetics and Inquiries into the Early Modern Era*, I (1994): 3–22.

15 J. G. Keysler, *Antiquitates selectae Septentrionales et Celtae* . . . *cum figuris* . . . (Hanover, 1720), pp. 369–510.

16 S. Pelloutier, *Histoire des Celtes, et particulièrement des Gaulois et des Germains depuis les tems fabuleux* . . . , 2 vols (La Haye, 1750), I: 509–16.

17 P.-H. Mallet, *Introduction à l'histoire de Dannemarc, où l'on traite de la religion, des lois, des moeurs, & des usages des anciens Danois* (Copenhagen, 1755). On Mallet, see H. Stadler, *Paul-Henri Mallet 1730–1807* (Lausanne, 1924); L. Gossmann, *Medievalism and the Ideologies of the Enlightenment: The World and Work of La Curne de Sainte-Palaye* (Baltimore, 1968), pp. 344–6.

18 Mallet, *Introduction à l'histoire de Dannemarc*, pp. 100–2.

19 *Ibid.*, pp. 199–201.

20 *Ibid.*, pp. 62–4, 198–9, 206, 212–14.

21 On Mallet's influence, see F. E. Farley, *Scandinavian Influences in the English Romantic Movement*, Studies and Notes in Philology and Literature, vol. IX (Boston, 1903), pp. 29–44.

22 R. B. Sher, *Church and University in the Scottish Enlightenment: The Moderate Literati of Edinburgh* (Princeton, 1985), chs 3, 6.

23 See J. L. Greenway, 'The gateway to innocence: Ossian and the Nordic Myth', in *Studies in Eighteenth-Century Culture*, vol. 4, ed. H. E. Pagliaro (Madison, 1975), pp. 161–70; F. Stafford, *The Sublime Savage: James Macpherson and the Poems of Ossian* (Edinburgh, 1988); H. Gaskill (ed.), *Ossian Revisited* (Edinburgh, 1991); J. Macpherson, *The Poems of Ossian and Related Works*, ed. H. Gaskill, with an introduction by F. Stafford (Edinburgh, 1996).

24 Kidd, *Subverting Scotland's Past*, p. 231; see also Weinbrot, *Britannia's Issue,* p. 519, and Weinbrot, 'Celts, Greeks and Germans'.

25 Kidd, *Subverting Scotland's Past*, pp. 219–39; J. Macpherson, *Introduction to the History of Great Britain and Ireland* . . . [1771], 2nd edn (London, 1772), pp. 268–77.

26 Macpherson, *Introduction*, p. 307.

27 For an important interpretation of Ossianic poetry in terms of enlightened representation of sensibility and feeling, see J. Dwyer, 'The melancholy savage: text and context in the poems of Ossian', in Gaskill (ed.), *Ossian Revisited*. Dwyer has also described the creation in late eighteenth-century Scotland of that 'virtuous discourse' of which Hugh Blair was a leading proponent, which aimed to chart a practical morality for the nation's leaders. One of its strategies was the relocation of virtue within the sensibility and feeling of domestic life. See Dwyer, *Virtuous Discourse, passim*, esp. ch. 5.

28 Yoshiaki Sudo, 'An unpublished lecture of Hugh Blair on the poems of Ossian', *The Hiyoshi Review of English Studies*, 25 (March 1995), 168; Blair, *Critical Dissertation*, in *Poems of Ossian*, ed. Gaskill, pp. 347–9. Ragnar Lodbrog was the ninth-century Danish

king whose funeral ode was partially translated in 1756 by Mallet, *Monumens de la mythologie et de la poesie des Celtes et particulièrement des anciens Scandinaves . . .* (Copenhagen, 1756), pp. 155–6. In 1763 both Blair and Thomas Percy published separate translations; see Farley, *Scandinavian Influences*, pp. 59–76.

29 T. Percy, *Northern Antiquities: or, a Description of the Manners, Customs, Religion and Laws of the Ancient Danes, and other Northern Nations; including those of our own Saxon Ancestors . . .* (London, 1770), vol. I, 'Translator's Preface. Proofs that the Teutonic and Celtic Nations were *ab origine* two distinct People', and vol. II, pp. v–xvii.

30 *Ibid.*, I: xii, 328–30n.

31 R. Henry, *The History of Great Britain, from the first invasion of it by the Romans, under Julius Caesar . . .* [1771–93], 2nd edn, 12 vols (London, 1788–95), I: 318–22, 333–5; II: 303–8, 320–8; III: 393–9; IV: 335–42, 345–51.

32 See Stuart's *Historical Dissertation on the English Constitution* (Edinburgh, 1768), especially 'Advertisement', Section I, and p. 108n.; and 'Character of Tacitus', *Edinburgh Magazine and Review*, I (1775), 22–4, 28. On Stuart, see W. Zachs, *Without Regard to Good Manners: A Biography of Gilbert Stuart 1743–1786* (Edinburgh, 1992), p. 24; Kidd, *Subverting Scotland's Past*, pp. 239–46.

33 *Edinburgh Magazine and Review*, I (February 1774), 203; Zachs, *Without Regard to Good Manners*, pp. 78–83.

34 G. Stuart, *A View of Society in Europe, in its Progress from Rudeness to Refinement: or, Inquiries concerning the History of Law, Government and Manners* [1778], 2nd edn (Edinburgh, J. Robertson, 1792, repr. with new intro. by W. Zachs, Bath, 1995), pp. 17–18.

35 *Ibid.*, pp. 28–34.

36 *Ibid.*, p. 15.

37 *Ibid.*, pp. 169–70, 244–5.

38 On these historians, see Sher, *Church and University*, esp. ch. 3; D. Stewart, 'Account of the life and writings of William Robertson D.D.' [1801], in *The Works of William Robertson D.D.*, 12 vols (London, 1818), vol. I; I. S. Ross, *Lord Kames and the Scotland of his Day* (Oxford, 1972); W. C. Lehmann, *Lord Kames and the Scottish Enlightenment* (The Hague, 1971); W. C. Lehmann, *John Millar of Glasgow* (Cambridge, 1960); Ignatieff, 'John Millar and individualism'.

39 This word was used in the singular in English, possibly for the first time, in 1771 by John Millar in his *Observations concerning the Distinction of Ranks in Society* (London, 1771, repr. as *Origin of the Distinction of Ranks . . .* , 3rd edn, London, 1779).

40 *Edinburgh Magazine and Review*, I (1773), 88–9; Zachs, *Without Regard to Good Manners*, pp. 42–3.

41 For their continuing rivalry, see *ibid.*, chs 5–6.

42 See Gossmann, *Medievalism and the Ideologies of the Enlightenment*, pp. 334–52.

43 Millar, *Origin of the Distinction of Ranks*, reprinted in Lehmann, *John Millar*, p. 176. See Kidd, *Subverting Scotland's Past*, part II; R. Meek, *Social Science and the Ignoble Savage* (Cambridge, 1976).

44 Meek, *Social Science*, ch. 2; J. F. Lafitau, *Moeurs des sauvages amériquains comparées aux moeurs des premiers temps*, 2 vols (Paris, 1724); P. Charlevoix, *Histoire et description générale de la Nouvelle France . . .* , 3 vols (Paris, 1744).

45 W. Robertson, 'A view of the progress of society in Europe', in *The History of the Reign of the Emperor Charles V* [1769], in *Works*, IV: 245–54, n. VI.

46 H. Home, Lord Kames, *Sketches of the History of Man* [1774], 2nd edn, 4 vols (Edinburgh, 1778), II: 69.

47 *Ibid.*, pp. 192, 195–6; see also *An Historical View of the English Government . . .* [1787], 4 vols (London, 1803), I: 53–4.

48 Millar, *Origin*, p. 219.

49 *Edinburgh Magazine and Review*, I (April 1774), 310–20.

50 Stuart to John Murray, 7 September 1774, Hughenden Papers, Bodleian Library, G/1/934, cited by Zachs, *Without Regard to Good Manners*, p. 100.
51 Stuart, *View of Society in Europe*, pp. 12, 177–8, 225–6.
52 Millar, *Origin*, pp. 198–203; see also Robertson, *History of America* [1777], in *Works*, IX: 152.
53 On Stuart's politics, see Zachs, *Without Regard to Good Manners*, pp. 125–30; Stuart, *An Historical Dissertation concerning the Antiquity of the English Constitution* (Edinburgh, 1768), pp. 126–7.
54 Millar, *Origin*, pp. 208–19.
55 *Ibid.*, pp. 206–7.
56 Kames, *Sketches*, I: 421–2, 450, 469–72, 480.
57 Gossmann, *Medievalism and the Ideologies of the Enlightenment*.
58 Blair, *Critical Dissertation*, in *Poems of Ossian*, ed. Gaskill, p. 376.
59 Stuart, *View of Society in Europe*, pp. 42, 61–2.
60 *Ibid.*, p. 129.
61 Robertson, 'View of the progress of society', in *Works*, IV: 78–98.
62 For the context of this interpretation, see Gossmann, *Medievalism and the Ideologies of the Enlightenment*, pp. 330–1.
63 Blair to Kames, 2 April 1774, in A. Fraser Tytler (ed.), *Memoirs of the Life and Writings of the Honourable Henry Home of Kames*, 2 vols (Edinburgh, 1807), II: 152–4; Kames, *Sketches*, II: 82–7 inserted into the second edition.
64 Millar, *An Historical View of the English Government* . . . [1787], 4 vols (London, 1803), I: 119–22; on the political parallels, see Burrow, *A Liberal Descent*, p. 33; Pocock, *Ancient Constitution*, pp. 384.
65 Millar, *Origin*, pp. 215–18.
66 Murphy's translation of the *Works* went through eight further British editions between 1807 and 1854, and was used in 1908 for the Everyman edition. John Aikin's translation of the *Germania, A Treatise on the Situation, Manners and Inhabitants of Germany* . . . (Warrington, 1777) was reprinted in 1805, 1815 and 1823. There were six further translations before 1860.
67 A. Murphy, *The Works of Cornelius Tacitus; with an Essay on the Life and Genius of Tacitus* . . . , 4 vols (London, 1793), 'Dedication'; Weinbrot, 'Politics, taste and national identity'.
68 Murphy, *Tacitus*, IV: 115.
69 S. Turner, *The History of the Anglo-Saxons* . . . , 4 vols (London, 1799–1805), I: viii; IV: 108.
70 For instance, W. Alexander, *The History of Women, from the Earliest Antiquity to the Present Time* . . . . [1779], 2 vols (London, 1782); A. Thomas, *Essay on the Character, Manners and Genius of Women in Different Ages*, enlarged from the French of M. Thomas by Mr Russell, 2 vols (London, 1773); J. Bennett, *Strictures on Female Education* . . . (London, 1787).
71 Elizabeth Hamilton to Dr S—, 29 May 1802, Miss [Elizabeth] Benger, *Memoirs of the late Mrs Elizabeth Hamilton* . . . , 2 vols (London, 1818), I: 44; J. Rendall, 'Writing history for British women: Elizabeth Hamilton and the *Memoirs of Agrippina*', in C. Campbell-Orr (ed.), *Wollstonecraft's Daughters* (Manchester, 1996).
72 L. Aikin, *Epistles on Women Exemplifying their Character and Condition in Various Ages and Nations* . . . (London, 1810), pp. v-viii, 57–9.
73 J. S. Mill, 'Modern French historical works', *Westminster Review*, VI (July 1826), 62–103, reprinted in J. M. Robson (ed.), *Essays on French History and Historians, Collected Works of John Stuart Mill*, vol. XX (Toronto and Buffalo, 1985), pp. 15–52, here pp. 45–8; H. Maine, *Ancient Law* [1861] (London, 1959), p. 99; F. Engels, *The Origin of the Family, Private Property and the State* [1884] (London, 1972), pp. 82, 132.

74 D. Stenton, *The English Woman in History* (1956), cited as an example of 'excellent good sense' in C. Fell, C. Clark and E. Williams, *Women in Anglo-Saxon England and the Impact of 1066* (Oxford, 1984), p. 13. For a discussion of the consequences of the 'golden age' view for scholarship on Anglo-Saxon women, see P. Stafford, 'Women and the Norman Conquest', *Transactions of the Royal Historical Society*, 6th series, IV (1994), 221–50; A. Klinck, 'Anglo-Saxon women and the law', *Journal of Medieval History*, 8 (1982), 118–19; B. Hanawalt, 'Golden ages for the history of medieval English women', in S. M. Stuard (ed.), *Women in Medieval History and Historiography* (Philadelphia, 1987).

The redeeming Teuton:
nineteenth-century notions of the 'Germanic' in
England and Germany

In both Britain and Germany in the nineteenth century the 'Germanic' was defined as part of the national identity. The nineteenth-century German notion of the Germanic has been widely discussed in the wake of two world wars, for which, in its compensatorily aggressive, separatist and hubris-ridden form that rejected what has become understood as the identity of the west, it has, explicitly or implicitly, been held responsible. A very crude, wholesale writing-off of German intellectual traditions from Herder to Hitler as dangerous Teutomania occurred, not surprisingly, under the immediate impression of the end of the Second World War.[1] But in more measured and sophisticated later investigations of the 'German disease', evaluations along similar lines proved long-lived and were put forward, for example, by Klaus von See in his *Germanenideologie*,[2] by Hans Kohn,[3] Fritz Stern[4] or George L. Mosse,[5] all of whom trace, in one way or another, the roots of German fascism to the German rejection of the rationalism of the Enlightenment and the democratic ideas of the French Revolution and to a retreat into a mystical Germanic identity. While the validity of the post-war construction of the German *Sonderweg* has been vigorously discussed, and questioned, by historians,[6] the notion of an un-western German tradition is widely agreed upon.[7] The idea of the inherently illiberal nature of the German traditions (and self-definition) still has considerable currency, as Jürgen Habermas's comments, made in the course of the German *Historikerstreit* of the mid-1980s, which debated the meaning and position of the Nazi regime in German historiography, demonstrate. Habermas asserted that 'unfortunately, a commitment to universalist constitutional principles rooted in conviction has only been feasible in the cultural nation of the Germans after – and through – Auschwitz. . . . Anyone wishing to recall the Germans to a conventional form of their national identity, destroys the only reliable basis of our bonds with the west.'[8]

The English notion of the Germanic as a vital ingredient, not of the national and cultural make-up of England's continental neighbour, but of its own, found expression in the nineteenth-century movement of Anglo-Saxonism, which united a group of Victorian historians through the shared ideas that the English nation was crucially shaped by the Germanic influences of the Anglo-Saxon immigrants who settled in England during the period of the Migrations, and that it still represented their ancestors' noblest traits in terms of legal, constitutional and generally social organization. The Anglo-Saxonist view of the English and their history has been treated from various perspectives, for example in relation to the Victorian effort to deny the Irish their national independence[9] or in relation to the 'Whig interpretation of history', Herbert Butterfield's influential term,[10] with which it shares the belief in the superior notion of freedom among the English,[11] which produced their superior political institutions.[12] Although both notions of the Germanic have been recognised separately, they have not been discussed in conjunction.[13] The benefits of a comparative approach to this phenomenon, which I undertake here, are the following: by comparing the two and grounding them in their nineteenth- and eighteenth-century contexts – where they originate as modern concepts – it should become possible to see what exactly the differences and similarities between them are and to decide to what extent they warrant a split into 'western' and 'German' Germanicness.

The roots of the nineteenth-century definition of the 'Germanic' lie in the eighteenth century. They grow out of contemporary attempts to loosen the exclusive hold of (neo-)classicism on thought and art, and to establish cultural origins through a historical perspective. The initial efforts in this direction involved the cautious suggestion that the original native cultures of non-Mediterranean Europe were not necessarily inferior to those of classical antiquity so celebrated since the Renaissance. It was mooted, for example, that the ancient Nordic lays or medieval romances might be of a cultural significance similar to that of the ancient Greek epics: the *Edda* or the *Nibelungenlied* might be comparable to Homer. While it may appear utterly ahistorical to the twentieth-century reader to group together works as culturally distinct as the *Liederedda* and the romances of Chrétien de Troyes, the mid-eighteenth century did not yet make clear distinctions between the early medieval, medieval and early modern periods: Bede and Shakespeare, *Beowulf* and the *Roman de la Rose*, all belonged to an undifferentiated and nebulous past of early European culture.

These early suggestions of comparability aimed at establishing analogies between the early phases of ancient and modern culture, and were eventually to lead to an assumption of equivalence. They originated as much in Britain as in Germany. As early as 1735, Thomas Blackwell pointed out in his *Enquiry into the Life and Writings of Homer* that there were striking similarities between the Homeric period and those of Dante and of Milton.[14] This notion was taken up by Richard Hurd in England and Johann Jakob Bodmer on the

Continent around mid-century. Hurd established parallels between 'gothic' and 'heroic' (i.e. ancient) times in his *Letters on Chivalry and Romance* in 1762.[15] Bodmer, in an essay of 1743, drew directly on Blackwell by applying the latter's social and cultural analysis of the Homeric period to the era of the Hohenstaufen emperors in twelfth- and thirteenth-century Germany, and explained the literary flowering of the latter period in terms which implicitly suggested a correspondence between the two.[16]

In the early nineteenth century these suggestions became more assertive, and the early cultural stage of modernity was described with increasing self-confidence. 'Modern', in this sense, comprised all of post-classical Europe as it evolved after the collapse of the Roman Empire, through the Middle Ages, up to the formation of modern nation-states. In his lectures on drama in Vienna in 1808, August Wilhelm Schlegel still advocated a parallelism of cultural stages between ancient and modern, as Bodmer and Hurd had done, but crucially defined a difference of content between classical and post-classical culture.[17] Classical consciousness, he argued, rested on the belief in the harmony between man and nature, which in the Greeks' case had led to a noble and dignified sensuality in taste and understanding, a sensuality rooted in a joyful appreciation of life in the here and now. Post-classical consciousness, shaped by the Christian religion, rested on the expectance of infinity, of redemption and eternal bliss in the beyond, and discarded this world as the irrelevant dross of a finite existence. Such a consciousness would necessarily produce art and thought dominated by a yearning for a lost past and a yet intangible future.[18] But, for Schlegel, Christianity was only one vital ingredient in the European identity. The other was ancient Germanicness, 'germanische Stammart':

> Apart from Christianity, the formation of Europe [*die Bildung Europas*] has since the beginning of the Middle Ages been decided by the Germanic identity of the Nordic conquerors . . . . The unrelenting nature of the north pushed the human being further and further back into itself, and what is withdrawn from the playful and free design of the senses [*spielende und freie Gestalt der Sinne*] must, in a noble disposition, benefit the earnestness of the mind [*Ernst des Gemüths*]. Hence the homely [*bieder*] heartiness with which the Germanic peoples adopted Christianity, so that it has not penetrated more deeply, nor proven more powerfully effective anywhere else. . . . Out of the uncouth, but faithful, heroic courage of the Nordic conquerors developed, through the admixture of the Christian attitude, chivalry.[19]

Christianity, the abstract religion of infinity and idealism, and ancient Germanness, characterised as a simple seriousness of mind, were eminently suited to each other, and merged during the Middle Ages, creating chivalry, the combination of Christian religion and warlike valour in the serious-minded pursuit of ideals. The idea of the two key elements was also discussed in Friedrich Schlegel's *Geschichte der alten und neuen Literatur* (1812).

Friedrich put additional emphasis on the notion of freedom, which he envisaged as innate to the Germanic essence: 'Christianity . . . from the one side,
and the free spirit of the north from the other, these were the two elements
which brought forth the modern world.'[20] As the merging of these elements –
and its evidence, chivalry – occurred near the beginning of the formation of
the modern culture, Friedrich Schlegel concluded that 'The Middle Ages were
quite properly the heroic age of Christianity',[21] an obvious analogue to the
heroic period of classical antiquity. In the conceptions of the two Schlegels
the ancient classical culture found a worthy and distinct successor in the
Germanic–Christian culture of the moderns. The two cultures were parallel
in structure, different in content, and equal in value. This evaluation of the
Middle Ages as the heroic age of the moderns would underpin the multifari-
ous manifestations of nineteenth-century medievalism – a movement fuelled
in many instances by escapist nostalgia, yet grounded at the same time in historicist research into cultural history.

Intellectual exchanges between Britain and Germany assisted the circulation of these ideas. In the later eighteenth century Johann Gottfried Herder
drew extensively on both Blackwell and Hurd, developing and assimilating
their ideas.[22] August Wilhelm Schlegel's lectures, for their part, were translated into English in 1815, and their reception was consolidated by generally
favourable reviews in both the *Edinburgh Review* and the *Monthly Review* the
following year.[23] More indirectly, but by no means ineffectively, Schlegel's
ideas were spread in Britain by Scott's *Essay on Drama*, which drew heavily on
the lectures, and his *Essay on Chivalry*, which took over Schlegel's definition
of the importance and effect of the Christian religion, but displayed, unlike
Schlegel's lectures, a decidedly anti-classical attitude. Both of Scott's essays
were appended to the widely read *Encyclopaedia Britannica* in 1814.[24]
Friedrich Schlegel's *Geschichte der alten und neuen Literatur* was equally
influential in Britain: it was translated in 1818 and widely reviewed.[25]

In the eighteenth century the emphasis, both in Britain and in Germany,
was on a contrast between a generally 'northern' modern European and a
southern and ancient classical culture. The idea of the Germanic occurred
within a European context, which it retained well into the nineteenth century.
Between 1805 and 1815, however, in Germany the need emerged to define a
more precisely German notion within this more general northern or European
framework. The need was occasioned by the Napoleonic occupation of large
areas of the recently abolished German Empire and by the extremely precarious positions of the major central European powers, Prussia and Austria.
National feeling was aroused for specific purposes: to end French occupation,
to abolish absolute rule in the many independent principalities that had made
up the Empire, and to replace it with constitutional rule – in short, to unite
and reform. What did this more specific German identity look like?

A. W. Schlegel's work is a useful example to demonstrate the hatching of a specific national identity within the larger context of the modern European identity. Against the political background of the Napoleonic victories in Europe, he gradually moves towards trying to define German and French identities as opposites and to cut out French influence on German culture. In his contributions to the *Deutsches Museum* of 1812, Schlegel can be seen to differentiate between German and French chivalry: 'In the twelfth century chivalry [*das Rittertum*] began to be modelled on foreign customs; in the wake of this a mass of French words was brought across the Rhine.'[26] Schlegel regrets the Franco-Romance influence on medieval German culture, which replaced the folksy element, a kind of original chivalry, with imported aristocratic courtly *Hofsitten* and 'educated chivalry' (*gebildetes Rittertum*).[27] When the origin of the modern identity was being considered, no differentiation was made, but when it came to carving out a specific national identity, distinctions were formulated that split up the European identity into segments (that neatly fit the current political situation).

Another response to the precarious political situtation before the battles of Leipzig and Waterloo are Johann Gottlieb Fichte's *Addresses to the German Nation*, given in Berlin in 1807–8. During the last fifty years, the *Addresses* have often been relegated to the contemptible nether regions of partisan nationalistic propaganda. Yet, though they certainly served political and nationalistic ends in their effort to instil a sense of superiority into their listeners and stir them into action, they still in some respects evinced the philosophical outlook of the author of the *Wissenschaftslehre*. In particular, they reflected some of Fichte's cosmopolitan concern for the improvement of the lot of humanity through education, offering as they did an outline of 'a means of education towards a new mankind'.[28] Initially Fichte acknowledged the homogeneity of all 'Germanic' peoples as the new historical force in Europe after the collapse of the Roman Empire. This quickly became a stock procedure in the early nineteenth century that is also found in the Schlegels', the Grimms' and Uhland's writings on literary and cultural history.[29] Soon, however, he made a distinction between the truly Germanic peoples and those originally Germanic peoples that in the course of their history had become Romance. This distinction was based not on race, as a late twentieth-century reader might suspect, but on language. For Fichte, the truly Germanic peoples – including the Germans, the Scandinavians and probably the English – were directly linked to their cultural and existential origin through a linguistic connection that provided them with an unbroken intellectual history:

> In a language that has remained alive without interruption, this super-sensuous [*übersinnlich*] part is metaphoric. It summarises in perfect unity at every stage the entirety of the sensuous [*sinnlich*] and intellectual [*geistig*] life of a nation. Thus it is possible to give a concept a name that is

not arbitrary, but grows necessarily from the entire previous life of the nation. From this concept, and its name, the circumspect eye, stepping backwards, ought to be able to reconstruct the nation's entire intellectual history.[30]

The Romance peoples – those that, though of Germanic stock, had adopted some form of Latin as their language – were, in Fichte's view, severed from their linguistic and intellectual origin. They could never fully understand the language they had taken on, because they had not lived through and, more crucially, *shaped* its development from the beginning, in particular the development of metaphors for abstract concepts. Their language was intellectually dead, having become, in its *übersinnlich* part, 'a shredded collection of arbitrary, inexplicable signs of equally arbitrary concepts, with which nothing can be done other than simply learning them [by heart]'.[31] The expression of abstract and spiritual notions was rendered problematic because the speakers had no grasp of the historically grown metaphoric containers of the abstract concepts they used to express themselves. While these problems of transferring metaphor and meaning from one language and cultural context to another are well known to translators of literature, it must be noted that Fichte's arguments were set forth in the context of anti-French propaganda, directed both against the immediate threat of Napoleon and more generally against the lingering effects of French cultural dominance over eighteenth-century Germany; hence the rather ludicrous implied denial of the possibility of any 'meaningful' development, in terms of conceptual shaping, within the French language since the very early Middle Ages.

The Germans, according to Fichte, were the most Germanic people of all, the *Stammvolk* ('trunk-nation'), with an *Ursprache* ('original language'), which predestined them to make a special contribution to history. Fichte argued that the Germans' special seriousness of mind and depth of feeling, the results of their continuous use of an original language, made them particularly suited to the initiation of intellectual and spiritual revolutions. The most important of these in the past had been, for Fichte, the Reformation, instigated by Martin Luther. 'This state of affairs [the corruption of late medieval religion] could no longer continue, once this light [of Renaissance clarity] fell into a mind [*Gemüt*] that was religious in true earnestness and in its approach to life, and when this mind was surrounded by a people to which it could easily communicate its more serious view of the matter.'[32] To Fichte, and to other Protestant thinkers of the period from Hegel to Heine,[33] the Reformation constituted the liberation of the mind from (Catholic) shackles, from a religious straitjacket that had lost its credibility and beneficial nature. In Fichte's view, it opened the way to realising reason (*Vernunft*) in freedom, which would ultimately lead to the perfect state of man on earth.[34] The idea that the Reformation was a world-historical event and that those who carried it out were making a world-historical contribution to history was rooted in the theories of history developed within German Idealism. Fichte, Schelling and Hegel all shared the notion that history was a teleological process within which unconscious reason proceeded gradually towards consciousness.[35] Once this was achieved, the historical process would end in the eternal equilibrium of fully realised reason and freedom.

In his *Philosophie der Geschichte* (lectures given between 1822 and 1831), Hegel applied this notion to what he perceived as world history. The world-historical process was advanced, in his view, by the idiosyncratic contributions of world-historical peoples. Each of these peoples possessed a *Volksgeist* – its specific national essence – which contained the innovative momentum required by the historical process in order to progress at a specific moment. This led it to challenge and to overthrow the current dominant people and its principle. In Hegel's understanding of history, successive contributions had been made by the oriental people, the Greeks, the Romans, and finally the Germanic peoples. The latter were the truly modern people, whose contribution marked the passing away of antiquity.

> The Germanic spirit [*Geist*] is the spirit of the modern world, the purpose of which is the realisation of absolute truth as the infinite self-determination of freedom, of that freedom which has as its content its own absolute form. It is the destiny of the Germanic peoples to function as the carrier of the Christian principle. The principle of intellectual [*geistig*] freedom, the principle of reconciliation, was laid into the still unselfconscious, uneducated minds of those peoples, and it was made their task, in the service of the world-spirit, not only to have the concept of true freedom as their religious substance, but also to produce it freely out of subjective self-consciousness.[36]

Again, the constitutive elements of Christianity and the Germanic are evident, which complement each other necessarily and perfectly, as Hegel outlines in a dialectic argument.[37] There is clearly a special quality to the Germanic contribution: it is consummate. Like Fichte, Hegel focused on the Reformation as a key event in world history, characteristically initiated by the German people:

> The old and thoroughly preserved emotional depth [*Innigkeit*] of the German people has to accomplish this revolution out of its simple, unrefined heart. . . . The human being is to have an immediate relationship with him [Christ] in spirit. . . . Thus the absolute immersion of the soul, which belongs to religion itself, and the freedom of the Church have been won. . . . Thus the new, the final banner has been unfurled, around which all peoples will assemble, the banner of the free spirit.[38]

Germanic has here become synonymous with German. The essentially Germanic nature of the Reformation was proven to Hegel by the fact that it only succeeded in Germanic countries – Germany, Scandinavia and England.

It did not succeed among Romance nations, he argued, because their essence and spirit were heterogeneous, divided by the combination of Germanic and Romance, which prevented them from possessing the 'totality of the spirit' required for the true comprehension of real (Protestant) Christianity.[39]

The notion of the Germanic that was entertained among German thinkers of the early nineteenth century could thus be summarised as follows. Ancient Germanicness – a love of liberty and a simple seriousness of mind – was perfectly suited to take on the spiritual essence of Christianity. The Germanic peoples brought about the end of antiquity and were the instigators and representatives of the modern phase in world history. Their original notion of freedom was elevated by the influence of the spiritually abstract religion of Christianity, thus becoming the carrier of the perfect realisation of conscious reason in liberty. Once the institutions of medieval Christianity, initially so beneficial, had become corrupt and untrue, this refined Germanic liberty and seriousness broke free from the corruption in order to realise this conscious reason. This liberation was instigated at the Reformation, which originated in and was only successful within the Germanic, rather than the Romance, regions of Europe. This view was fully developed and greatly favoured by Protestant thinkers. Their Catholic counterparts, such as the Catholic convert Friedrich Schlegel, tended to take a modified view, focusing on the achievements of the (Catholic) Middle Ages, which produced chivalry, the initial fusion of Christianity and Germanic qualities, rather than the Reformation. In general, however, they did not disagree regarding the fusion and importance of the Germanic essence and Christianity in world history. Neither can a strict division between a Catholic and Prostestant view be maintained: Protestant thinkers and artists showed interest in what was considered the cultural significance of the Middle Ages, too. A distinction between the Germanic, a potentially European denominator, and the German is emphasised when a differentiation from the French, and by extension from the Mediterranean south, which, by one sleight of hand, could be extended to classical antiquity, is to be achieved. In this context it is useful to remember that this understanding of the Germanic was broadly developed in the context of an intended emancipation from forms of eighteenth-century classicism associated with French influence.

This conception of the Germanic may be compared with its English counterpart. The notion that the English were thoroughly Germanic – or, as it was usually put, 'Teutonic' – culminated in the phenomenon of Anglo-Saxonism – the stress on Anglo-Saxon descent – whose zenith coincided with that of British imperial power in the mid- to late nineteenth century. Anglo-Saxonism, however, was part of a broader emphasis on the 'northern' or the 'Germanic'. Thomas Macaulay – no Germanophile in his politics – wrote in the introductory chapter of his *History of England*, published in 1848 and soon widely disseminated both in Britain and in Germany:[40] 'Early in the fourteenth century the amalgamation of the races [in England] was all but complete: and it was soon made manifest . . . that a people inferior to none existing in the world had been formed by the mixture of three branches of the great Teutonic family [Anglo-Saxon, Danish and Norman] with each other, and with the aboriginal Britons.'[41] The Celtic influence was here evidently seen as minor, as it is not associated with the adjective 'great'. A clear, and early, indication that, in England as in Germany, such self-definitions were made in the context of a general conceptual opposition between the Mediterranean south and the Germanic north is given in Scott's already mentioned *Essay on Chivalry*, in which the entirety of northern culture, contrasted with classical culture, is throughout the essay repeatedly referred to as 'German'.[42]

The Hegelian notion of the world-historic nation as the motor of the teleological progression of history was replicated in the lectures on *Comparative Politics* given in 1873 by the future Oxford Regius Professor of History, Edward Augustus Freeman. Fifty years after Hegel's lectures on the philosophy of history, Freeman's lectures occur within the context of the British reception of Hegel. 'The Greek, the Roman, and the Teuton, each in his own turn, stands out above the other nations of the Aryan family. Each in his turn has reached the highest stage alike of power and civilization that was to be had in his own age, and each has handed on his own store to be further enriched by successors who were at once conquerors and disciples.'[43] The Teutonic contribution was the development of the concept of the nation-state, which to Freeman, and to many others, seemed the most advanced concept of human social organisation. The idea of the constitutional nation-state as the goal of history and the salvation of mankind is the red thread of nineteenth-century English theorising about history. For Freeman, the English were the 'truest representatives' of the Teutonic race, because they alone had preserved the ancient Germanic traditions in their pure form.

> Alone among the political assemblies of the greater states of Europe, the Parliament of England can trace its unbroken descent from the Teutonic institutions of the earliest times. There is absolutely no gap between the meeting of the Witan of Wessex which confirmed the laws of Ælfred . . . and the meeting of the Great Council of the Nation which will come together in a few days within the precincts of the home of the confessor. . . . No other nation, as a nation, can show the same unbroken continuity of political being. In this way we may claim to have preserved more faithfully than any of our kinsfolk the common heritage of our common forefathers.[44]

Evidently the English, as well as the Germans, considered themselves to be the true preservers of the Germanic essence. Once again, it was the notion of unbroken descent from the origin that formed the basis of the claim: for Fichte the descent was linguistic, for Freeman it was constitutional.

The notion that the modern Teuton was defined by the combination of ancient Germanic essence with the Christian religion, and that the combination was of world-historic importance, was elaborated by Charles Kingsley in his series of lectures *The Roman and the Teuton*, given at Cambridge in the 1860s, during his tenure as Regius Professor of Modern History. While Kingsley was never fully accepted by the establishment of historians even during his professorship, and is nowadays remembered chiefly as a novelist, he was an extremely popular lecturer with the students,[45] a much-read writer of essays and sought-after public speaker, whose ideas were widely disseminated. In his lectures he stated:

> They [the Teutons] never learnt the lesson [to unite their various tribes into one force] until after their final victory, when the Gospel of Christ . . . came to unite them into one Christendom. . . . Had they destroyed Rome sooner, what would not they have lost? What would not the world have lost? Christianity would have been stifled in its very cradle; and with Christianity all chance – be sure of it – of their own progress.[46]

Again, one notes the decidedly redemptive – if not, in this case, precisely consummate – qualities of the Christianised Teuton. Like Fichte, Kingsley saw the Teuton as the original European. Germany was the 'mother of all European life', hers the 'root-history of Europe'.[47] Kingsley, despite being an intense Germanophile, was still glad to be English, because he thought the English had made the greatest success of their Teutonicness. 'Happy for us Englishmen, that we were forced to seek our adventures here, in this lonely isle, . . . to till the ground in comparative peace, keeping unbroken the old Teutonic laws, unstained the old Teutonic faith and virtue.'[48] And again:

> And if our English law, our ideas of justice and mercy, have retained, more than most European codes, the freedom, the truthfulness, the kindliness of the old Teutonic laws, we owe it to the fact that England escaped, more than any other land, the effete Roman civilization; that she therefore, first of the lands, in the twelfth century rebelled against, and first of them, in the sixteenth century threw off the Ultramontane yoke.[49]

Teutonic northernness was favourably contrasted with classical Mediterraneanness and with Romanised Europe. The focus on legal institutions – also noticeable in Freeman's interest in parliamentary history – is also significant. Kingsley, like Fichte and Hegel, marked the Reformation as a turning-point. For him, however, it is an important step on the road towards the formation of the modern nation-state, rather than towards the realisation of absolute freedom and reason: 'The antagonism of the Church to the national and secular law remained for centuries. It died out first perhaps in England, after the signature of Magna Carta. For then the English prelates began to take up that truly Protestant and national attitude which issued in the Great Reformation.'[50] In another chapter Kingsley remarked: 'The monastic organization indeed had to die, in many countries, in order that national life might develop itself, and the dissolution of the monasteries marks the birth of a united and powerful England.'[51]

An even more striking instance of the presentation of British constitutional institutions as the weal of the world was contained in Charles Wentworth Dilke's significantly named book *Greater Britain* (1868): 'The ultimate future of any section of our race, however, is of little moment by the side of the triumph of the whole, but the power of English laws and English principles of government is not merely an English question – its continuance is essential to the freedom of mankind.'[52] Not surprisingly, these ideas were shared by Freeman, who held that all people who came to live under English laws in the colonies, even those long independent such as the USA, were in a sense 'English', as they had been liberated by the redemptive nature of constitutional Englishness.[53] Here, just as in Fichte and Hegel, generally accepted national boundaries were transcended by one nation's claim to possess the means of international redemption.

Through their Teutonic-minded Anglo-Saxonism, these English writers concurred with the notion, developed by the German thinkers, that the Germanic essence had made and was making a vital contribution to world history, and that, to a considerable extent, it determined the welfare of mankind. They also assented to the notion that this Germanic essence was made up of the blending of an ancient tribal Germanic character, seriousness and independence, with the Christian faith. There is also the same element of antagonism towards the Mediterranean south and towards the Catholic: Christianity has to be of the Teutonised, Reformed kind. In striking contrast to the Germans, however, the English writers were preoccupied with constitutional and legal developments and contributions. It was through *these* developments – the setting-up of an independent national church, the binding of the sovereign into a system of law (which forms a line in nineteenth-century English historiography from the Magna Carta of 1215 to the Glorious Revolution of 1688), and, crowningly, the early development of a nation-state based on a constitutional monarchy – that the Germanic essence manifested itself, in the English view.

The Germans, on the other hand, were preoccupied with the definition and existence of this essence within a teleological scheme of history. This difference can be partly explained by pointing to the quite different philosophical traditions of the two countries in the earlier nineteenth century. Whereas in Britain the legacy of empiricism and political philosophy exerted a powerful influence, the more recent German tradition developed from Idealist thought, which was far more abstract in nature. Just as influential in determining the difference, however, were the actual historical circumstances of the two nations, which can only be described as diametrically opposed. The English definitions, although no doubt partly inspired by German thought, were based on an interpretation of actual historical experience: Magna Carta, Henry VIII's Act of Supremacy, the Glorious Revolution and the Empire all proved the point. The German definitions, on the other hand, could only be said to outline a potential. The reality in Fichte's day was lamentable: no unified state, no constitutional safeguards, French occupation. Even in Hegel's later life, the Metternichian Restoration did not bode well for achieving political and constitutional unity, although German *culture* was clearly in the ascendant. Endeavours to bring about political union were to fail again in 1849. It is therefore against a background of difficulty and endeavour that Fichte's appeal to his audience at the end of his *Addresses* must be set: 'Among all modern nations it is you in whom the seed of human perfection lies most prominently and to whom the task has been given to be the vanguard of its development. Should you, and with you the modern essence, perish, then humanity's hope for rescue from the depths of its predicament perishes too.'[54] Fichte was clearly worried that it might indeed perish, rather than assert itself, and that Germany might become a French colony. Again the problem surfaces: on the one hand, the German nation has the potential to be supreme among nations, to be the redeemer of mankind, but at the same time it is the nation most beset with alienating foreign influences, which impede its self-realisation and its consummate contribution to history. While Hegel was quietly confident that the *Weltgeist* would inevitably realise itself in history, Fichte feared it might need prompting. Whereas the Teutonic English could look back on 'real' achievements, the Germanic Germans had to make do with the hope of realising their Germanic essence in the future.

When these similarities and dissimilarities between the German and English conceptions of the Germanic are weighed up, the limitations of any theory that relates specific characteristics of the German conception – its redemptive features, for example – to some kind of German *Sonderweg*, or to some line of intellectual descent connecting Herder forward to Hitler and to little else, become apparent. It may be that the English notion of the Germanic, rooted as it was in the historical experience of an actual nation-state, possessed a kind of 'realism', whose absence in the German case facilitated Nazi abuse. But the very difference of historical circumstance itself undermines one of the key arguments in the German-specific interpretation – the suggestion that the redemptive elements in the ideology, the ones lending themselves most obviously to the excesses of a mystical nationalism, were essentially compensatory. For these redemptive features were not peculiar to a vulnerable and politically fragmented Germany; they were shared by the British at the peak of their imperial power. The comparative approach strongly suggests that a fundamental reason for the development of the nine-teenth-century notion of the Germanic lies in the positive evaluation of the Germanic and the northern from the eighteenth century onwards, which is a European phenomenon, and that to leave this circumstance out amounts to telling the story without its beginning and hence out of context.

This investigation also suggests that it would be interesting to probe in more detail the extent to which the English diverged from what has often been seen as the standard 'western' path of development in political culture – one based on rationalistic notions of liberty, on constitutional democratic con-tracts and laws that have international acceptance, and on the ideas that informed the constitutions of the French Revolutionary Republic and the USA. It has traditionally been asserted that the nineteenth-century German notions of freedom and the state are different from their 'western' counter-parts, because they are based on a Romantically organic idea of a historically grown cultural community, the *Volksgemeinschaft*, which subordinates the individual and cherishes laws that are the result of historical organic growth rather than of rational consideration of civil rights. It might be illuminating in this context to consider whether there are not elements of this organic notion in the English worship of parliament and its organically developed history, in the British pride in the lack of a written constitution – matters are decided by organically grown, traditional methods – and in the veneration of many other national institutions that have acquired their representativeness by organically surviving: Oxford and Cambridge, Eton, Westminster Abbey, the monarchy. Leopold von Ranke wanted to see a German state develop 'wie er dem Genius der Nation entspricht' ('that corresponds to the nation's genius').[55] Kingsley and Freeman assured their readers that nineteenth-century England was such a place. The difference remains nevertheless: while the Germans took the essence of the historically grown identity to lie in cultural, intellectual and lin-guistic fields, the English took it to lie in constitutional and institutional struc-tures – structures which, of course, supplied the basis for Britain's claim to belong to the 'western' tradition. It is important, however, to recognise the common elements of a 'Romantic' belief in organic growth and particularity. It should also be noted that the anti-French orientation whose prominence in German political thought and culture has encouraged the identification of 'German' with 'anti-western' was also a common element in the political think-ing and national self-definitions of the supposedly more 'western' British in the nineteenth century.

It is well known that German thinkers who concerned themselves with the definition of a German identity, culturally and politically, saw parallels between themselves and the English, suggesting some kind of shared tradi-tion. They often looked admiringly across the Channel.[56] By mid-century, some did not hesitate to consider the English and the Germans as Teutonic brethren. This illustrates a forgotten closeness in thought and attitude between English and German writers and thinkers.[57] Max Müller, the Oxford don of German extraction, observed in 1858:

> There is no country where so much interest is taken in the literature of Germany as in England, and there is no country where the literature of England is so much appreciated as in Germany. . . . In recent times, the literature of the two countries has almost grown into one. . . . And the strong feeling of sympathy between the best classes in both countries holds out a hope that, for many years to come, the supremacy of the Teutonic race, not only in Europe, but all over the world, will be maintained in common by the two champions of political freedom and of the liberty of thought – Protestant England and Protestant Germany.[58]

Politically, many preferred being on the German side to supporting the French: both Kingsley and Freeman applauded the outcome of the Franco-Prussian war in 1870. This closeness, unthinkable today, has been obliterated by the events of the first half of the twentieth century.

Since the German collapse in 1945, the German notion of the Germanic has been inspected and rejected, with great emotion, with even greater embarrassment and pain. In Britain, the notion of the Teutonic fared differently. No political revolution has disturbed England's relationship with its past and identity since the seventeenth century. Although for obvious reasons no longer labelled 'Teutonic', the patriotic pride that fiercely protects parliament as the bedrock from which all (proper) political life grows, the suspicious rejection of popish Catholicism and the teasing antagonism towards the French and Mediterranean nations seen as 'other' suggest the perennial existence of these nineteenth-century ideas. They are also evident in the political debate about 'Europe' today, in which the call for self-exclusion on the grounds of an organically grown historical superiority can be clearly heard.

Notes

1 See I. Kershaw, *The Nazi Dictatorship,* 2nd edn (London, 1988), p. 7.
2 K. von See, *Deutsche Germanenideologie* (Frankfurt-on-Main, 1970).
3 H. Kohn, *The Mind of Germany: the Education of a Nation* (London, 1960).
4 F. Stern, *The Politics of Cultural Despair: a Study in the Rise of Germanic Ideology* (Berkeley, 1961).
5 G. L. Mosse, *The Crisis of German Ideology: the Intellectual Origins of the Third Reich* (New York, 1964).
6 See Kershaw, *The Nazi Dictatorship,* or J. Hiden and J. Farquarson, *Explaining Hitler's Germany* (London, 1983).
7 See Kershaw, *The Nazi Dictatorship,* pp. 18ff.
8 J. Habermas, 'Eine Art Schadensabwicklung. Die apologischen Tendenzen in der deutschen Zeitgeschichtsschreibung', *Die Zeit,* 11 July 1986. Unless otherwise indicated, all transactions from the German are by the present author.

9 See L. P. Curtis, *Anglo-Saxons and Celts: a Study of Anti-Irish Prejudice in Victorian England* (Bridgeport, 1968).

10 H. Butterfield, *The Whig Interpretation of History* (London, 1931).

11 See J. Burrow, *A Liberal Descent: Victorian Historians and the English Past* (Cambridge, 1981).

12 Efforts in conservative revisionism in Britain in the 1980s, not dissimilar to those in Germany that prompted Habermas's comments, were directed towards a revival of this view of British history via new education policies. See R. Samuel, 'Continuous national history', in R. Samuel (ed.), *Patriotism: the Making and Unmaking of British National Identity*, 3 vols (London, 1989), I: 9–17.

13 Throughout his book Burrow makes numerous references to scholarly influences from Germany, but the notion of related ideas on the Germanic, the investigation of which is in no way the purpose of his study, does not emerge.

14 T. Blackwell, *Enquiry into the Life and Writings of Homer* (London, 1735, repr. Menston, 1972), pp. 65–6.

15 R. Hurd, *Moral and Political Dialogues with Letters on Chivalry and Romance*, ed. E. J. Morley, 3 vols (London and Cambridge, 1911), III: 95–106.

16 Bodmer refers to Blackwell at the beginning of his essay 'Von den vortrefflichen Umständen für die Poesie unter den Kaisern aus dem schwäbischen Hause' [1743], reprinted in M. Wehrli (ed.), *Das geistige Zürich im 18. Jahrhundert: Texte und Dokumente von Gotthart Heidegger bis Heinrich Pestalozzi* (Zurich, 1943), pp. 67–76.

17 August Wilhelm's brother Friedrich concerned himself with a definition of the ancient, or classical, in contrast with the modern, or Romantic, from his early writings onwards and modified his evaluations repeatedly, as did August Wilhelm (see A. Grosse-Brockhoff, *Das Konzept des Klassischen bei Friedrich und August Wilhelm Schlegel* (Cologne and Vienna, 1981)). August Wilhelm's efforts have been chosen here, because they present the simpler discussion that, crucially, enjoyed enormous popularity and hence influence in the course of the nineteenth century (see Grosse-Brockhoff, *Das Konzept*, p. 245).

18 A. W. Schlegel, *Vorlesungen über dramatische Kunst und Literatur*, ed. G. V. Amoretti, 2 vols (Bonn and Leipzig, 1923), I: 10–13. A. W. Schlegel had already begun to develop this difference in his earlier Berlin lectures on 'Klassische Literatur' and 'Romantische Literatur' in 1801–4, repr. in *Kritische Schriften und Briefe*, ed. E Lohner, 7 vols (Stuttgart, 1962–74): III, IV.

19 Schlegel, *Vorlesungen über Dramatische Kunst und Literatur*, I: 11.

20 F. Schlegel, *Kritische Ausgabe*, ed. E. Behler *et al.*, 35 vols (Munich, Paderborn and Vienna, 1958–), VI: *Geschichte der alten und neuen Literatur*, p. 150.

21 *Ibid.*, p. 197.

22 In his essay *Würkung der Dichtkunst auf die Sitten der Völker*, for example, Herder takes up the notion of analogy between Homeric and medieval poets: see J. G. Herder, *Sämtliche Werke*, ed. B. Suphan, 33 vols (Berlin, 1877–1913), VIII: 399.

23 See V. Stockley, *German Literature as Known in England 1750–1830* (London, 1929), pp. 263–9.

24 Both essays reprinted in W. Scott, *Essays on Chivalry, Romance and Drama* (London, 1887), pp. 1–65 (*Chivalry*) and 109–226.

25 Stockley, *German Literature*, pp. 266–7. Stockley puts forward the intriguing thesis that the translator was J. B. Lockhart, Scott's son-in-law, which emphasises the crucial influence of Scott and his circle on the dissemination of Schlegelian ideas in Britain, long after Scott had supposedly turned his back on German influences.

26 A. W. Schlegel, 'Über das Lied der Nibelungen', *Deutsches Museum*, ed. F. Schlegel (Vienna, 1812–13, repr. in 4 vols, Hildesheim, 1973), I: 26.

27 *Ibid.*, p. 24.
28 *Fichtes Werke*, ed. I. H. Fichte, 11 vols (Berlin, 1834–46, repr. Berlin, 1971), VII: 311 (4. Rede). On Fichte's combination of cosmopolitanism and a national outlook, see C. Prignitz, *Vaterlandsliebe und Freiheit: Deutscher Patriotismus 1750–1850* (Wiesbaden, 1981), pp. 75–6, 85–6. Prignitz carefully outlines the complex cultural and political situation that generated a harmonious coexistence of the two concepts, but may – in view of the decided anti-French polemic which Fichte's *Reden* contain – be going too far in asserting a completely non-aggressive innocence for the notions which they outline.
29 See A. W. Schlegel, *Romantische Literatur* (1803) and *Dramatische Literatur und Kunst* (1808); F. Schlegel, *Geschichte der alten und neuen Literatur* (1812); G. W. F. Hegel, *Philosophie der Geschichte* (lectures given throughout the 1820s); W. Grimm, *Die deutsche Heldensage* (1829); L. Uhland, *Sagengeschichte der germanischen und romanischen Völker* (1831–32).
30 *Fichtes Werke*, VII: 325.
31 *Ibid.*
32 *Ibid.*, p. 346 (6. Rede).
33 See, for example, Hegel, *Philosophie der Geschichte* ('Die germanische Welt'), and Book 1 of H. Heine, *Die Romantische Schule* (1835).
34 See *Fichtes Werke*, VII: 354–5 (6. Rede).
35 See Fichte, *Grundzüge des gegenwärtigen Zeitalters* (1803–4); F. Schelling, *System des Transzendentalen Idealismus* (1800).
36 G. W. F. Hegel, *Werke*, ed. E. Moldenhauer and K. M. Michel, 20 vols (Frankfurt, 1970–79), XII: 415.
37 See esp. *ibid.*, XII: 422–8.
38 *Ibid.*, pp. 494–6.
39 *Ibid.*, pp. 499–502. Fichte made a similar point in his sixth address, *Fichtes Werke*, VII: 351ff.
40 See M. Müller, 'German literature', in his *Chips from a German Workshop*, 4 vols (London, 1870), III: 1.
41 T. B. Macaulay, *The Works of Lord Macaulay*, 12 vols (London, 1898–1907), I: 14.
42 Scott, *Essays on Chivalry, Romance and Drama*, pp. 1–65.
43 E. A. Freeman, *Comparative Politics: Six Lectures given before the Royal Institution in January and February 1873*, 2nd edn (London, 1896), p. 25. Freeman uses the term 'Aryan' and also speaks of Christianity itself as the 'Semitic faith' (p. 28). This illustrates the general move towards a more racially based outlook in the second half of the nineteenth century. Freeman appears, however, to use the terms descriptively, reflecting the advances in scientific linguistics and anthropology, as he is not hostile to Christianity.
44 *Ibid.*, p. 30.
45 See G. Kendall, *Charles Kingsley and his Ideas* (London, 1947), pp. 160–1.
46 C. Kingsley, *The Roman and the Teuton*, new edn (London, 1889), pp. 11–12.
47 *Ibid.*, p. 322.
48 *Ibid.*, p. 16.
49 *Ibid.*, p. 266.
50 *Ibid.*, p. 263.
51 *Ibid.*, p. 217.
52 C. W. Dilke, *Greater Britain: a Record of my Travels through English-Speaking Countries*, 2 vols (London, 1869), II: 407.
53 See Freeman's *Some Impressions of the United States* (1883), quoted in W. R. W. Stephen, *Life and Letters of Edward A. Freeman*, 2 vols (London, 1895), II: 179–81.
54 *Fichtes Werke*, VII: 498–9.
55 Quoted in W. Weidenfeld, *Der deutsche Weg*, 2nd edn (Berlin, 1991), p. 40.

56 For a succinct summary of German Anglophilia see H. James, *A German Identity 1770–1990* (London, 1989), pp. 21–5.
57 For a differentiated assessment of the German view of England in the first half of the nineteenth century, see C. E. McClelland, *The German Historians and England: a Study in Nineteenth-Century Views* (Cambridge, 1971), parts 2 and 3.
58 Müller, 'German literature', pp. 1–2.

Paving the 'peculiar path':
German nationalism and historiography since Ranke

There is really nothing so very novel about recognition of the 'invented', 'forged' or simply constructed quality of national traditions and identities. Nationalist historians of the nineteenth and earlier twentieth centuries frequently demonstrated a consciousness that patriotic national histories did not simply reflect nations and their continuities as established facts. National histories were written also to sustain and develop national identities and allegiance to the nation-state. In central Europe, historians' awareness of what Milan Kundera has termed the 'unobviousness' of nations was pivotal to their approach to creating national histories.[1] Nationalist historical narratives could, in their authors' perception, provide correctives and perhaps substitutes for an absent continuity of nation-statehood. Thus, Ranke's complacent assertion that the history of Germany possessed to an unparalleled degree 'the outstanding characteristic of traversing all the centuries in unbroken continuity' was qualified in a more reflective moment by his observation that historical continuity as such could be 'narrated' but never 'proved'.[2] It may therefore be instructive to reflect on the interconnectedness of the emergence of history as an academic discipline and the legitimation of modern nation-states. A great deal has been written about the general political engagement of professional historians. However, surprisingly little attempt has been made to locate their politics in the context of nation building, let alone to read their works as imaginative exercises in the construction of nations.[3] The continuing rumblings of the *Historikerstreit* (historians' dispute) of the 1980s, the emphasis placed by some of its protagonists on deriving national meanings from the past, and the high political profile of the debate itself, add a specifically German dimension to the importance of coming to terms with the past of one's own discipline.[4] And while representations of the past played an important part in the production of nationalist symbols and discourses across Europe, the role played by the German historical profession as custodians of national history was in many ways paradigmatic. This arose in part from the early professionalisation and rapid expansion of the discipline. It was expressed in the high social status of the occupants of established Chairs in History, and the authority with which they could address an educated public.

This essay will argue that, in Germany, an imagined community of historical scholarship first foreshadowed and then celebrated the formation of the nation-state. Education in history was held to promote the shaping of people into autonomous individuals contributing to the life of their 'fatherland',[5] while the prospects of the discipline were seen as being contingent on the power of the nation. The uniqueness of national progression along a 'German path', too, was perceived at once as indicating the proper direction of research and (in its modern forms) also as being in part an outcome of nationalist historical writing. Finally, I will suggest that German nationalist historians repeatedly addressed a potentially unsettling and ambiguous relationship between the state on the one hand and the nation and *Volk* on the other. An uneven, incomplete and merely relative shift from *Staat* to *Volk*, from conservative to mobilising conceptions of German history, ensued. At stake was the question of how, exactly, the historical imagination should construct 'Germany'. Embittered controversies could and did arise, whether over the origins of German nationhood or over the dynamics and objectives of contemporary German domestic and foreign policy. However, neither approach threatened the paradigmatic idea of a 'German path' *per se*. When, after 1945, both statist and *völkisch* approaches faced conceptual crises, advocacies of a 'German path' could turn into remarkably similarly framed denunciations.

In virtually every generation of German historians, an abundance of programmatic statements made by a proselytising professoriate has underscored both the dependence of the nation on memory and the unique qualifications of the historians to shape that memory as well as to reveal and disseminate it. Ranke himself set out not only 'to reveal the content of German history and to experience the effective vital spirit of the nation within it' but also 'to give body to an otherwise vague national consciousness'.[6] In the Weimar Republic, the Tübingen medievalist Johannes Haller preached patriotism precisely because he understood it to be the 'calling' of the universities to act as the 'plantations' of the 'German spirit', to 'cultivate' it.[7] Within the universities themselves, that burden must fall primarily on the historians' shoulders since 'Political education is historical education. Without knowledge of modern history, there can be no political judgement!'[8] And at the height of the *Historikerstreit* in the Federal Republic of Germany in the 1980s, arguments about such questions as whether an historical legitimation for a more adventurous German foreign policy could be found brought professional historians back on to the front pages of 'quality' newspapers. This time, the obsessive search for moral meanings embedded in the past threatened at worst not only to distort research but to displace it.

The 1960s and 1970s witnessed a remarkable and, however fleetingly, successful challenge to the supremacy of nationalist history within the academy in West Germany. By the mid-1970s, the new social scientific history associated with the work of the Bielefeld School could even be hailed as the new orthodoxy of German professional historical opinion. Its hallmark was the identification – and denunciation – of a purported German *Sonderweg*: a peculiar aberrant German path of historical development. Germany, the Bielefelder maintained, in failing to push through a bourgeois revolution, had evaded the processes of parliamentarisation undergone in Britain, France and 'the west' in general. It had maintained a political system at odds with modern industrial society. Until 1918, the argument ran, preindustrial elites, in collusion with a 'feudalised' and supine bourgeoisie, propped up the monarchical system. And the end result of the *Sonderweg* was the Third Reich. The Bielefelder, in their structuralist approach to history no less than in the Social–Liberal politics they espoused, understood themselves to represent in microcosm Germany's route back to the west after a long deviation.

In the wake of trenchant criticisms ventured especially by Geoff Eley and David Blackbourn, much of the intellectual edifice of the thesis of a *Sonderweg* has crumbled.[9] Its proponents, sometimes traduced as unpatriotic by statist historians still concerned to rescue the good name of the Bismarckian Reich, may be accused of having produced a mirror-image of the nationalist historiography they had set out to debunk. Certainly, their break with the older paradigm was highly self-conscious, and gave rise to a series of biographical essays critically reappraising the history of German historiography.[10] Arguably, their necessarily sharp encounter with nationalist historiography encouraged them to exaggerate the extent of the existence of a supposed norm of western development and of German singularity.

Few of the prestigious institutions of nineteenth-century Germany can in fact have undergone as complete a process of embourgeoisement as the universities. Yet it is precisely within them that some of the most startling evidence of a German *Sonderweg* may be encountered. What emerges is not so much a real, structural *Sonderweg* capable of being tested through comparisons with western European national experiences, as an imaginary *Sonderweg* proclaimed by contemporary German intellectuals in conscious repudiation of what they understood to be a western pattern. The peculiarly German path with which this essay is concerned is a mentality. It was construed above all in historical terms and gained its ascendancy in tandem with the advance of institutions which could maintain and encourage it.

To claim that, at any point, the bourgeois historians were themselves 'feudalised' would be misleading. A handful had genuinely aristocratic credentials. Many more claimed a kind of spiritual and intellectual kinship with the aristocracy, though this turned out to be chiefly a means of expressing their sense of belonging to an elite. According to Haller, the universities were themselves 'aristocratic in origin and purpose, that is to say a selection from among the better people'.[11] Monarchy and aristocracy were certainly admired, but the historians also demonstrated real pride in their own roots within the *Bildungsbürgertum* (one of those curious German compound nouns, its individual parts respectively conveying cultivation as well as education and a notion of active citizenship as well as bourgeois class-consciousness). As a rising social class, the *Bildungsbürgertum* found itself in something of a dilemma throughout the nineteenth century. On the one hand, its members were keen to turn their backs on the class of craftsmen and artisans from which most of them had emerged and who, at a remove of only a generation or two, remained too close for comfort. On the other hand, their desire for social assertion tempted them into researching their family trees, presumably on the assumption that a long family tree would somehow confirm their relatively new-found status.[12] Historians, whose self-perception encouraged them to seek to act as the opinion formers of their class, evinced a considerable scholarly interest in its nature and functioning. This was pretty much as close as the Prussian School historians ever got to social history.[13]

Much of the *Bildungsbürgertum* in general, and all the professional historians in particular, owed advancement, prestige and influence in the first place to the state. The first Chairs in History in Germany were established in the aftermath of the French Revolution and the Napoleonic Wars. The German states, including and especially those which owed their territorial expansion to Napoleon's rationalisation of the map of Germany, sought to benefit from the historian's craft: their legitimacy was to be historically certified. Myths and the romantic literary imagination gave way progressively to historical documents and the historical imagination towards the middle of the nineteenth century. As the politics of state formation grew more hard-headed, so the demand for historians and their facts increased. It was in this climate that the 'Rankean' obsession with archival evidence and fetishisation of sources came to be the hallmarks of academic history.[14]

The appeal of Prussian-led German nationalism to the bulk of historians had nothing whatever to do with resignation, or with a betrayal of Liberal values on their part. On the contrary, Bismarck's accomplishment of the *kleindeutsch* solution won approval precisely because it appeared to be liberating. It offered more scope to the historian, for whom national history was surely a more stimulating undertaking than the study of petty dynasties or principalities. The history of regions within Germany was encouraged only as long as regions were represented as 'nurseries' or as microcosms of the nation at large. Otherwise, regional history was held to be a risky business capable of lending sustenance to particularist attempts at state formation and so threatening Germany's integrity.[15]

To anyone at the top of the academic hierarchy, the state was a generous paymaster. But historians who became genuinely wealthy owed their fortune only indirectly to the state. There were indeed modest fortunes to be made, whether from publications which reached wide sections of the *Bildungsbürgertum* or from the ability to charge an entrance fee to students attending some lectures. The state acted as a facilitator in all this. Without the prestige it could attach to the historian, and without the privileged access to archives which lay in its gift, the possibilities of exerting influence on the public or of attracting a market for the products of scholarship were severely constrained. The state could confer honorific civil service titles on the incumbents of established Chairs. It could bring historians into close relations with political elites, and it could make or break young historians' careers. Nevertheless, historians liked to conceive of themselves as belonging to an autonomous community of practitioners of their craft: to a guild (*Zunft*). In part at least, this was a useful fiction, providing a source of professional identity. Even as historians imaginatively represented the contents of archives as evidence of a national past, they constructed a sense of their own corporate identity. This rested on improved communications networks and on organisational and institutional innovations masked by mock-medieval nomenclature in much the same way as the nationalist movements themselves did.

The *Zunft* was the self-proclaimed guarantor of academic liberty. But professional historians' definition of academic liberty had little to do with an individual's freedom of thought or with the toleration of intellectual diversity. Rather, it had to do with *Zunft* members' perception of themselves as a self-regulatory body entitled to define the basis of entry into its ranks. In Imperial Germany, where the reality was of massive ministerial interference in the faculties' stated preferences for appointments, this aspect of the *Zunft* was little short of pure fantasy.[16] It no doubt contributed, however, to the self-esteem of professors who were in fact political appointees but who would have hated to admit it. In the Weimar Republic, the myth was fostered further, and ministerial overruling of shortlists for Chairs was ritually denounced as a denial of academic liberty. On the rare occasions on which the Republican authorities sought, through involuntary early retirement, to rid themselves of unrepentant anti-democrats, the latter were able to mobilise colleagues and students, but also parliamentarians and the wider Protestant, bourgeois–nationalist milieu in their defence.[17] The professoriate did exert considerable influence over its own succession. The length of time normally required to be considered for an appointment to a full Chair made the 'apprentice' historian heavily reliant on his supervisor's patronage. For the young historian to step out of line academically or politically was to place his career at risk. Even in the period 1918–33, a scholar was far more likely to find his career blighted if his patriotism could be impugned than if his loyalty to the Republic was called into question.[18]

But the *Zunft* comprised more than an agglomeration of professors and those angling for the combined influence and financial security which nothing short of a full Chair could bring an historian working within the universities. It embraced archive directors and other auxiliary servants of the discipline (*historische Hilfswissenschaftler*) as well as staff employed in research institutes or working for journals. Historians' sense of belonging to a single working community of scholars was enhanced by the voluminous correspondence generated within the *Zunft*. Eminent and not so eminent historians carefully preserved their academic and political correspondence, especially with colleagues and favoured students. By the inter-war years at the very latest, they did so with a view to having their letters filed away in university or national archives after their deaths. Such bodies of correspondence, which must frequently have been written (or subsequently selected for preservation) with half an eye to posterity, are problematic as sources for the politics of German historians. But they afford material evidence of networks of clientage, political communication and internal university politics. Hundreds of collections of historians' papers are gathered in dozens of state and university archives in Germany, and the fact that archivists were (and are) anxious to secure them is itself suggestive. The historiographical record has long been regarded as an important part of the national historical record.

Thus, the development and longevity of a discrete historical methodology and ideology – German 'historism' – cannot be fully understood within the framework of a narrow history of ideas. The nationalist paradigm in German historical scholarship came into being, and endured, because it enjoyed the favour of the state, and because the historical profession was capable of policing its members with striking efficiency.[19] The historical profession was itself an imagined community which purveyed an imagined history and prefigured the nation. Personal and professional career trajectories and interpretations of the fate of the nation became deeply intertwined. So much so in the case of the maverick (but deeply nationalist) grandee of the Wilhelmine academic elite Karl Lamprecht that – as Roger Chickering has acidly remarked – his '*German History* . . . was his account of his own personal growth. The progress of Germany through the successive periods of its history was a metaphor for his own emancipation from the constraints on his intellectual development.'[20] Periods of national confidence inspired general professional optimism. Defeats and crises such as those of 1918–19 were correspondingly internalised as crises of historism.[21]

What George Iggers has called 'the German conception of history' had clear contours.[22] It concerned, first, the welding of peoples into nation-states through the actions of great men, and, second, the identification of a German mission abroad. Historism developed simultaneously as an historical methodology and as an ideology of German nationalism. In and of itself it constituted

a core element of the 'German path'. This is manifest not simply in its practitioners' veneration of the state, but more particularly in their associated critique of western European concepts of civil society, natural rights and social
contracts. If it was only during the First World War, and in the aftermath of
the Treaty of Versailles, that German historians fully articulated an ideology
of the 'German path', and if their assertion that western Europe held out a
model of political development alien to Germany was conveyed with a degree
of aggression peculiar to that period, the direction had already been strongly
indicated by the historians of the Prussian School (most notably Heinrich von
Sybel, Friedrich Dahlmann, J. G. Droysen and Heinrich von Treitschke) in the
third quarter of the nineteenth century. Later historians acknowledged their
debt to this tradition. Thus, in 1922 Paul Joachimsen attributed to historism
the achievement of having put the Humanist conception of the People 'into a
firm and increasingly important relationship to the notion of the German state
. . . and so given it a direction . . . which conclusively divided it from western
development'.[23] Thus historism could be represented simultaneously as an
inspiration and as an integral feature of the German path. Writing in the same
period as Joachimsen, Hermann Oncken repeatedly stressed the role played
by German historiography in providing a vitally important 'building-block' of
the nation-state, whose nineteenth-century 'renewal' had been inspired by historically derived imagery. Far from merely reflecting the development of the
Bismarckian Reich, historism had, in disseminating 'consciousness of the
great collective heritage of the past', been a *sine qua non* for the accomplishment of national unity, and this in itself marked Germany out from the other
European nations.[24] This curious train of thought enabled German nationalists' dependence on the stories concocted by historians to be transformed from
a weakness into a strength.

Echoing their German counterparts' view of the First World War as a
confrontation as much between world-views as between combatant states,
British historians were exercised in particular by what they saw as the German
historians' culpable role in providing a moral imperative for the pursuit of the
war. In 1914 and 1915, a string of publications named Heinrich von Treitschke
as the epitome of German bellicosity and overweening ambition.[25] It may be
suggested that Treitschke himself was not a major influence on the German historians of the Wilhelmine period. Wolfgang J. Mommsen has argued that the
mobilising thrust of Prussian School historiography, with its emphasis on the
nation and on nationalist dynamism, was supplanted in Wilhelmine scholarship
by a more stabilising trend which, in its focus on legitimising the state, looked
back to the calmer tones of Ranke.[26] But the 'Rankean Renaissance', associated
with historians such as Erich Marcks and Friedrich Meinecke, neither had as
dominant a voice within the *Zunft* as Mommsen seems to imply, nor was fundamentally opposed to the tradition of Treitschke. Historians like Dietrich Schäfer

and Richard Fester carried on the Prussian School's impetus through their support for radical nationalist interest groups. Furthermore, while German historians were bitterly divided by their participation on opposite sides of debates on German war aims and over whether domestic reforms would serve the war effort, Treitschke was not disowned by the relatively moderate 'governmental' nationalists associated with the Rankean revival. The rejuvenated interest in Ranke had never involved more than a shift in emphasis. In the circumstances of the World War, when the mobilisation of the nation appeared to historians to be a task to which they should all contribute, the distinctions between the approach of the Prussian School and that of the neo-Rankeans lost its pertinence. In a letter of October 1914, Friedrich Thimme, the historian and librarian of the Prussian *Herrenhaus*, conveyed the nationalist enthusiasm which had overrun the hitherto sedate language of the neo-Rankeans: 'We historians now wish to be the prophets of the new Germany. . . . If one cannot serve the Fatherland with the sword, then at least it should be done with the pen.'[27] This was undertaken very much in the spirit of Treitschke. As Thimme put it to Meinecke in May 1917, 'It is precisely we historians, who are more responsible than others for administering the heritage of Bismarck and of Treitschke, who now belong on the fronts both of foreign and of domestic policy.'[28] Meinecke himself understood the meaning of the war as a battle between the 'German spirit' and the values of the west.[29] Historians sought to act not only as the analysts of Bismarckian power politics as it had been practised in the past, but as its exponents in the present.

As in the wars of unification, the fact that Germany seemed set to reach a 'far higher world-historical level' cemented the relationship between national power-political assertion and historical scholarship. Willi Andreas excitedly looked forward to new opportunities for his discipline. 'Historical studies will flower mightily after the war; the broadest perspectives are opening up before us.'[30] The expansion of German territory and enhancement of German power would, it was anticipated, provide a substantial intellectual return for the historians' investment of their energies in national propaganda campaigns. The shocks of defeat and of the November Revolution thus had a particular poignancy for historians. To many who had added an academic gloss to the glorification of Imperial Germany, the twin catastrophes took on dimensions which were as much professional as personal or political, and their responses were conditioned by the temptation to compare the past with an unpromising present. Fritz Hartung, a young constitutional historian who had served in the war, felt that his entire intellectual world had collapsed with the German front lines: 'As an historian, devoting his efforts to explaining the present out of the past, I now find myself standing before an expanse of ruins. For everything which we have hitherto felt to be the firm foundation of our statehood now lies prostrate.'[31] Haller, too, gave a professional inflection to his experiences of the material miseries of post-war Germany: 'It may well be that it is precisely we academics who, given the general privation of which we are surely now experiencing only the beginning, will find it hardest to assert our estate. Where we were wont to draw out of abundant resources, we will now have to save, to do without.'[32]

Despite this sense of desolation, for Hartung, Haller and the bulk of their colleagues the perceived threat to German identity was to be combated by a reversion to a purportedly German tradition and a resolution, in Haller's words, 'to awaken the German spirit to new life and new creativity'.[33] 'As an historian', Hartung wrote, 'I cannot make up my mind to burn all that I had previously worshipped. Even now [20 November 1918], the age of Bismarck still seems to me to have been the high point of German history, and not a regrettable aberration, a detour into power politics.'[34] The Wilhelmine professoriate was virtually unanimous in denying the Weimar Republic historical and, by extension, national legitimacy. A significant minority within it (drawn chiefly from the ranks of neo-Rankeans and erstwhile supporters of the 'moderate' war aims of Chancellor Bethmann Hollweg) was prepared at least to tolerate, and at most conditionally to support, the Republic. Even for this group, however, the experiment with parliamentary democracy was, *a priori*, un-German. Hans Delbrück, whose fierce denunciation of Ludendorff certainly assisted the Republic, was still wholly unwilling to commit himself to it in principle:

> I may say of myself that I can see the sins of the old regime with the same clarity as I can see the achievements of the Republic. Nevertheless, I cannot celebrate the Republic, nor can I give allegiance to the black, red and golden flag. I can affirm only that the Republic is the only form in which Germany may live today. But even so I cannot forget that it was the victorious enemy who pressed this form of the state upon us and that the national assembly had no option but to pour the will of the enemy into the paragraphs of the constitution. And that, however highly one may prize republican idealism, was certainly a vital factor.[35]

Just as Fritz Hartung felt the creeping on German public opinion of internationalism and of belief in a 'world conscience' to have been a more important factor than the admitted errors of the old regime in bringing about Germany's defeat, so parliamentary democracy, once it had been identified as a western imposition on Germany, was now held also to have a debilitating influence on the nation's capacity to renew its power political ambitions. Party political pluralism was regarded as a modern form, or continuation, of the particularism of states which was now uniformly regarded as the tragic misadventure of German history between the medieval and the Bismarckian Reich.

Hagen Schulze has recently suggested that a fundamental problem for the

Weimar Republic was that its supporters were unwilling to couple their democratic commitment with a German nationalist one.[36] In the case of the historians, the problem was rather that those who were prepared to give the Republic any kind of backing at all tended to subordinate the defence of democracy to a defence of nationalist traditions. Friedrich Thimme was enraged by the role played by Social Democratic and Roman Catholic Centre Party politicians in influencing the Republic's decision to sign the Treaty of Versailles. He announced that he would give up his long-standing attempts at healing the political divisions between the Christian denominations in Germany and berated the Social Democratic leaders with whom, throughout the war, he had sought to build bridges. He was now 'very much inclined to seek contacts further to the Right again, and in any event will see my chief task as raising national consciousness out of its present rock-bottom condition'.[37] If, once his anger had subsided, Thimme dropped his threat to turn so very sharply to the Conservatives, he stuck leech-like to his nationalist commitment. Paradoxically, the Weimar Republic itself furnished him with the wherewithal to put it into practice. Through the massive edition of German Foreign Office documents on the long run-up to the First World War, Thimme sought not just to vindicate the German nation from the accusation of responsibility for the causes of the war, but to give the monarchy and ruling elites a clean bill of health.[38]

For many more overtly anti-democratic historians, the defence of 'German' traditions of authoritarianism, militarism and power politics was utterly incompatible with any dalliance with the Republic. Johannes Haller, who defined true patriotism as 'love of the past', counterposed adventures in the creation of new political forms to the necessary preservation of a value system embedded in history: 'We must cry out to the loquacious and overly busy heralds of the so-called new era: innovation is not rejuvenation! Whoever wishes to renew what has been spoiled must reach back to the original. Our hope for a better future lies only in a return to the true, old essence of our being. Only if it draws juice from the root may the plant produce new shoots.'[39] Bismarckian virtues were paraded to students and to the reading public by an array of revanchist historians. The dilemma which Haller and like-minded colleagues found themselves in was that they could now find little to say for Bismarck's successors. There was no consensus about what exactly had been wrong with the social and economic development of Wilhelmine Germany, but all were agreed that it had been fatally flawed. Haller identified an excess of bourgeois capitalism (and so also an increasing proximity to 'western' trends) as the fundamental problem of the era;[40] Fritz Rörig, also a medievalist, diagnosed too much feudalism as the cause of the disease.[41] But however far the routes which their analyses took diverged, their conclusions were essentially alike. State and nation had failed to grow together in this period, and the 'spirit of 1914' had thus rested on too insecure a basis to endure the trials of a long war. Haller himself, with several of his most successful students as well as the bulk of historians of his own generation, stuck to statist historiographical precepts and (albeit with less and less hope, and with repeated dalliances with fascism) to Conservative politics.[42] In many respects, the outcome of the war and the establishment of the Weimar Republic confirmed them in their confidence in the statist and nationalist paradigm.

To some historians, however, the ignominious ending of the monarchy in Germany and the acknowledged failings of the imperial political system suggested the desirability of departures from established lines of historical inquiry and of political engagement. Younger historians, and more particularly Sudeten, Baltic, Austrian and other Germans who (in origin at least) came from beyond the borders of the Reich, contributed to a shift in the emphasis of scholarship which was simultaneously an attempt at defining a rather different basis for nationalism. One initiative was launched by the Austrian historian Heinrich Ritter von Srbik, who appealed for a new pan-German (*gesamtdeutsch*) historiography capable of transcending the now archaic quarrels between proponents of *Klein-* and *Großdeutschland*. Since dynastic loyalty no longer constrained them, the separation of Austrian Germans from the Reich no longer made sense to them. Srbik's ambition dovetailed with the promotion of 'folk history' or history written 'from the perspective of the *Volk*' (*vom Volke her*). The territorially truncated Weimar Republic could now be measured against a vision of a new Reich based on ethnicity – that is to say, on *völkisch* principles. If the vision was to be realised, then an expanded nation-state had to be created through the efforts of the *Volk* itself. These political impulses demanded an historical elaboration which statist historism by itself was perceived to be ill-equipped to offer. 'Folk historians' complained that Germany's advisers in peace negotiations after the First World War, though they included for instance the eminent military historian Hans Delbrück, had had no answer to the efforts of Polish historians who could produce ethnic maps to bolster their territorial claims. Ethnocartography became one of the hallmarks of 'folk history'. So, too, did interest in the hitherto neglected history of the peasantry. Although research agendas were framed within parameters which dictated an avoidance of evidence of class conflict and were designed to accomplish the retrospective nationalisation of the peasantry as a long-term reservoir of German blood, they did produce a kind of social history.[43]

To claim that 'folk history' introduced a paradigm shift in German historiography would be going too far. Its practitioners saw state formation as the necessary outcome of *völkisch* endeavour and explicitly proclaimed an interpretation of history at once '*völkisch* and statist'.[44] For statist historians the *Volk*, however passive its role, had always constituted the bedrock upon which power political designs should be forged. (It was, for instance, a commonplace to denounce medieval German emperors who, neglecting their 'task' within Germany, embarked on adventures on Italian soil.)[45] In many respects, the statist majority and 'folk historical' minority coexisted perfectly amicably, and certainly without any structured debate about methodology.

There were, however, moments of tension between the two perspectives. 'Folk history' could all too readily degenerate into ahistorical, biological racial determinism. Furthermore, since the *Volk* was now supposed to provide a dynamic element in nation building, a lineage for *völkisch* dynamism had also to be constructed. Some 'folk historians' inverted the historists' proposition that the state predated the people,[46] finding the first Germans amidst the ancient forests and asserting sweeping continuities between these Germanic tribesmen and modern Germans.

In the Third Reich, these tensions were manifest in the very different pedigrees historians attempted to establish for Nazism. The controversies which ensued were always ultimately about the nature of German identity. Statist historians, often in spite of some private misgivings about Nazism, were for the most part pleased to pronounce the Weimar Republic an unfortunate interlude and to hail the Third Reich as a return to traditional routes of national development. Encouraged by the Hitler–Hindenburg relationship, and by the bows Hitler publicly made to totems of the old order, they presented Nazism with a family tree reaching back through Bismarck to Frederick the Great. They struggled also to rehabilitate aspects of nineteenth-century German Liberalism, and especially of Liberal historiography.[47] Their support for an authoritarian regime entailed no populist pandering to the power of the *Volk*, but was predicated on a belief in its political immaturity and incapacity for autonomous action. *Völkisch* priorities, in contrast, concerned the continuity of Germanic forces either irrespective or in spite of processes of state formation. Statist responses derided the claims that German history could be rewritten 'on a racial basis', that the Germans were a Nordic race, even that they were Aryans.[48] The potential for collision between the two approaches is illustrated by the contested history of the foundations of the Carolingian Reich. 'Folk' historians' celebration of the Saxon tribal revolt led by Widukind against Charlemagne caused consternation among historians for whom the achievements of Charlemagne (or rather of Karl der Große: whether the French or German form of the name was used in itself constituted a statement!) remained integral to German national history.

Fritz Rörig, himself an exponent of a variant of *Volksgeschichte* – though of a brand which saw not Germanic tribesmen or peasants but entrepreneurial, urban medieval burghers as the carriers of *völkisch* values – was among those who rushed to Charlemagne's defence. He was at pains to emphasise that he felt both professionally and politically bound to do so. In bringing his 'serious anxieties' to the attention of the Rector of the University of Kiel in June 1934, he stressed that he was writing in his 'capacity as the permanently appointed representative of Medieval History at the University [. . . and] at the suggestion of men in leading positions'.

> Regarding my personal competence in this matter, I would refer to the fact that I have always consciously declared myself to be the representative of a conception of history which does employ value judgements in work relating to the past. It arrives at these judgements through addressing the question of whether particular developmental sequences in our German past advanced or damaged the *völkisch* and statist development of our German *Volk*. . . .
>
> It is from this very perspective that the anxieties I have indicated arise – when I see the impression growing ever more firmly fixed in the German public mind that Karl der Große was alien to the *Volk* and a slaughterer of Saxons.
>
> This conception has already had the consequence that the Kiel *Nordische Rundschau* has published a picture of the felling of the *Irminsul*[49] on which Karl is described as a 'French Emperor'. Should such an impression become established in the German mind, then I would in the first place see a serious danger for our foreign policy therein. I fear that we could do no greater favour to French historiography, but also to French propaganda, than simply to resign all claim to Karl. Karl was of German blood and, among other things, had heroic German songs collected and the rights of German tribes set down in writing. From such careless behaviour on the part of the Germans, it would be possible to construct a renewed Franco-Belgian claim to Aachen and even to the ancient German and Frankish Rhineland.

There were implications also for domestic policy:

> There can scarcely be a doubt that, without the conclusion of the *circa* one hundred years' struggles between Saxons and Franks through the incorporation of the Saxons, the continental tribes would not have formed a single statist and *völkisch* entity in the time that followed. Nor would they do so today. This development of state and *völkisch* unity was, as early as a hundred years after Karl's death, already so strong that political leadership within the Reich could go over to the Saxon counts. There is a danger that, through a revival of a Frankish–Saxon antithesis, particularist antagonisms might return to life within our *Volk*. This cannot, after all, accord with the direction indicated by our Führer's goals.

Here Rörig came perilously close to rendering Charlemagne/Karl as an Aryan. He even contrived to imply that not Karl, but the Saxon leadership, was guilty of racial treason, since it had attacked the Frankish part of Karl's army 'at a point at which both were marching together against the alien threat on their borders: the Sorbs'. Rörig further justified his position by drawing on the authority of Dietrich Schäfer ('a man of thoroughly Lower Saxon sensibilities'), the historian whose Pan-German circle had been instrumental in the founding of the early Nazi Party. 'Without the incorporation of the Saxon tribe into the Frankish state', Rörig quoted Schäfer as having written, 'our present Reich is unimaginable. When its consequences are added up, that act appears as Karl's greatest achievement.'

Rörig also feared that the clash of opinion over Karl was not an isolated incident. Rather, it was characteristic of a problematic relationship between the regime and professional historians 'entirely infused with the German spirit':

> I am very pleased by the fact that leading men from the world of politics repeatedly make reference to the history of our *Volk*, whether to give warnings or to raise spirits. However, I do believe that such appeals to the conscience of the nation would work better in the long run were they not sometimes to occasion tensions between German historical scholarship and the slogans and views spread among the *Volk*. I regret such tensions profoundly. Perhaps occasional meetings between men in the political leadership and representatives of the discipline would be in order, so that historical problems might be discussed prior to their political evaluation. Respecting my own field of work, I should be pleased to place myself at the disposal of such an undertaking.[50]

Rörig found precisely such an outlet for his political ambitions in the *Nord- und Ostdeutsche Forschungsgemeinschaft* (NODFG).[51] Through that and other channels he was to continue to contribute to nationalist propaganda until the final year of the Second World War. Even while he made increasing use of racist language in his academic work, he continued to protest against at least one Nazi attempt to redefine German national identity. The very concept *deutsch*, he warned, was in danger of being displaced by references to *Germanen*.[52]

'Folk historians' were in general far more prominent as participants in Nazi war propaganda than their statist colleagues. Whereas Haller and Hartung found themselves either uninspired by the war itself or out of sympathy with the kind of propaganda expected of them, 'folk historians' made the proud claim that the profession was far better prepared to contribute to the national cause than it had been in 1914–18. The categories, 'facts' and figures they employed were at worst capable of being turned to deadly purpose by the regime.[53] After 1945, some of them were able to put their skills – and knowledge of eastern Europe – at the service of western Cold Warriors. Rapidly and crudely, they de-Nazified their terminology, substituting the words 'social' or 'structural' for *Volk* and *völkisch*.[54] In many respects, however, the tainted past of this segment of the discipline probably retarded the eventual breakthrough of social history in the Federal Republic. The statist tradition lumbered on, meanwhile, under the aloof leadership of Gerhard Ritter. Ritter's incarceration in a Nazi concentration camp, a consequence of his activities in the

Conservative Resistance, now provided him with what he thought a firm foundation from which to mount a defence of German national history and historians.[55] Nevertheless, in a divided country whose population had, in the estimation of nationalist historians, lost all sense of its own history, statist as well as 'folk' historical traditions emerged weakened at the end of the war and of the Nazi dictatorship. Even before the work of Fritz Fischer and of the Bielefeld School had shattered what remained of confidence among nationalist historians, the idea of a German path began to show signs of turning into its opposite – into the notion of a derailed *Sonderweg*.

Fritz Rörig, the last 'bourgeois' Professor of History to have retained his Chair in the German Democratic Republic, now located the root of the evil in the division of the Empire on the death of Charlemagne. In the absence of a strong, centralised state, particularism operating in tandem with the ambitions of princes had crushed all bourgeois political initiatives and finally broken the civic spirit of the bourgeoisie. From the advent of the 'absolutist state' of Frederick William I of Brandenburg–Prussia, the bourgeoisie could display no more than 'the narrow, petty posture of the urban "subject"'. Rörig underscored his argument in what was to become the classic manner: by measuring German shortcomings against English standards of presumed accomplishment. 'If one calls to mind the contemporary position of the English bourgeoisie . . . with its ever-expanding gaze across the seas, with its stirring activities in parliament, the antithesis is self-evident.' In neither 1815 nor 1848 was the German bourgeois able to achieve 'the unity of nation and state', so that 'responsible collaboration in the great tasks of a spacious and liberal state remained closed to it'. Thereafter, it subordinated itself to the 'demonic greatness' of Bismarck. Finally, though Rörig characterised the Third Reich as a 'falsification', a direct line to Hitler was strongly indicated.[56]

Haller, the old warhorse of statist nationalism, rather outdid Rörig in an embittered denunciation of overweening German ambition and aggression, a *Sonderweg* which he traced from the sixteenth century to Hitler.

> Ambition strives for the possible; conceit always wishes to be taken for more than one is or can be. It did not awaken among the Germans only with Wilhelm II. It speaks to us from the writings of the German Humanists at the beginning of the sixteenth century. They declared their *Volk* to be the first in the world, superior to all others, even to the Romans who had ruled the world. We encounter its voice in the eighteenth century, from the patriotic wasteland of a Klopstock. And it broke out unrestrainedly in the days of the Revolution of 1848.[57]

A 'German path' remained as evident to these authors after 1945 as it had ever been before. Its construction had always depended on a high degree of eclecticism. Now, they ornamented it with very different signposts.

Notes

1 M. Kundera, 'Speech made at the Fourth Congress of the Czechoslovak Writers' Union June 27–9, 1967', in D. Hamšik, *Writers Against Rulers* (London, 1971), p. 169.

2 Quoted in L. Krieger, *Ranke: The Meaning of History* (Chicago, 1977), pp. 163, 137.

3 D. Deletant and H. Hanack (eds), *Historians as Nation-Builders: Central and South-East Europe* (London, 1988) is more useful in relation to the first than the second of these undertakings.

4 On the *Historikerstreit* itself, see R. Evans, *In Hitler's Shadow: West German Historians and the Attempt to Escape from the Nazi Past* (London, 1989); C. S. Maier, *The Unmasterable Past: History, Holocaust, and German National Identity* (Cambridge, Mass., 1990); on more recent developments, see S. Berger, 'Historians and nation-building in Germany after reunification', *Past and Present*, 148 (1995), 187–222.

5 Krieger, *Ranke*, p. 72. Women were as comprehensively excluded from the pursuit of professional historical scholarship as they were from nineteenth-century nationalist associational life. See B. Smith, 'Gender and the practices of history: the seminar and archival research in the nineteenth century', *American Historical Review* (1995), 1150–76.

6 Quoted in Krieger, *Ranke*, p. 162.

7 J. Haller, 'Der bildende Wert der Neueren Weltgeschichte', in his *Reden und Aufsätze zur Geschichte und Politik* (Stuttgart, 1934), p. 181. Unless otherwise indicated, all translations from the German are by the present author.

8 J. Haller, 'Von Tod und Auferstehung der deutschen Nation', in his *Reden und Aufsätze*, pp. 337–8.

9 D. Blackbourn and G. Eley, *The Peculiarities of German History: Bourgeois Society and Politics in Nineteenth-Century Germany* (Oxford, 1984); see also R. Fletcher, 'Recent developments in West German historiography: the Bielefeld School and its critics', *German Studies Review*, 7 (1984), 451–80.

10 H.-U. Wehler (ed.), *Deutsche Historiker*, 9 vols (Göttingen, 1971–82).

11 Bundesarchiv Koblenz, Haller Papers: from the manuscript of the unpublished part of Haller's memoirs written c. 1946, part IV: 'Im Strom der Zeit', p. 244.

12 A. Thimme, 'Biographische Einführung', in A. Thimme (ed.), *Friedrich Thimme 1868–1938: ein politischer Historiker, Publizist und Schriftsteller in seinen Briefen* (Boppard, 1994), pp. 16–17.

13 U. Haltern, 'Geschichte und Bürgertum: Droysen – Sybel – Treitschke', *Historische Zeitschrift*, 259:1 (1994), 59–107.

14 See R. Chickering, *Karl Lamprecht: A German Academic Life* (Atlantic Highlands, 1993), pp. 24–37, 75.

15 Archiv der Hansestadt Lübeck, Rörig Papers no. 40, Rörig to Wilhelm Engel, 5 July 1935.

16 B. vom Brocke (ed.), *Wissenschaftsgeschichte und Wissenschaftspolitik im Industriezeitalter: Das 'System Althoff' in historischer Perspektive* (Hildesheim, 1991).

17 P. Lambert, 'Generations of German historians: patronage, censorship and the containment of generational conflict 1918–1945', in M. Roseman (ed.), *Generations in Conflict: Youth Revolt and Generation Formation in Germany 1770–1968* (Cambridge, 1995), pp. 172–3.

18 P. Lambert, 'The politics of German historians 1914–1945', unpublished D.Phil. thesis (University of Sussex, 1986), pp. 29–51.

19 W. Weber, 'The long reign and final fall of the German conception of history: a historical–sociological view', *Central European History*, 2:4 (1988), 385–95; Lambert, 'Generations of German historians'.

20 Chickering, *Karl Lamprecht*, p. 138.

21 Lambert, 'The politics of German historians', pp. 136ff.

22 G. G. Iggers, *The German Conception of History: The National Tradition of Historical Thought from Herder to the Present* (Middletown, 1968; 2nd edn, 1971).

23 Quoted in B. Faulenbach, *Ideologie des deutschen Weges: Die deutsche Geschichte in der Historiographie zwischen Kaiserreich und Nationalsozialismus* (Munich, 1980), p. 135.

24 *Ibid.*, p. 36.

25 See S. Wallace, *War and the Image of Germany: British Academics 1914–1918* (Edinburgh, 1988), pp. 67ff.

26 W. J. Mommsen, 'Ranke and the neo-Rankean school in Imperial Germany: state-oriented historiography as a stabilizing force', in G. G. Iggers and J. M. Powell (eds), *Leopold von Ranke and the Shaping of the German Historical Discipline* (New York, 1990), pp. 124–40.

27 Thimme to Karl Thimme, 24 October 1914, in Thimme (ed.), *Friedrich Thimme*, p. 122.

28 Geheimes Staatsarchiv preußischer Kulturbesitz, Meinecke Papers no. 46, Thimme to Meinecke, 22 May 1917.

29 Faulenbach, *Ideologie des deutschen Weges*, p. 170.

30 Universitätsbibliothek Göttingen, A. O. Meyer Papers no. 12, Andreas to Meinecke, 4 April 1915.

31 Bundesarchiv Koblenz, Fester Papers no. 249, Hartung to Fester, 20 November 1918.

32 Haller, 'Von Tod und Auferstehung', p. 335.

33 *Ibid.*, p. 337.

34 Fester Papers no. 249, Hartung to Fester, 20 November 1918.

35 Bundesarchiv Koblenz, Wilhelm Solf Papers no. 99, Delbrück to Theodor Wolff, 11 August 1925 (carbon copy).

36 H. Schulze, 'Fragen die wir stellen müssen. Keine historische Haftung ohne nationale Identität', in R. Augstein *et al.*, *'Historikerstreit': Die Dokumentation der Kontroverse um die Einzigartigkeit der nationalsozialistischen Judenvernichtung* (Munich, 1987), p. 149.

37 Niedersächsisches Staatsarchiv, Oldenbourg, Hermann Oncken Papers no. 588, Thimme to Oncken, 27 June 1919.

38 Lambert, 'The politics of German historians', pp. 200–19; A. Thimme, 'Biographische Einführung', pp. 39–47.

39 Haller, 'Von Tod und Auferstehung', p. 340.

40 J. Haller, *Die Ära Bülow* (Stuttgart, 1922), p. 75; J. Haller, *Die Epochen der deutschen Geschichte* (5th edn, Stuttgart, 1942), p. 388; Faulenbach, *Ideologie des deutschen Weges*, p. 247.

41 Archiv der Hansestadt Lübeck, Rörig Papers no. 44, Rörig to Joseph Hansen, 5 November 1930; no. 52, Rörig to Oncken, 6 October 1933.

42 See P. Lambert, 'Between Conservatism and Nazism: Führer, Volk and foreign policy in the politics and historical scholarship of Johannes Haller, 1914–1947' (forthcoming).

43 On Srbik's role, see O. J. Hammen, 'German historians and the advent of the National Socialist State', *Journal of Modern History*, 13:2 (1941), 161–88, which also suggests that German historians' experience at Versailles was a spur to innovation. The same point is made by E. Vollert, 'Albert Brackmann und die ostdeutsche Volks- und Landesforschung', in H. Aubin *et al.* (eds.), *Deutsche Ostforschung: Ergebnisse und Aufgaben seit dem ersten Weltkrieg*, vol. I (Leipzig, 1942), pp. 3–11. This may have been Hammen's source. For interpretations of *Volksgeschichte* as a kind of social history, see W. Oberkrome, *Volksgeschichte: Methodische Innovation und völkische Ideologisierung in der deutschen Geschichtswissenschaft 1918–1945* (Göttingen, 1993); H. Lehmann and J. van Horn Melton (eds), *Paths of Continuity: Central European Historiography from the 1930s to the 1950s* (Cambridge, 1994).

44 Rörig Papers no. 33, Rörig to the Rector of the University of Kiel, 6 June 1934. Cf. O. Höfler, 'Volkskunde und politische Geschichte', *Historische Zeitschrift*, 162 (1940), 17–18.

45 See G. Althoff, 'Die Beurteilung der mittelalterlichen Ostpolitik als Paradigma für zeitgebundene Geschichtsschreibung', in G. Althoff (ed.), *Die deutschen und ihr Mittelalter: Themen und Funktionen moderner Geschichtsbilder vom Mittelalter* (Darmstadt, 1992), pp. 148–9.

46 The terms of the debate are clearly established in a series of statist contributions penned by Haller's former supervisee and then successor at Tübingen, Heinrich Dannenbauer: see, for example, his *Germanisches Altertum und deutsche Geschichtswissenschaft* (Tübingen, 1935) and *Indogermanen, Germanen, Deutsche: Vom Werden des deutschen Volkes* (Tübingen, 1935).

47 K. Schönwälder, *Historiker und Politik: Geschichtswissenschaft im Nationalsozialismus* (Frankfurt-on-Main, 1992), pp. 20–8; P. Lambert, 'German historians and Nazi ideology: the parameters of the Volksgemeinschaft and the problem of historical legitimation, 1930–1945', *European History Quarterly*, 25 (1995), 555–82.

48 J. Haller, *Der Eintritt der Germanen in die Weltgeschichte* (Berlin, 1939), p. 13.

49 The sacred tree trunk venerated by the Saxon tribes and sole symbol of their unity.

50 Rörig Papers no. 3, Rörig to the Rector of the University of Kiel, 6 June 1934.

51 *Ibid.*, no. 50, Rörig to Albert Brackmann, 2 March 1934; no. 66, Rörig to Ahasver von Brandt, 22 February 1942. On the role of the NODFG see M. Burleigh, *Germany Turns Eastwards: A Study of Ostforschung in the Third Reich* (Cambridge, 1988).

52 Rörig Papers no. 50, Rörig to Martin Lintzel, 15 January 1935.

53 See Burleigh, *Germany Turns Eastwards*.

54 See, e.g., Van Horn Melton, 'From folk history to structural history: Otto Brunner (1898–1982) and the radical-conservative roots of German social history', in Lehmann and Van Horn Melton (eds), *Paths of Continuity*, pp. 263–92.

55 Ritter to Werner Jäger, 5 March 1946, in K. Schwabe and R. Reichardt (eds), *Gerhard Ritter: Ein politischer Historiker in seinen Briefen* (Boppard, 1984), p. 412.

56 F. Rörig, 'Die Stadt in der deutschen Geschichte' [1952], reprinted in his *Wirtschaftskräfte im Mittelalter: Abhandlungen zur Stadt- und Wirtschaftsgeschichte* (Cologne, 1959), pp. 676ff.

57 Haller, 'Im Strom der Zeit', p. 63.

PART III

THE NATION IN SPACE

Mapping national identities: the culture of cartography, with particular reference to the Ordnance Survey

To imagine a nation is to envision its geography. Borders, scenery, routeways, regions, a capital city, provincial towns, historic landmarks, sites for future development, help define a sovereign territory. A nation's internal geography is articulated in terms of a wider world, its various frontiers, agreed or disputed, with other territories – states, federations or empires – its avenues of trade and migration, its outposts of economic power and cultural identity, its actual or projected spheres of influence. There is seldom a secure or enduring consensus about a nation's geography, about which places are representative, which central, which peripheral, and about how they are co-ordinated both within the nation and in relation to the world at large. Disputes about a nation's geography reflect competing interests – court, country, merchants, clergy, intellectuals – and competing notions of citizenship.[1]

A number of discourses and disciplines have been commandeered to envision and re-vision a nation's geography, to describe, design and physically reshape it: landscape painting, topographical poetry, architecture, archaeology, town and country planning, tourism, schoolteaching, civil engineering, military conquest. In this essay I will examine the role of maps in framing these discourses and disciplines and projecting the interests they serve. I will emphasise the power and complexity of maps as artefacts – their scales, spatial projections, conventional signs, texts, cartouches and cover art – and the culture of cartography which they define, the world of map-making, publishing and marketing, map-reading, display and reproduction. While official authorities, not least state ministries, have been intent to control and co-ordinate cartography, the conventions of map-making, even the very maps comissioned by the state, have been appropriated for a variety of civilian interests.[2] In the main part of this essay I shall examine a particular state-sponsored cartographic programme, the British Ordnance Survey, focusing on the military, commercial, educational and recreational use of Ordnance Survey maps.

Maps at a scale to show the nation as a whole portray it as a place of identifiable, characteristic size and shape. Advances in geodesy in Europe

Figure 1 Jan van Doetecum, *Leo Belgicus*, 1598, reissued 1650

from the sixteenth century, especially in the calculation of latitude and longitude, and the acceptance of Mercator's projection from a curved to a planar surface, helped to standardise orientation, surface areas, the configuration of coasts, courses of rivers, the distribution of highlands, and the position of major towns.[3] With the drawing of borders, the nation took on a consistent look, the body politic expressed in a characteristic physiognomy. This function was reflected in the production of a variety of artefacts, from medals to wall maps, inscribed with the portrait of the nation. The prospect of partition or territorial losses provoked images of a fragmented map, a dismembered national body. Propaganda maps used the shape of national territories as a basis for drawing heroic or demonic human or animal figures.[4] Cartographic shape appears as important to the identity of those nations which were carved out for the convenience of others, as to that of those which have largely controlled their own borders.[5] Benedict Anderson points out that the practice of colouring colonies on maps with an imperial dye – British pink–red, French purple–blue, Dutch yellow–brown – helped to promote a highly abstract image, a logo-map detached from other geographic information, which has proved indispensable upon independence, not least for the suppression of the cultural divisons which colonial regimes bequeathed.

> In this shape, the map entered an infinitely reproducible series, available for transfer to posters, official seals, letterheads, magazine and textbook covers, tablecloths, and hotel walls. Instantly recognizable, everywhere visible, the logo-map penetrated deep into the popular imagination, forming a powerful emblem for the anti-colonial nationalism being born.[6]

State-sponsored trigonometrical, topographical and toponymical surveys are key instruments for the expansion and consolidation of central government. Such surveys aid the internal colonisation of the nation-state as well as the incorporation of its overseas territories.[7] Commissioned by the Crown, with the royal arms on each sheet, and Elizabeth I enthroned on the frontispiece, Christopher Saxton's great collection of county maps of England and Wales (1574–79) projected the dominion of central government over the regions.[8] But in refining the portrayal of county, politically dominated by the landed gentry, Saxton's atlas projected a political 'country' which was to subvert the authority of the Crown.[9] In eighteenth-century France the Cassini Survey (1750–89), based on a chain of triangulations extending the length of France through a meridian passing through Paris, projected the space of the nation as a uniform, extended surface, transcending local landforms and loyalties, which might be reshaped for the reform of government. Within this framework, the topographical survey reflected commercial and military interests concerned with road building, fortification and the exploitation of natural resources, projecting an image of France no less centred on Paris, but manifested in a concrete, physiographic portrayal of the national territory.[10]

From the early nineteenth century onwards, European nations tabulated statistics in cartographic form. Thematic maps displayed a variety of social indices such as literacy, disease, poverty, language, birth-rates, land use and economic performance. These maps produced new, sometimes troubling, patterns of the nation's regional constitution, often as part of various policy initiatives to reform it. By the twentieth century, professional geographers were producing more complex choropleth maps charting correlations between a number of physiographic and demographic variables – climate and race, landforms and religion – which extended beyond national boundaries. These were deployed to chart the *Lebensraum* both of established imperial nations like Britain and France, anxious to map out lands fit for full white settlement or merely for imperial rule, and of small, sometimes emergent, nations like Estonia, which were concerned about the broader federal affiliations, the broad regional formations of land and life, in which their national life might best be sustained.[11]

Cadastral maps, showing the ownership of property, are powerful instruments of statecraft, for reforming revenue through land taxation, evaluating resources, monitoring agriculture, reclaiming land, rationalising landholding and organising the extension of settlement into new lands. State-commissioned or state-controlled cadasters are highly contentious, for under the authority of central government, they transfer power between various interests – from commoners to capitalists, from aristocrats to small farmers, from aboriginal inhabitants to pioneer settlers – as well as creating a powerful new layer of bureaucracy concerned with the management of the land. Some cadasters, such as English enclosure maps or Dutch polder maps, are maps of individual communities, but provide the blueprint for a kind of landscape widely recognised as an emblem of national pride. Others are systematic surveys of whole territories, numbering thousands of maps, which provide a comprehensive framework for constructing new kinds of citizenship.[12] Established prior to the the the sale, settlement or development of new land, the grid of the US Federal Land Survey was intended to produce a post-colonial polity of small, independent owner-occupiers. The aim was not achieved – in parcelling land so conveniently for sale, the grid offered prospects of engrossment and speculation – but when the method was later combined on the prairies with policies offering small parcels very cheaply, and eventually free, to homesteading farmers, it had an enduring impact on the physical landscape and cultural imagination. Promoters of county atlases offered subscribers the opportunity to have their name and the exact position of their home on the Federal grid, their stake in the nation, inscribed on the map, with the opportunity for a vignette of their farmhouse and fields. Thousands of such atlases were published in the late nineteenth century, and with the Bible and family photo album, had pride of place in the home parlour.[13]

Globes and planispheres, inscribed with the terrestrial and celestial pretensions of government, have long been part of the panoply of state power.[14] Mercator's projection provided a lasting template for world maps. With its fidelity to compass bearings, it served the interests of European exploration and colonisation, but it has endured beyond all practical considerations as an image of Europe and the North Atlantic world as privileged centres of world affairs. The international agreement of 1884 to take Greenwich as the prime meridian positioned Britain on the *axis mundi*. This position was eagerly exploited by wall maps commemorating the spread of British influence, showing a small island at the centre of a red-tinted empire on which the sun never set, framed at the margins by vignettes of peoples, flora and fauna which flourished under British dominion.[15] In the present century large corporations have deployed the same imagery, portraying sources of raw materials, views of cheerful overseas workers, and trade routes animated by old-fashioned clippers and galleons blown by the exhalations of the Winds.[16] Recent projections, notably that of Arno Peters, have tried to redress the Eurocentrism of

Mercator, by giving a more accurate impression of the size of countries to the south of the equator, and so pushing Europe and North America to the upper margins of the world map.[17] The most profound revision of the global image in recent times, the photographs of the earth taken from space, have challenged the very authority of the atlas. The product of an imperial venture, the American Apollo missions, they have yet promoted an image of the earth as One World, or Whole Earth, an icon of a world freed from the political apparatus of the map – its grids, frontiers and place-names – an icon both to internationalist activists and to multinational corporations.[18]

The extension of map-reading and map-making has been part of the democratisation of citizenship in the twentieth century. Military training in field surveying and map interpretation was extended to many ranks.[19] Maps

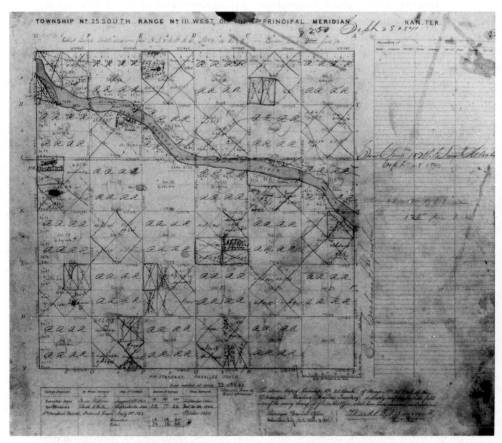

Figure 2 **Local office plat of township 25, south range 3 west, Kansas, annotated with names of landowners**

were a key part of the kit of various organisations, such as the Boy Scouts and Girl Guides, rambling and cycling clubs and youth hostelling associations, which sought to extend access to the countryside for ordinary people. In so doing they promoted a culture of health and fitness, a healthy bonding of body and land.[20] Schools encouraged pupils not only to trace the capes and bays of official atlases, but to make local field surveys and sketches of rocks and soils, plants and house-types, land use and settlement. Combining these materials in collage with postcards, relief models, and shaded, cut-up and mounted sheets of published maps, pupils produced portraits of the land and life of their neighbourhood.[21] Such conventions of parish study or *Heimatkunde* took much of their inspiration from the anti-imperial, internationalist patriotism of Kropotkin, Le Play and Patrick Geddes, yet were liable to be enlisted

Figure 3 **Gilbert Walldroff's farm, Leoni Township, from** *Illustrated Atlas of Jackson County, Michigan* **(1874)**

Figure 4 *Imperial Federation: The British Empire in 1886*

for nationalistic ends, as a basis for an insular love of homeland, and a semi-mystical blending of race and place.[22]

Cartography continues to represent a terrain of contending interests, not only framing different versions of national identity, but questioning the very idea of the nation as a cultural formation. In contrast to official or commercial plans which threaten to redevelop localities, English artists and community activists produce so called 'parish maps', in a variety of media, portraying the places – footpaths, wildlife habitats, allotments, village greens – which make up the community's heritage, its common ground.[23] Artists and writers from the former British imperium, from Ireland, Australia, Canada, the Caribbean, rework the conventions of cartography to envision post-colonial identities.[24] 'Alternative cartographies' are recovered by ethnological research depicting the day-to-day journeying and cosmic views of peoples who trangress the containing, controlling vision of the nation-state.[25]

The British Ordnance Survey had its impetus in the military survey of Scotland (1747–55), undertaken to pacify the Highlands and secure the unified

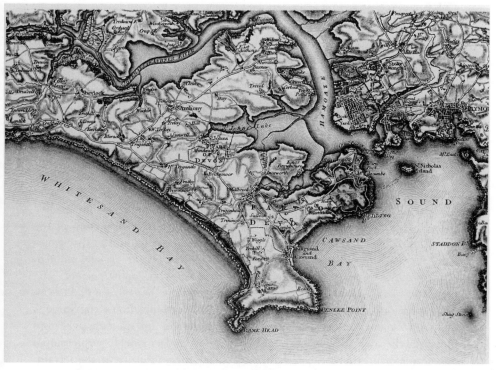

Figure 5 **Plymouth Sound, from** *General [Ordnance] Survey of England and Wales, Devon* (1809)

kingdom from Jacobite threats. The maps of the survey displayed features such as relief, hydrography, land cover, roads, bridges and castles, relevant to the deployment of troops in a newly mobile form of warfare.[26] With the outbreak of war with France in 1756, it became apparent that the mapping of England and Wales lagged well behind that of much of mainland Europe. Saxton's atlas still provided the basis for map-making. There were some new mathematical-based county surveys in the eighteenth century, eagerly promoted by the patriotic Society of Arts, but these only served to show how cartographically uncoordinated Britain was as a whole.[27] During a brief period of co-operation with France, after the American War of Independence, the Royal Society initiated a trigonometrical survey in south-east England co-ordinated with that of the second Cassini Survey in northern France. With the outbreak of the Napoleonic Wars, the state-controlled Ordnance Survey took responsibility for extending the trigonometrical survey and initiating a new topographical one.[28]

The first regions surveyed were in southern England, along the strategically important routes along the coast and overland to London. The first map which the Ordnance Survey took full responsibility for drawing, engraving and publishing was that of Essex, surveyed in the 1790s and issued in 1805. If the maps initially took their names from counties, the county as a social formation did not define their territories. At a scale of one inch to a mile, England and Wales were re-visioned in terms of a new national grid and a series of regions unified in and through movement and circulation. There were differences in style and technique as the survey progressed. The maps for the West Country, for example, present a highly morphological image of the terrain, with densely hachured hills and cliffs and a detailed signalling and naming of places, including small farms, mines and antiquities. What was depicted was a land long shaped by a people as well as by nature, and a bulwark against foreign aggression.[29]

The Ordnance Survey was part of a new programme of state intelligence which included the first national census and the Statistical Section of the Board of Trade.[30] It also fitted well with the dispersal of authority from a landed, county-based aristocracy to that metropolitan, commercially minded, professionally respectful and highly patriotic formation, 'polite society'. The very expertise of surveying, drawing and engraving the maps was upheld as an object of national pride. Private map publishers were quick to use the Survey's maps and name before the government tightened up on copyright and increased the scale of its marketing. The maps offered a model for professional artists to expand the scope of landscape as a genre, to describe the terrain, history and economic prospects of regions. They encouraged tourists to explore English regions while the Continent was closed (though maps were withdrawn from sale in 1811 because their circulation was considered to jeopardise national security), merchants to speculate about new markets, engineers to envisage new and improved roads and waterways. The maps provided a framework for new disciplines like geology and for evolving ones like archaeology. The Ordnance Survey displayed new dimensions of national power.[31]

In the course of the nineteenth century, the Ordnance Survey extended its reach and expanded its scope, to provide the framework for a variety of interests. A geological survey was undertaken from 1835 with the aim of charting resources for industry, agriculture and road making. From the 1840s, as the census went into greater detail about individual households, and as the condition of burgeoning cities captured the imagination of professional reformers, so the Survey produced town plans on vast scales, sometimes as much as ten feet to a mile. These clarified neighbourhoods which had been shrouded in the lurid literary imagery of the slum: Boards of Health could plot the minutiae of the urban fabric – drains, privies, cesspits, dustbins, lamps, water taps and wash houses – and make their plans accordingly.[32] Charles Booth's massive survey of the 'life and labour' of London transcribed information from the 1881 census and notebooks from home visits of School Board visitors on to the twenty-five-inch-to-a-mile map of the city, classifying streets in various colours 'according to the general condition of the inhabitants'.[33] From the 1850s, there were schemes to empower the Ordnance Survey to map every property in the country, but a full cadastral survey of owners and occupiers was never undertaken, and in consequence a full picture of the concentration of landownership and the enduring power of the gentry, which so alarmed liberal reformers, was never produced.[34]

In 1824 the Survey was extended to Ireland to fix the boundaries and names of the 60,000 townlands which were the basis of local taxation. Nothing in the choice of the scale of six inches to a mile 'was dictated by a close knowledge of peculiarly Irish circumstances', notes J. H. Andrews; 'It should rather be regarded as a cartographical expression of the union of the two kingdoms, comparable with the act (passed while the committee was at work) for extending statute measure to Ireland.'[35] A separate department was set up for the place-name survey. This employed civilian Irish-speaking scholars to consult documents and interview local people *in situ* about place-name pronunciation and spelling. While the place-names that eventually appeared on the maps were Anglicised and standardised to suit the sponsors of the Survey, the process itself was upheld at the time by Irish nationalists as one of cultural recovery. This aspect was more evident in an ancillary aspect of the Survey, the production of written memoirs on places. If the economic and topographical material was often marshalled by the improving ethos of the statistical movement, the cultural and historical material sometimes assumed an alarming independence. The volume for Londonderry gave less space to the Protestant defence of the city in 1689 than to approving comment on the recent ban on celebrating it. Whatever the reasons for the British government abandoning the memoir project (and there were fears of an unreliable department exacerbating political tensions), it was seen by nationalists as an act of suppression.[36] For Alice Stopforth Green, writing in 1911, the place-name and memoir survey was

> the first peripatetic university Ireland has seen since the wanderings of her ancient scholars . . . Passionate interest was shown by the people in the memorials of their ancient life – giant's rings, cairns, and mighty graves, the twenty-nine thousand mounds or moats that have been counted, the raths of their saints and scholars – each with a story on the lips of the people . . .[37]

Despite the expansion of the Ordnance Survey's activities, by the later nineteenth century it could scarcely keep pace with the material changes to the landscape or with fresh demands from a new mass market. Some maps had not been revised for half a century or more, showing places braced for the Napoleonic Wars, but no evidence of railways, industrial development or urban expansion. A new audience for geography found maps of their localities or of those they wished to visit difficult to come by, expensive when they were available, and often poorly printed. A new series of cheap, coloured one-inch maps was announced in 1914, but production was postponed until the end of the war.[38]

After the war, for which it produced some 33,000,000 maps, plans and diagrams, the Ordnance Survey helped to frame the reform of national identity, in replanning Britain as a bright, healthy homeland, and in promoting a youth-oriented, modern-minded rediscovery of the countryside. The Ordnance Survey itself underwent radical reconstruction. In a drive for public accountability, the government demanded drastic cutting of costs, especially staff costs, and called for the raising of revenue, notably by a more commercial and competitive marketing of maps. The military culture and organisation of the Ordnance Survey were reformed. Civilian demands, both official and informal, increased sharply, for large-scale plans to support legislation on land registration, slum clearance and town and country planning, and for smaller-scale maps for touring by motorists, cyclists and hikers. Map techniques were modernised. Engraving was abandoned. Redrawn and reproduced through new techniques, maps were made clearer and more colourful. The new Popular Edition, which first appeared from 1918, had finely drawn orange contours and picked out first-class roads in red. Accompanying the Popular Edition was a series of Tourist Maps, the first for 'Snowdonia', which helped hikers by combining contours with hachures and layer tints. The next edition, in the 1930s, used a range of layer tints, modernised lettering, added new symbols for modern features such as National Trust areas and included a grid for a public now trained in using co-ordinates. Comprehensive, comprehensible guides to the use of Ordnance Survey maps were issued and the whole enterprise was promoted with posters and showcards.[39]

Map covers were transformed. From 1919 Ellis Martin was employed as the Survey's artist and designer. Martin had worked for the military in Flanders, drawing sketch maps to aid the movement of heavy artillery, and joined the Ordnance Survey as a map-maker, but it was his pre-war training as a magazine and advertising illustrator which shaped his career. His picture of a cyclist in a cap and Norfolk jacket, smoking his pipe, reading his map to scan a panoramic stretch of countryside, became the standard cover illustration for the Popular Edition, to be replaced for the Fifth Edition in the 1930s by a more up-to-date figure of a shirt-sleeved hiker. For Tourist Maps Martin's covers were more colourful and site-specific. In that for the Cotswolds, the hiker leans on a limestone wall, with the map open to plot his way up Cleeve Hill (figure 6). The landscape, panoramically displaying a farmhouse and the pattern of the land, its paths, walls, fields and woodlands, echoes the map. The image was disseminated in advertising cards of the 1930s for the whole series

Figure 6 Ellis Martin, Cleeve Hill, Glos., illustrated cover to *The Cotswolds* Ordnance Survey District Map (1931)

Figure 7 **J. M. W. Tucker,** *Hiking* (1936)

of one-inch maps, 'The Complete Guide to the Countryside'.[40] It was reworked in J. W. Tucker's 1936 painting, *Hiking* (figure 7). Here three young women consult the OS Cotswolds map, positioning themselves in terms of the landscape below. Along with the map, much in the picture is a measure of modernity: travel, leisure, youth, the bright dress and athletic demeanour of the young women.[41]

Sales of Ordnance Survey maps soared as rural tourism became a mass pursuit. On annual holidays, now enjoyed by most employees, and on summer weekends, thousands of ramblers took to the hills. Urban masses staked a claim for rural England as the grip of its traditional custodians, the landed gentry, visibly weakened in the post-war agricultural depression. Conflicts between ramblers and landowners culminated in organised mass trespasses.[42] Ordnance Survey maps were no respecters of property; for the new mobile army of urban ramblers they displayed the opportunities for moving through the landscape, by road, bridleway, footpath or any other way indicated by the physical relief of the landscape. Maps were not regarded by ramblers of any persuasion as a licence to roam in any way they wanted. The discipline of map-reading, along with the rules and regulations of hiking organisations, promoted a strict code of country conduct. Map use distinguished the rambler from loutish urban visitors, like those from noisy, litter-dropping charabanc parties. It also distinguished them from backward rural labourers.[43] Batsford's *How to See the Country* declared:

> Country folk are generally not map conscious. . . . You can astound the company of the village bar by telling them the message of the map for you of any piece they like of the surrounding landscape, and if you produce a map measurer you are likely to be suspected of black magic. . . . Maps are your charter to the countryside and its innermost recesses. . . . With an Inch Ordnance sheet of your selected area you are master of the countryside: it lies symbolically before you.[44]

The Director-General of the Ordnance Survey, Sir Charles Close, who promoted the post-war reforms, was particularly keen to deploy Ordnance Survey maps as documents for the reconstruction of national history. Not only did existing maps reveal regions with a dense network of antiquities, but the Survey's collection of aerial photographs, produced for military reconaissance and for further revisions to existing maps, revealed large-scale earthworks, in striking patterns. Close appointed an Archaeological Officer, O. G. S. Crawford, founder of the journal *Antiquity*, who pioneered what he called the 'distributional method' of 'field archaeology', the plotting of the spatial as well as chronological significance of archaeological sites, in particular the relation with topography, geology, soils and natural vegetation. Using both fieldwork, by bicycle, and specially commissioned flights for aerial photography, Crawford assembled an archive for the production of 'period maps' which proved hugely popular with the public. *Roman Britain* and *Neolithic Wessex* charted cultures already esteemed respectively for roads and towns and for long barrows and stone circles; the deserted villages and field systems mapped in *Britain in the Dark Ages* shed light on a period presumed to be without culture at all.[45]

Charles Close's own guide to Ordnance Survey maps, *The Map of England* (1932), envisaged the map user as a time-traveller, moving through different cross-sections of the nation's history. For Close, England's history came to an end in the seventeenth century, before the dominion of large property owners, enclosing and emparking, curtailed the freedom to roam. Walks along the line of ancient ridgeways, using some modern roads and lanes, but cutting across country in other places, revealed ancient freedoms. A respect for the geographical imagination of ancient Britain carried over to one for tribal cultures elsewhere: 'in the less visited parts of Africa, natives will draw for you in the sand a diagram of the position of the neighbouring villages and of the bush paths joining them. The idea of a map is quite familiar to such people.'[46]

The Ordnance Survey map was the primary document for an unofficial yet hugely popular archaeological pursuit, the survey of so-called ley lines. Ley hunting was inspired by the works of Alfred Watkins, especially *The Old Straight Track* (1925). Watkins drew lines on Ordnance Survey maps between various landmarks – earthworks, megaliths, beacon sites, notches in hills, moats, crossroads, castles, churches, ponds, holy wells (see figure 8). Combining these maps with collages of photographs, showing sites and views at key points in his transects, and descriptions of folklore and place-name evidence, Watkins argued that ley lines were a prehistoric system of communication and social organisation.[47] Some ley hunters went further, to argue that they were lines of tellurgic force which converged on ancient transmitter stations like Stonehenge. Watkins and his followers detected an indigenous culture more refined than had been hitherto presupposed.[48] The country's ancient inhabitants were not barbarous savages, or isolated farmers, waiting to be civilised from the Mediterranean, but the possessors of a highly organised, highly unified culture – members of just the sort of planned society that progressive experts of the time envisioned. A progressive figure himself, an innovative industrialist, pioneering photographer, enthusiast for town planning and large-scale engineering schemes, a supporter of women's suffrage and education,[49] Watkins attributed to ancient surveyors the professionalism and authority of modern planners. It is perhaps not coincidental that at the time when ley hunters roamed the land, the National Grid of electricity was being constructed, its lines and pylons the very symbol of the the clarity, harmony and order of the modern age.[50]

The Ordnance Survey sold its maps at a discount to schools as a basis for learning about local areas, for pupils to trace or shade with their observations. These exercises seized the imagination of the geographer Dudley Stamp, from the London School of Economics (LSE). Alarmed at the decline in agricultural production in the 1930s and concerned that the country was far less informed about the use and misuse of its land than other European nations, Stamp instituted the Land Utilization Survey (1931–38), to record the use of every acre of land in Britain. Schoolchildren, a quarter of a million of them from 10,000 schools, supervised by their geography teachers, carried out the survey on six-inch sheets according to a standard sevenfold classification (see figure 9). They were encouraged to make notes in map margins, indicating the nature and condition of the land. For Stamp, this was above all an exercise in citizenship. 'The work of recording land use is a magnificent educational exercise involving accurate observation and map reading, and, being done as part of a national scheme, inculcated an early appreciation of the unit in a democracy and induced a local pride in achievement.'[51] The completed maps were sent to the LSE to be transcribed on to one-inch scale sheets, and then passed on to the Ordnance Survey to be printed in attractive colours, mounted on

RADNOR VALE—EASTERN END

MOUND ◯ STONE ◖ CHURCH ◔ CROSS ROAD ◌ INITIAL POINT ◯

Figure 8 Radnor Vale, from Alfred Watkins, *The Old Straight Track* (1925)

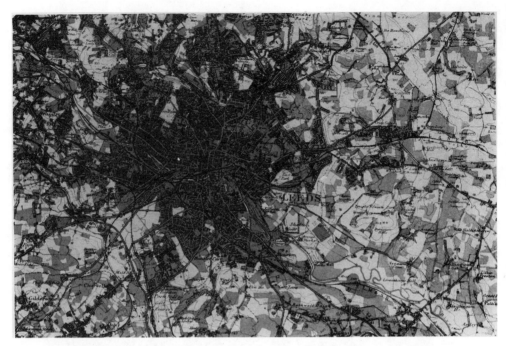

Figure 9 *Leeds and Bradford*, **Land Utilization Survey of Britain, Sheet 31 (surveyed 1932)**

linen and waterproofed. The Land Utilization Survey was a highly agrarian vision. The seven land-use categories were weighted towards agricultural production; non-agricultural, usually urban, uses were categorised as 'non-productive'. Heavily populated areas displayed like an X-ray scan the condition so many planners feared, the cancerous spread of urban land use, coloured deep scarlet, into the countryside.[52]

The mass popularity of cartography in inter-war Britain conditioned a variety of consciously modern cultural pursuits. British artists surveyed landscapes with diagrammatic clarity, finding in maps and aerial photographs the flatness and functional precision which were hallmarks of the modern movement.[53] The work of British writers is filled with allusions to maps. 'Watching and mapping and traversing landscapes couldn't be more fundamental to the '30s literature's sense of itself,' notes Valentine Cunningham, 'to the '30s writers' typical envisaging of their art as being on the road, on the way, into or across a new country.'[54] British culture was, in the words of Gavin Ewart, 'an over-charted countryside'.[55]

This essay has demonstrated the capacity of cartography to represent a range of information and to project a variety of political claims. Maps have the power to transform discourses of national identity, to chart history as a sequence of settlement patterns or distribution of antiquities, economy as a topography of peaks and depressions, citizenship as a pattern of property ownership or rights of way. Moreover, maps have the potential materially to realise political claims and have proved powerful instruments of statecraft. In an age of mass citizenship, map-making and map-reading have had the democratic potential of reading and writing written texts. Even official maps have proved more powerful than the authority which commissioned them. They have been interpreted, used and reinscribed to represent many forms of cultural identity, some of which put the nation as a social formation into doubt.

Notes

1 C. Williams and A. D. Smith, 'The national construction of social space', *Progress in Human Geography*, 7:4 (1983), 502–27; S. Daniels, *Fields of Vision: Landscape Imagery and National Identity in England and the United States* (Cambridge and Princeton, 1993); D. Hooson (ed.), *Geography and National Identity* (Oxford, 1994); A. Godlewska and N. Smith (eds), *Geography and Empire* (Oxford, 1994).

2 J. B. Harley, 'Maps, knowledge and power', in D. Cosgrove and S. Daniels (eds), *The Iconography of Landscape* (Cambridge, 1988); N. Alfrey and S. Daniels (eds), *Mapping the Landscape: Essays on Art and Cartography* (Nottingham, 1990); D. Buisseret (ed.), *Monarchs, Ministers and Maps: the Emergence of Cartography as a Tool of Government in Early Modern Europe* (Chicago, 1992); D. Wood and J. Fels, *The Power of Maps* (London, 1993).

3 C. W. J. Withers, 'How Scotland came to know itself: geography, national identity and the making of a nation, 1680–1790', *Journal of Historical Geography*, 21:4 (1995), 384–6.

4 P. Barber and C. Board, *Tales from the Map Room: Fact and Fiction about Maps and their Makers* (London, 1993), pp. 78–84; J. Pickles, 'Texts, hermeneutics and propaganda maps', in T. J. Barnes and J. S. Duncan (eds), *Writing Worlds: Discourse, Text and Metaphor in the Representation of Landscape* (London, 1992).

5 S. A. Radcliffe, 'Imaginative geographies, postcolonialism, and national identities: contemporary discourses of the nation in Ecuador', *Ecumene*, 3:1 (1996), 1–22.

6 B. Anderson, *Imagined Communities: Reflections on the Origin and Spread of Nationalism*, rev. edn (London and New York, 1991), p. 75.

7 A. Godlewska, 'Map, text and image: the mentality of enlightened conquerors: a new look at the *Description de l'Egypte*', *Transactions of the Institute of British Geographers*, new series, 20:1 (1995), 5–28; T. J. Bassett, 'Cartography and empire building in nineteenth-century West Africa', *Geographical Review*, 84:4 (1994), 316–35.

8 S. Tyacke and J. Huddy, *Christopher Saxton and Tudor Map-Making* (London, 1980).

9 V. Morgan, 'The cartographic image of "the country" in early modern England', *Transactions of the Royal Historical Society*, 5th series, 29 (1979), 129–54; R. Helgerson, 'The land speaks: cartography, chorography and subversion in Renaissance England', *Representations*, 16 (1986), 51–86.

10 J. W. Konvitz, *Cartography in France 1660–1848: Science, Engineering and Statecraft* (Chicago and London, 1987); J. W. Konvitz, 'The nation-state, Paris and cartography in eighteenth- and nineteenth-century France', *Journal of Historical Geography*, 16:1 (1990), 3–16.

11 D. N. Livingstone, 'Climate's moral economy: science, race and place in post-Darwinian British and American Geography', in Godlewska and Smith (eds),

Geography and Empire; A. Buttimer, 'Edgar Kant and Balto-Skandia: *Heimatkunde* and regional identity', in Hooson (ed.), *Geography and National Identity*; P. Gruffudd, 'Back to the land: historiography, rurality and the nation in inter-war Wales', *Transactions of the Institute of British Geographers*, new series, 19:1 (1994), 61–77.

12 R. J. P. Kain and E. Baigent, *The Cadastral Map in the Service of the State* (Chicago and London, 1992).

13 H. Johnson, 'Towards a national landscape', in M. P. Conzen (ed.), *The Making of the American Landscape* (London, 1990).

14 V. Morgan, 'The literary image of globes and maps in early modern England', in S. Tyacke (ed.), *English Map-Making 1500–1650* (London, 1983); P. Wombell, *The Globe: Representing the World* (York, 1989); Barber and Board, *Tales from the Map Room*; D. Cosgrove, 'Contested global visions: One-World, Whole-Earth and the Apollo space photographs', *Annals of the Association of American Geographers*, 84:2 (1994), 270–94.

15 Wombell, *The Globe*, pp. 14, 20–1.

16 Wood and Fels, *The Power of Maps*, pp. 72–5.

17 P. Stalker, 'Map wars', in Wombell, *The Globe*, pp. 28–33.

18 Cosgrove, 'Contested global visions'.

19 S. Daniels and S. Rycroft, 'Mapping the modern city: Alan Sillitoe's Nottingham novels', *Transactions of the Institute of British Geographers*, new series, 18:4 (1993), 460–80.

20 D. Matless, '"The art of right living": landscape and citizenship 1918–39', in S. Pile and N. Thrift (eds), *Mapping the Subject: Geographies of Cultural Transformation* (London and New York, 1996).

21 *Ibid.*

22 Buttimer, 'Edgar Kant'.

23 D. Crouch and D. Matless, 'Refiguring geography: parish maps of common ground', *Transactions of the Institute of British Geographers*, new series, 21:1 (1996), 236–55.

24 G. Huggan, 'Decolonizing the map: post-colonialism, post-structuralism and the cartographic connection', *Ariel*, 20:4 (1989), 115–31; C. Nash, 'Remapping and renaming: new cartographies of identity, gender and landscape in Ireland', *Feminist Review*, 44 (1993).

25 H. Brody, *Maps and Dreams* (London, 1983); J. B. Harley, 'Rereading the maps of the Columbian encounter', *Annals of the Association of American Geographers*, 82:3 (1992), 523–41; R. G. Paulston (ed.), *Social Cartography: Mapping Ways of Seeing Social and Educational Change* (New York, 1996).

26 J. Christian, 'Paul Sandby and the military survey of Scotland', in Alfrey and Daniels (eds), *Mapping the Landscape*.

27 J. B. Harley, 'The re-mapping of England, 1750–1800', *Imago Mundi*, 19 (1965), 56–123.

28 W. A. Seymour (ed.), *A History of the Ordnance Survey* (Folkestone, 1980).

29 J. B. Harley and Y. O'Donoghue, *The Old Series of Ordnance Survey Maps of England and Wales*, vol. 2 (Lympne Castle, 1977).

30 E. J. Yeo, 'The social survey in social perspective, 1830–1930', in M. Bulmer, K. Bales and K. K. Sklar (eds), *The Social Survey in Historical Perspective* (Cambridge, 1991).

31 Seymour, *History of the Ordnance Survey*, pp. 67–78; N. Alfrey, 'Landscape and the Ordnance Survey', in Alfrey and Daniels (eds), *Mapping the Landscape*; Daniels, *Fields of Vision*.

32 Seymour, *History of the Ordnance Survey*, pp. 99–164.

33 J. Elliott, *The City in Maps: Urban Mapping to 1900* (London, 1987).

34 Kain and Baigent, *The Cadastral Map*, pp. 260–1.

35 J. H. Andrews, *A Paper Landscape: the Ordnance Survey in Nineteenth-Century Ireland* (Oxford, 1975), p. 24.

36 *Ibid.*, pp. 144–79; M. Hamer, 'Putting Ireland on the map', *Textual Practice*, 3:2 (1989), 185–201.

37 A. S. Green, *Irish Nationality* (London, 1911), pp. 245–6.

38 Seymour, *History of the Ordnance Survey*, pp. 178–232.

39 *Ibid.*, pp. 230–56; T. Nicholson, 'Ordnance Survey ephemera to 1939', *The Map Collector*, 54 (Spring 1991), 1–40; 'The one inch to the mile Ordnance Survey map of England', *Geographical Journal*, 78 (1931), 353–6.

40 J. P. Browne, *Map Cover Art: a Pictorial History of Ordnance Survey Cover Illustrations* (London, 1990), pp. 60–107.

41 Matless, '"The art of right living"', pp. 104–5.

42 J. Lowerson, 'Battles for the countryside', in F. Gloversmith (ed.), *Class, Culture and Social Change: a New View of the 1930s* (Brighton, 1980), pp. 268–77.

43 D. Matless, 'The English outlook: a mapping of leisure', in Alfrey and Daniels (eds), *Mapping the Landscape*; Matless, '"The art of right living"'.

44 H. Batsford, *How to See the Country* (London, 1945–46), pp. 60, 63–4.

45 Seymour, *History of the Ordnance Survey*, pp. 237–40.

46 C. Close, *The Map of England, or About England with an Ordnance Map* (London, 1932), p. 1.

47 A. Watkins, *The Old Straight Track* (London, 1925).

48 T. Williamson and T. Bellamy, *Ley Lines in Question* (Kingswood, 1983).

49 R. Shoesmith, *Alfred Watkins: a Herefordshire Man* (Little Logaston, 1990).

50 D. Matless, '"Ordering the land": the "preservation" of the English countryside, 1918–39', unpublished Ph.D. dissertation (University of Nottingham, 1990), pp. 429–33.

51 L. D. Stamp, *The Land of Britain: Its Use and Misuse* (London, 1962), p. 4.

52 S. Rycroft and D. Cosgrove, 'The stamp of an idealist', *Geography* (October 1994), 36–9; S. Rycroft and D. Cosgrove, 'Mapping the modern nation: Dudley Stamp and the Land Utilization Survey', *History Workshop Journal*, 40 (1995), 91–105.

53 I. Jeffrey, *The British Landscape 1920–50* (London, 1984); D. Mellor, *A Paradise Lost: the Neo-Romantic Imagination and Britain 1935–55* (London, 1987).

54 V. Cunningham, *British Writers of the 1930s* (Oxford, 1988), p. 226.

55 *Ibid.*, p. 228.

'All ocean is her own': the image of the sea and the identity of the maritime nation in eighteenth-century British art

Benedict Anderson's proposed definition of the nation as 'an imagined polit-ical community' admits a potential for the functioning of non-verbal and non-literary signs and discourses in the construction of the idea of 'nation'. The conclusion that the nation must be at some level imagined begs the question of what media and cultural channels provide the means for such an imagin-ing to take hold. Bernard Smith's book *Imagining the Pacific* plays on the lin-guistic proximity of the words 'imagine' and 'image' to suggest that eighteenth-century western imagery of geographical discovery in the Pacific operated at the centre of an hermeneutic circle in which the imagery was informed by pre-existing values of western cultural *imagination about* the Pacific, but served to provide a detached 'scientific' appraisal, an apparently objective *image*, of the newly discovered regions, upon which the imagination could feed. It is the premise of this essay that the pictorial image of navigation and the sea func-tioned similarly in imagining the nation in eighteenth-century Britain, giving visual form to a growing sense of political, economic and cultural community, but simultaneously stimulating its growth.[1]

The connection between the rise of British art and the emergence of a coherent national identity in the second half of the century was taken as vir-tually axiomatic by critics from the late eighteenth century on. From early in the century it was commonplace to associate the ambitions of the unified and prospering nation with the virtuous examples of classical Greece and Rome, asserting British claims as the true and uncorrupted heir of classical civilisa-tion, as well as establishing the norm in British commentary on art of using the arts of the nation as an index of its constitutional health. Writers from Richardson to Blake, but perhaps most influentially Winckelmann, stressed that the political perfection of the classical republic had produced the most perfect art known to the world, because it was created under conditions of individual political freedom.[2] The progress of the arts in Britain would recip-rocally improve and secure the well-being of the nation, in two main ways. The adherence, in painterly practice, to classical principles of art, through the form of history painting and sculpture, would provide models of virtue for the edification of the governing members of society, which would constitute 'the tests by which the national character will be tried in after ages, and by which it has been, and is now, tried by the natives of other countries'.[3] Equally importantly, the development of a national school of art would contribute to the country's commercial prosperity in real terms, the rise of commerce and entrepreneurialism itself being taken as a mark of the liberty of the 'free-born Englishman'.[4] The result of the impact of constitutional freedom upon commercial and artistic progress would be a day when

> commerce round the world
> Has winged unnumbered sails and from each land
> Materials heaped that, well employed, with Rome
> Might vie our grandeur, and with Greece our art![5]

In 1762, at the apogee of British military conquest and colonial and commercial expansion, that day appeared to have dawned:

> whatever has been the complaint formerly, we have ground to hope that a new era is receiving its date. Genius is countenanced and emulation will follow. Nor is it a bad indication of the flourishing state of a country, that it daily makes improvements in arts and sciences. They may be attended by luxury, but they certainly are produced by wealth and happiness . . . . At this epoch of common sense, one may reasonably expect to see the arts flourish to as proud a height as they attained at Athens, Rome, or Florence. . . . Our eloquence and the glory of our arms have been carried to the highest pitch. The more peaceful arts have in other countries generally attended national glory. If there are any talents among us, this seems the crisis for their appearance.[6]

The character of the connection between British art and national development has in recent years been the subject of much critical and historical scrutiny. The development from the first half of the century of a critical theorisation of aesthetics and aesthetic sensibility has itself been taken as a paradigm of the bourgeois subject's civic participation in an 'imagined political community', whereby subjectivity is defined according to the individual's membership of a 'republic of taste':

> Like the work of art as defined by the discourse of aesthetics, the bourgeois subject is autonomous and self-determining, acknowledges no merely extrinsic law but instead, in some mysterious fashion, gives the law to itself. In doing so, the law becomes the form which shapes into harmonious unity the turbulent content of the subject's appetites and inclinations. The compulsion of autocratic power is replaced by the more gratifying compulsion of the subject's self identity.[7]

In this critique aesthetic sensibility may be taken as a measure of, or even as synonymous with, social harmony, as conceived by bourgeois ethics. But the 'aesthetic law' was not wholly self-determining. It corresponded to universal values of good and evil, beauty and ugliness, virtue and vice. In this connection Eagleton cites Adam Smith's visualisation of human society 'like a great, immense machine, whose regular and harmonious movements produce a thousand agreeable effects', and in which 'whatever tended to render its movements more smooth and easy would derive a beauty from this effect, and, on the contrary, whatever tended to obstruct them would displease'.[8] In its implication that there can be no such thing as a neutral social position, that the individual either contributes to the greater social good, or, in Smith's term, 'obstructs' it, this vision of society corresponds to the classical aesthetic doctrine that whatever does not add to the work of art, detracts from it. As Eagleton comments, 'The whole of social life is aestheticized; and what this signifies is a social order so spontaneously cohesive that its members no longer need to think about it. Virtue, the easy habit of goodness, is like art beyond all mere calculation.'[9]

If we accept this diagnosis of the imagining of the nation as fundamentally an aesthetic construction, it assumes an extremely complex function for the pictorial image both in it and of it. This is not the place to enter into detailed analysis of this proposition. But methodologically it presents two immediate advantages. First, the connection between aestheticisation and nation offers a parity between political and economic factors and other less statistically tangible but no less influential practices in the arts or social sciences as ingredients in the construction of national consciousness. Second, it facilitates an understanding of the nation as a discourse, rather than as a fixed and objective presence. Thus both eighteenth-century aesthetics, with its own internal discourse of, for example, the beautiful and the sublime, and the discourse of the nation as a political or socio-economic community, may be seen to operate within an overarching 'discursive network' of the nation, within which each is inflected by and interacts with the other.[10] This allows discussion of the nation to some extent to pre-empt the difficult problems of causation and development, which so often determine the analysis of nationalism. While, for example, E. J. Hobsbawm rightly disavows the view of the nation as a 'primary' or 'unchanging social identity' but with Gellner stresses 'the element of artefact, invention and social engineering which enters into the making of nations', he then goes on to assert that 'for the purposes of analysis nationalism comes before nations'; and adopts Hroch's 'division of the history of national movements' into three phases, from a minority and 'purely cultural' phenomenon to a mass political ideology.[11] Such a developmental approach to the nation, even for the purposes of analytical convenience, is highly problematic. Firstly, it gives undue priority to the identity of the nation in its purely political character, marginalising other salient factors. Second, one might sensibly ask how nationalism could in any meaningful way precede nations. It might be equally productive to treat them as complementary discourses, whereby 'More than a style and doctrine of politics, nationalism is a *form of culture* – an ideology, a language, mythology, symbolism and consciousness – that has achieved global resonance, and the nation is a type of identity whose meaning and priority is presupposed by this form of culture.'[12] Third, and perhaps most importantly for the purposes of this essay, such an approach restricts the variety of ways by which a nation may be defined, especially vis-à-vis citizens' defining criteria of their own national affiliation. One of the principal contentions of this essay will be that mass support for a national ideal might not be expressed solely, or even principally, in political terms. In eighteenth-century Britain, an ideology of mythic origin, of religious destiny, and geographical identity functioned to endow a disparate and fluctuating political community with a quasi-coherent sense of nationhood, often cutting across class and other distinctions.[13]

This essay offers a case study of the connection between the aesthetic and the nation, by considering some of the ways in which pictorial imagery reiterated and reinforced the long-standing nationalistic idea of the island of Britain being defined by its providential affinity with the sea. At one level this concern permeated imagery very discreetly and extensively. John Runciman's 1760s painting of *King Lear in the Storm*, for instance, removes the scene from the theatrically proper heath to a painterly, imaginative, clifftop from which Lear looks out over a raging sea and shipwreck, as though into a mirror of his own psychological and constitutional turmoil.[14] But the specific genre of marine painting was also openly connected with national glory and the rise of a distinctive 'English school' of art. As one contemporary commentator put it:

> Marine painting in Vandervelt's taste is a branch of the art in which one need not be afraid to affirm that the English excel. And yet we must not imagine that there are a great number of artists in this, any more than in other branches. But when one or two hands become as eminent, as those who are now distinguished for marine pictures in England, are they not capable of giving a character of superiority to their country?

> Every thing that relates to navigation, is so well known in England, and so interesting to that nation, that it is not at all surprizing to see them greatly pleased with marine pictures.[15]

This essay will propose that the explicit subjects of the sea and of navigation recur in images of the period more consistently and more significantly than has generally been supposed, that they can be closely related to ideologies of commerce and patriotism, and that they figured importantly in the construction of a multifaceted and complex, but homogeneous, idea of nation. I shall conclude by remarking an instance in painting and poetry of the early years of the nineteenth century in which the image of the sea becomes a transparent sign for patriotic identification with the nation.

At the same time as witnessing the rise of urbanised institutions, the 'revolution in communications', the increasing homogenisation of language, the geographical integration of the country through surveys and road building, and the fact of continuous warfare – some of the features by which Linda Colley characterises the emerging sense of British nationhood – the eighteenth century saw a systematic theorisation of the benefits of commerce for the prosperity and power of the country at every level.[16] While political unity had been encouraged by the 1707 Act of Union and the defeat of the Jacobite threat in 1745, the ideology of commerce presented a structure by which society could be organised vertically through different classes. It predicated a social structure in which everyone found their proper place according to their merits, and formed connections based upon mutual help and dependence. In the commercial society, it was held, self-interest was inseparable from the interest of others, and thereby of the public nation at large, or even of the world. As a treatise of 1728 put it:

> [commerce and navigation] enlarge our Knowledge of Persons and Things, relieve our Wants, and give us the Advantage and Benefit of every Climate. They join the most distant Regions, to their mutual Profit: they make even our Antipodes to be our Neighbours . . . we have the Advantage of Inventions and Improvements of every Nation: And every Man is enabled, according to his Ingenuity, to do something for his own Benefit; and to assist his Neighbour in doing what may make his Life more happy and easy.[17]

The character of the emerging nation was therefore a commercial one, by which it would be aggrandised, and its unique constitution and freedom preserved. Through the association of the fundamental principles of the state with an ideology of commerce, the national identity implicitly acquired a global and maritime dimension. Despite being tainted, in the civic humanist tradition, with ideas of luxury, corruption and civic debilitation,[18] commerce's increasing ideological sway as the century progressed could thus be easily grafted on to the pre-existing mythology of the country as the 'sceptr'd isle', a state providentially defined by its natural geography. To advocate a policy of commerce was simply to submit to the scheme of nature. Bolingbroke put it succinctly:

> The situation of Great Britain, the character of her people, and the nature of her government, fit her for trade and commerce. Her climate and her soil make them necessary to her well being. By trade and commerce we grow a rich and powerful nation, and by their decay we are growing poor and impotent. As trade and commerce enrich, so they fortify our country. The sea is our barrier, ships are our fortresses, and the mariners, which trade and commerce alone can furnish, are the garrisons to defend them.[19]

Figure 10 **Anon., *Saint George for England***

Such rhetoric of patriotism received reciprocal popular support in prints such as *Saint George for England* of 1781, after an original picture exhibited in the 1762 Society of Sign Painters exhibition, where it was one of seven depictions of titular saints of European nations, *The Renowned Seven Champions of Christendom, from an entire New Design* (figure 10). It was the only one which refrained from indulging in pejorative national stereotyping. In the opinion of a contemporary reviewer, the whole series was

> A Capital Piece. – . . . St. George is an English Sailor, mounted on a Lion, with a Spit [by Way of Lance] bearing a Sirloin of Beef in one Hand, and a full Pot of Porter, marked *Only Threepence a* QUART, in the other. By the Lion's Foot are two Scrolls, like Ballads, the one inscribed, O the Roast Beef of Old England; the other, Hearts of Oak are our Men.

By contrast, among the other saints, 'St. David is a Taff, mounted on a Goat brandishing Leek in one Hand, and bearing a Cheese, by Way of Target, in the other.' But the greatest satire is of course reserved for the French: 'St. Dennis is a Frenchman, mounted on a Deer, a timorous swift-footed Animal, with a small Sword, in one Hand, on which a Frog appears to be spitted, and a Dish of Soup Maigre in the other.'[20]

The context for such imagery was an exhibition which, whatever its satirical intent, was obviously staunchly lower middle-class and artisanal in character, and patriotic in ideology. Its unequivocal espousal of popular patriotism is exemplified by *Saint George for England*, where the traditional chivalric (land-based) martial knight is transformed into one of Bolingbroke's 'garrisons', an ordinary Jack Tar mounted on the British lion, and armed not with a lance but with a pot of porter and the Roast Beef of England. It is a remarkably open identification of popular patriotism with the figure of the mariner and the sea, as well as a surprising inversion of the usual aesthetic identification of the hero by aristocratic or classical attributes. Similar conflations of the aristocratic and the vulgar, contingent upon the maritime national identity, occur elsewhere in the visual expression of popular patriotism. Gillray's 1793 engraving *The French Invasion; or John Bull, Bombarding the Bum-Boats* (figure 11) develops a complex compound image in which the map of England and Wales (though interestingly not of Scotland or Ireland) is anthropomorphised into John Bull, who is in turn given the regal features of George III, the figure engaged in the far from delicate and refined act of repelling the republican invasion by shitting on it. But beneath the scatological surface of the joke lies an involved pictorial construction of national character and definition, which purports to be all-inclusive, both socially, by integrating the King with the commoner John Bull, and geographically, by identifying this compound figure with the topographical limits of the kingdom. By exaggerating the disposition of the map for naturalising the idea of nationhood, Gillray turns it into a rhetorical public address on a patriotic level. The synthesis of both the figural symbol and head of state with the popular typification of the ordinary Englishman, and then of these two with the map of England and Wales, addresses both a larger corporate public but also the individual within it, and thus invokes the viewer's patriotic affiliations as such a figure within the nation. The important point here for the identity of the nation is that its symbolic or imagined character is held to be coterminous with its physical topography, as defined by the sea, over which the exaggeratedly uninhibited physicality of the English character has dominion.

When coupled with the ideology of commerce, such a construction of national identity became inevitably endowed with a global dimension. The national character depended upon 'the conquest of Ocean'. And this was both a commercial and military necessity. The colonial and maritime triumphs of the Seven Years War were celebrated in numerous images, such as Hayman's *Triumph of Britannia* (figure 12), which shows a common typology of Britannia

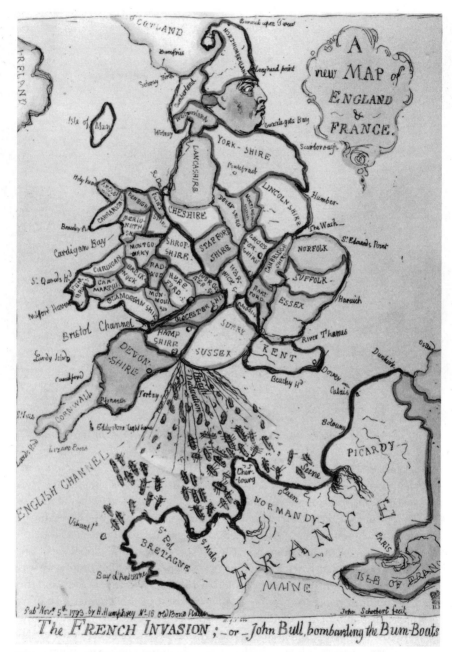

Figure 11 **James Gillray, *The French Invasion; or John Bull, Bombarding the Bum-Boats***

Figure 12 **S. F. Ravenet after Francis Hayman, *The Triumph of Britannia***

as the consort of Neptune. The chariot is flanked by Nereids holding up
roundel-portraits of the naval commanders of the war. This rhetorical structure even gained legal guise. Blackstone's *Commentaries on the Laws of
England* pronounces that 'the main or high seas are part of the realm of
England, for thereon our Courts of Admiralty have jurisdiction'.[21]

A less belligerent and more consistent expression of the global aspect of
the nation is provided by the image of the Thames, in which emphasis was
generally placed on the river below London Bridge as both the starting and the
finishing point of maritime commerce. The interest in the Thames as a literary topos, throughout the eighteenth century and beyond, in forms ranging
from Augustan epic to topographical description, testifies to its cultural significance. It is consistently seen both as the embodiment of British liberty, and
as the umbilical link between the territorial island and commercial globalism.
Verse and prose accounts from early in the century onwards stress the seamlessness between the river's source in the heart of England, and its expansive

entrance into the oceans of the world. The grand modernity of the commercial metropolis is exemplified by the Pool of London, typically populated with forests of masts, 'On whose each tide, glad with returning sails, / Flows in the mingled harvest of mankind', as Thomson writes. At the same time as it brings in the 'harvest of mankind', it exports British commercial and constitutional liberty. 'The day shall come', writes Pope in *Windsor Forest*, 'when, free as seas or wind, / Unbounded Thames shall flow for all mankind', a sentiment echoed almost a century later in Thomas Love Peacock's *The Genius of the Thames*.[22] For Peacock, the Thames *is* the national identity, flowing 'in freedom's sacred light'. It is the witness not just to the topography through which it passes, but to the temporal sequence of events which have made the land Britain. It is the memorial repository of every act of every 'peasant, warrior, prince, and sage' who 'Upheld their ancient heritage'. And British identity will cease only with the death of the river:

> Still shall thy power its course pursue,
> Nor sink, but with the world's decay.
> Long as the cliff that girds thy isle
> The bursting surf of ocean stems,
> Shall commerce, wealth and plenty smile
> Along the silver-eddying Thames.[23]

From about 1740 the mythical identity of the Thames became entwined with commercial theory, presenting the poetic ideal as a realisable social policy. Visual imagery was vital in forming this new image. Not only did the Pool of London and the docks become increasingly acceptable painterly subjects, but by dwelling on the bridge-building projects between the 1740s and 1760s at Westminster, London Bridge and Blackfriars (figures 13 and 15), or on riverside commercial developments such as the Adelphi, painters confirmed the Thames as a paradigm of modernity. Marlow's painting of *The Adelphi, London, under Construction* (figure 14) places the processes of building directly in the foreground, denoting the river as the economic and material provider of magnificence. Simultaneously, a mass of literature treated the Thames in a prosaic register, subjecting it to analytical and statistical description, legislative proposals and topographical recording, whereby its symbolic identity was overlaid with discourses of political economy, social improvement, and what David Solkin has termed 'commercial humanism'.[24] Images commonly present the combined identity by showing the commercial activity of the river below the nationalistic icons of St Paul's or Westminster, naturalising the river's association with national commercial progress. Marlow's *Blackfriars Bridge and St Paul's Cathedral, London* (figure 13) is typical in providing a compositional continuity between the classical structures of the cathedral and the bridge, eliding both foreground and background into a

Figure 13 William Marlow, *Blackfriars Bridge and St Paul's Cathedral, London*

Figure 14 William Marlow, *The Adelphi, London, under Construction, with York Water Tower and the River Thames towards Westminster*

Figure 15 **Samuel Scott, *The Building of Westminster Bridge***

harmonious whole, within which the church provides the national moral context for the modernity of the bridge, and vice versa. In this sense the very structure of the imagery can be directly related to the discursive structure of commercial theory.

We can demonstrate, for example, how the iconography of Scott's *The Building of Westminster Bridge* of 1747 (figure 15) conforms to the essays on commerce, taste and other social themes which were being published in contemporary journals. In an essay entitled 'The Benefits of Human Society', Johnson puts forward a vision of a society made harmonious by what might be termed a 'division of consumption'. It is exemplified by London:

> Not only by . . . popular and modish trifles, but by a thousand unheeded and evanescent kinds of business, are the multitudes of this city preserved from idleness, and consequently from want. In the endless variety of tastes and circumstances that diversify mankind, nothing is so superfluous but that someone desires it; or so common but that someone is compelled to buy it. As nothing is useless but because it is in improper hands, what is thrown away by one is gathered up by another; and the refuse of part of mankind furnishes a subordinate class with the materials necessary to their support.[25]

It is commerce, the Thames, which is the agent of this 'trickle-down' effect whereby every commodity and everybody finds their natural and proper place in a hierarchy of consumerism.

The 'mingled harvest of mankind' is stowed in the metropolitan 'shops and warehouses, . . . immense stores of every kind of merchandise piled up for sale, [containing] all the manufactures of art and products of nature'. Johnson contrasts the lot of even the most prospering North American savage, in unsocial isolation, with 'the conveniences which are enjoyed by the vagrant beggar of a civilized country':

> To receive and communicate assistance constitutes the happiness of human life: man may indeed preserve his existence in solitude, but can enjoy it only in society: the greatest understanding of an individual doomed to procure food and clothing for himself will barely supply him with expedients to keep off death from day to day; but as one of a large community performing only his share of the common business, he gains leisure for intellectual pleasures, and enjoys the happiness of reason and reflection.[26]

The performance of each individual's share of the 'common business' cumulatively creates a common good which is, ingeniously, not commercial at all, but consists of the leisure for reflection and reason, presumably to contemplate the merits of human society under a system of commerce.

Scott's image has a discernibly similar structure, serving similar ideological ends. The viewer is placed at river level, and enters the picture by following it upstream from the bottom right-hand corner. At the right edge are a group of lightermen and a barge laden with cargo. The principal foreground focus, however, is at the centre left, where a supply of timber has arrived at one of the many timber yards on the south bank. The stark tonal contrast and repoussoir of the crane and its hook act as a pictorial 'hook' to catch the eye, as well as providing, in the narrow horizontal composition, a balance to the dominating structure of the sunlit abbey, which is itself thrown into an almost equal tonal contrast by a bank of stormy clouds behind it. But these two visual centres are connected compositionally by the arches of Westminster Bridge under construction, providing a very effective device for uniting the two halves of the image. It takes the viewer by progression from the timber yard across to the Houses of Parliament and Westminster. The act of viewing over the picture surface is synonymous with traversing the river, a move made possible by the new bridge in both cases. Moreover, the structure of the image, as a continuous linear movement along a chain of different represented elements on the picture surface and into the pictorial space, invites an analogous thematic or narrative interpretation. The huge raw timbers turn into the masses of the timber crane. An association is then invited between this frame and the juxtaposed wooden scaffolding supports of the stone arches of the bridge. The linkage by material may be pursued from the stone bridge to the great stone structures of Westminster. Just as the bridge when complete will unite the political and constitutional centre of the nation, sited on the north bank, with the commercial wharves and yards of the south (as well as with the naval centres further east at Deptford and Greenwich), so it also unites the mechanical activity of the boatmen in the foreground with the virtuous ideal of the 'commonweal' connoted by the abbey beyond. Indeed, the implication is that without the provision of timber from the lightermen and the merchants accomplishing their 'share of the common business', the bridge could not be built at all. The ideological structure of the image, as of Johnson's essay, is one which completes a seamless shift from the particular to the general, the material to the abstract, the mechanical to the philosophical and political, from private commercial interest to publicly virtuous impartiality: a transition which, in Scott's painting, is associated with the Thames.

The river workers, engrossed in the task at hand, do not see the result of their labour (which, as the right-hand group shows, is not excessively intensive, and allows scope for leisure, as well as the consumption of luxury commodities produced in the colonies, in this case, tobacco). And the structure connecting the low labour of the timber yard with the elevated political and patriotic significance of Westminster is tellingly similar to that by which Johnson moves from a base culture of 'popular and modish trifles' and 'a thousand unheeded and evanescent kinds of business' to the 'happiness of reason and reflection'. So, in Scott's painting, the construction of the bridge, the material symbol of modern life realised by commerce, affiliates the private industry of the yard to the political public of Parliament. The bridge may be seen as a symbol of enfranchisement, similar to the natural meritocracy supplied by Johnson's vision of commercial society. Such a connection is explicitly made in Hume's essay 'Of Refinement in the Arts', published in 1752. Hume is particularly concerned to dissociate the refinement of the arts from a pernicious sense of luxury. He writes:

> where luxury nourishes commerce and industry, the peasants, by a proper cultivation of the land, become rich and independent; while the tradesmen and merchants acquire a share of the property, and draw authority and consideration to that middling rank of men, who are the best and firmest base of public liberty. . . . They covet equal laws, which may secure their property, and preserve them from monarchical, as well as aristocratical tyranny.

> The lower house is the support of our popular government; and all the world acknowledges, that it owed its chief influence and consideration to the increase of commerce, which threw such a balance of property into the hands of the Commons. How inconsistent, then, is it to blame so violently a refinement in the arts, and to represent it as the bane of liberty and public spirit![27]

Not only is the connection between mechanical industry and political liberty made explicit, but it is seen as effected by refinement in the arts, the kind of refinement of which Westminster Bridge was a celebrated manifestation. By extension, the image which depicts it in such a refined and elegant style may itself be viewed as a promotion of 'liberty and public spirit'.

There is, therefore, a correspondence between Hume's appeal to an ideal of 'popular government', which he sees as being directly related to the effects of commerce on the independence of the middle and lower orders of society, and the analogous structure of Scott's image. This perhaps gives a clue to the conspicuous contrast in the painting between the bank of lowering cloud and the radiant sunlight which appears to dispel it. The date of the picture, 1747, is only a little later than the decisive repulsion of the Jacobite claim to the throne, a claim which was popularly identified with absolutism and arbitrary power. The emergence of a shining Westminster and calm river from a storm perhaps invites an analogy with the preservation from 'monarchical, as well as aristocratical tyranny' brought by commerce allowing the 'Commons' political representation through their acquisition of property and independence.

Clearly the characterisation of commerce that I have given has been of its positive side. The building of Westminster Bridge, for instance, was politically contentious.[28] But I am concerned to concentrate specifically on its meaning for the formation of a national identity. Of course, neither commerce nor patriotism was a universally accepted or uniformly fixed set of values; both were widely and vigorously contested. The complexities of the discourse of patriotism of the late eighteenth and early nineteenth centuries cannot be dealt with here. It should be noted, however, that the triumphalist linkage of patriotism and commerce, exemplified by images such as Hayman's *Triumph of Britannia*, was subjected to the social and ideological disruptions of the late 1760s and 1770s. When Wilkes and the reforming 'mob' could proclaim their cause under the names 'True Briton' and 'Patriot', and the American War introduced a fundamental division of patriotic loyalty, the sense of patriotism as a single value with straightforward connections to the constitution and to global commerce became untenable. As the *London Evening Post* put it in 1778, 'Merchants and genuine patriots are *not* synonymous terms.'[29]

Yet while the discourse of patriotism could become appropriated by a radical agenda, in which its Roman republican derivation was brought to the fore, and therefore by the 1790s could paradoxically be held to indicate sympathy for the regicide and democratic reform of the French Revolution, I want to end by suggesting that the sense of loyalty to the nation, so frequently invoked in loyalist propaganda of the 1790s and 1800s, was in part expressed by bypassing the question of the propriety of the term 'patriotism' (even though the term continued to be used by both loyalists and radicals), entrenching instead a cultural naturalisation of the national identity, in which art and aesthetics, and particularly the image of the sea, played a crucial role, and which transformed the national identity from an area of political contest to a cultural fact.

Likewise, by the beginning of the nineteenth century, the image of the sea had become largely detached from the radical connotations of patriotism. If

Figure 16 **James Gillray, *Britannia between Scylla and Charybdis***

the discourse of patriotism had taken on a threatening meaning, then the highly politicised naval mutinies of the 1790s, particularly those of 1797, rendered the patriotic associations of the sea even more unstable.[30] Instead, the sea, divested of a specific political character, was transformed into a *natural* demonstration of the maritime basis of national identity, by which its providential and traditional character could become a subject of the perceptual study of nature within the terms of high art and aesthetics. Prints such as Gillray's *Britannia between Scylla and Charybdis* of 1793 (figure 16) maintained the emphasis on the indivisibility of the maritime character and national security and liberty, above all when Pitt the Younger was at the helm of the ship of state, to steer Britannia between the rock of Democracy, to the port side, and the whirlpool of Arbitrary Power, to the starboard. But the increasing interest in the sea in the realm of high art provided a subject not only suitable for the expression of a naturally and quintessentially British art, but appropriate also to an individual sympathy with the nation which such art 'imagined'.

Figure 17 **J. M. W. Turner, *The Sun Rising through Vapour***

Turner's painting *The Sun Rising through Vapour* of *c.* 1809 (figure 17) shows an almost supernaturally tranquil scene of a shore populated with local fishermen and women laying out their catch. In the distance is a man-of-war, its sails struck, emerging, like the sun, out of the dissolving mist. It appears to be a scene of security, plenty and optimism on the natural frontier of the nation, a sense encouraged by the fact that the painting was probably bought as the pendant to an earlier, explicitly patriotic image by Turner, of *The Victory Returning from Trafalgar*.[31] Significantly, the premise of the image is visual revelation: the scene is in the process of emerging to the viewer's sight.

Similarly, William Lisle Bowles, in a poem of 1803 (a few years before Peacock's *Genius of the Thames*), presents the marine view, like Turner's to the east, this time from Stoke's Bay, in the same metaphorical guise, but with an undisguisedly patriotic interpretation. The two share the same idea of nationalistic involvement in the image of the sea. Bowles, like Turner, describes the undisturbed calm on the shore. His personal cares are dispelled like the mist:

> every cross
> Of upland life, and every heartfelt loss
> No more the mind with dark suffusion blot,
> But, like the clouds of the aerial haze,

Silent and soft, and fading as we gaze,
Stray o'er the spirit, and disturb it not!
So, scarcely felt, the cares of life subside!
But prouder feelings swell the PATRIOT's heart,
When, stately o'er the morning tide,
He sees the tall ships in their glory ride!
Each partial thought, e'en like the passing wind,
Is gone – new triumphs flash upon his mind –
Whilst to each meaner object senseless grown,
He for HIS COUNTRY breathes, and lives, and feels, alone.

Just as Bowles's particular thoughts dissipate like mist to reveal the existential truth of the nation in the vision of the sea and ships, so in Turner's image the ships emerge in the distance to form the central focus of the composition, around which the 'particular' foreground activities of industry and business revolve like satellites. Patriotic sympathy is not simply a revelation of a natural form, but resides in the visual – or, we might say, imaginative – faculty of the beholder, and perhaps more importantly, via the sense of sight, in the moral sensibility of the loyal individual. Turner around this time began to see his own act of painting as a form of navigation and voyage, investing the idea of the sea with his own personal aesthetic sentiment.[32] And aesthetic expression is for both Bowles and Turner the realisation of civic and patriotic sympathy. This takes us back to Eagleton's analysis of the aesthetic: the 'compulsion of the subject's self-identity', in which 'The whole of social life is aestheticized' and 'Virtue . . . is like art beyond all mere calculation', is united in this case with the self-identity of the nation, defined by the sea. National identity and the individual's membership of the nation is here less of a political definition than an aesthetic one. On the contrary, the construct of the sea offered by Bowles and Turner, a litmus test of patriotic sentiment, marginalises the political, in favour of an appeal to the universal and universalising moral forces of nature and, by implication, of God.[33] Loyalty to the nation is an act of sentiment and faith, indeed an experience of revelation, and the expression of the identity of the maritime nation has changed, to become ineffably naturalised in the sea. No longer is the sea just a metaphor or vehicle for the commercial and global destiny of the nation. It is the verifiable fact of the national character. For every loyal citizen the sea is the demonstration of civic existence. And every individual's own national identity is not simply the sea, but the way s/he sees it.

Notes

1 B. Anderson, *Imagined Communities: Reflections on the Origin and Spread of Nationalism* (rev. edn, London and New York, 1991), p. 6; B. Smith, *Imagining the Pacific: in the Wake of the Cook Voyages* (New Haven and London, 1992). The terms

'image' and 'imagine' signify, of course, within a deep history of aesthetic and
philosophical thought in western culture, discussion of which is beyond the scope of
this essay, although it is highly relevant to understanding the ideological basis of global
exploration and visual classification in the Enlightenment. See W. J. T. Mitchell,
Iconology: Image, Text, Ideology (Chicago, 1986).

2 The prime text is Winckelmann's *History of the Art of Antiquity* (Dresden, 1764): see
A. Potts, *Flesh and the Ideal: Winckelmann and the Origins of Art History* (New Haven
and London, 1994), pp. 54–60 and *passim*. For sources, see J. Draper, *Eighteenth-
Century English Aesthetics* (New York, 1968); a useful selection is contained in S.
Copley (ed.), *Literature and the Social Order in Eighteenth-Century England* (London,
1984). For a comprehensive discussion of art's theoretical relation to civic society in
eighteenth-century Britain, see J. Barrell, *The Political Theory of Painting from
Reynolds to Hazlitt: the Body of the Public* (New Haven and London, 1986), pp. 10–64
and *passim*.

3 J. Barry, cited in A. D. Smith, *National Identity* (Harmondsworth, 1991), p. 86.

4 This, for example, was the main line of argument of John Boydell's 1793 speech to the
Guildhall, proposing the pictorial programme for the Egyptian Hall. John Pye, in his
retrospective survey of British art in the eighteenth century, also considers the integration of the practices of art and commerce to be undeniably the main motive behind the
creation of a thriving British school: *Patronage of British Art, an Historical Sketch*
(London, 1845, facsimile repr. London, 1970).

5 J. Thomson, *Liberty* (London, 1738), Book V, ll. 570–3.

6 H. Walpole, *Anecdotes of Painting*, 3 vols (London, 1888), Preface [1762], pp. xi–xii,
xiii.

7 T. Eagleton, *The Ideology of the Aesthetic* (Oxford, 1990), p. 23.

8 A. Smith, *The Theory of Moral Sentiments* (1759), cited in *ibid.*, p. 37.

9 Eagleton, *The Ideology of the Aesthetic*, p. 37.

10 This is, of course, a schematised application of some of the methods adopted by Peter
De Bolla's *The Discourse of the Sublime* (Oxford, 1989), pp. 4–27.

11 E. J. Hobsbawm, *Nations and Nationalism since 1780: Programme, Myth, Reality* (2nd
edn, Cambridge, 1992), pp. 10, 12, citing E. Gellner, *Nations and Nationalism* (Oxford,
1983) and M. Hroch, *Social Preconditions of National Revival in Europe* (Cambridge,
1985).

12 Smith, *National Identity*, pp. 91–2.

13 See particularly L. Colley, *Britons: Forging the Nation 1707–1837* (New Haven and
London, 1992); G. Newman, *The Rise of English Nationalism: a Cultural History
1740–1830* (London, 1987). Of relevance here, also, especially to the function of class
mythology and ideology in 'imagining' the nation, is D. Wahrman, *Imagining the Middle
Class: the Political Representation of Class in Britain, c. 1780–1840* (Cambridge, 1995).

14 W. M. Merchant, 'John Runciman's "King Lear in the Storm"', *Warburg and Courtauld
Institute Journal*, 17 (1954), 385–7.

15 M. Rouquet, *The Present State of the Arts in England* (London, 1755, facsimile repr.
London, 1970), pp. 60–1.

16 Colley, *Britons*, pp. 1–85.

17 *Some Thoughts Concerning Government in General: and Our Present Circumstances in
Great Britain and Ireland* (Dublin, 1728), quoted in R. C. Wiles, 'Mercantilism and the
idea of progress', *Eighteenth-Century Studies*, 8:1 (1974–75), p. 69.

18 See particularly the discussions in J. G. A. Pocock, *Virtue, Commerce and History:
Essays on Political Thought and History* (Cambridge, 1985), pp. 37–50, 103–23, and J. G.
A. Pocock, *The Machiavellian Moment: Florentine Political Thought and the Atlantic
Republican Tradition* (Princeton, 1975), pp. 462–505; on luxury, see J. Sekora, *Luxury:
the Concept in Western Thought, Eden to Smollett* (Baltimore, 1977).

19 Henry St John, Viscount Lord Bolingbroke, *The Idea of a Patriot King*, in *The Works of Lord Bolingbroke, in Four Volumes* (London, 1844, repr. 1967), II: 414.

20 *St James's Chronicle*, 29 April–1 May 1762, p. 3.

21 Blackstone, *Commentaries on the Laws of England*, 4 vols (Oxford, 1765, facsimile repr. London, 1966), I: 107.

22 Thomson, *Liberty*, Book V, ll. 58–9; A. Pope, *Windsor-Forest* (London, 1713), ll. 397–8; T. L. Peacock, *The Genius of the Thames: a Lyrical Poem in Two Parts* (London, 1810).

23 Peacock, *The Genius of the Thames*, p. 111.

24 Among the most important mid-century descriptions and analyses of London and the Thames were those by Strype (1755), Maitland (1756) and Entick (1766). Besides paintings, there was a wealth of related printed imagery, by Bowles and Boydell among others, as well as maps, the most illustrious being John Rocque's 1746 map of London. See also H. Phillips, *The Thames around 1750* (London, 1951). On 'commercial humanism', see D. Solkin, *Painting for Money: the Visual Arts and the Public Sphere in Eighteenth-Century England* (New Haven and London, 1993), p. 19 and *passim*.

25 S. Johnson, 'The benefits of human society', *The Adventurer*, 67 (26 June 1753), in D. Greene (ed.), *The Oxford Authors, Samuel Johnson* (Oxford, 1984), p. 262.

26 *Ibid.*, pp. 264–5.

27 D. Hume, 'Of refinement in the arts', in *Of the Standard of Taste and Other Essays*, ed. J. W. Lenz (Indianapolis and New York, 1965), pp. 48–59 (quotation p. 57); see also D. F. Norton (ed.), *The Cambridge Companion to Hume* (Cambridge, 1993), pp. 230–8.

28 See Phillips, *The Thames*; M. Hallett, 'Framing the modern city: Canaletto's images of London', in M. Liversidge and J. Farringdon (eds), *Canaletto and England* (exhibition catalogue, Birmingham Gas Hall Exhibition Gallery, 1993–94), p. 47.

29 The literature on this subject is vast; see notably J. Brewer, *The Common People and Politics 1750–1790s* (in the series The English Satirical Print 1600–1832) (Cambridge, 1986); J. Brewer, *Party Ideology and Popular Politics at the Accession of George III* (Cambridge, 1976); N. Rogers, *Whigs and Cities: Popular Politics in the Age of Walpole and Pitt* (Oxford, 1989); Colley, *Britons*, pp. 80–5, 105–45, 178–81; L. Colley, 'Whose nation? Class and national consciousness in Britain 1750–1830', *Past and Present*, 113 (1986), 169–87; L. Colley, 'Radical patriotism in eighteenth-century England', in R. Samuel (ed.), *Patriotism: the Making and Unmaking of British National Identity: Vol. I: History and Politics* (London and New York, 1989), pp. 169–87 (quotation, p. 182); H. Cunningham, 'The language of patriotism, 1750–1914', *History Workshop Journal*, 12 (1981), 8–33.

30 J. Dugan, *The Great Mutiny* (London, 1965); E. Royle and J. Walvin, *English Radicals and Reformers 1760–1848* (Brighton, 1982), pp. 80–92. For a revealing analysis of mutiny as cultural discourse, see G. Dening, *Mr. Bligh's Bad Language: Passion, Power and the Theatre of the Bounty* (Cambridge, 1992).

31 Exhibited 1806?, oil on canvas, 67 x 100.3 cm, Yale Centre for British Art, Paul Mellon Collection; M. Butlin and E. Joll, *The Paintings of J. M. W. Turner* (rev. edn, New Haven and London, 1984), cat. no. 59, pp. 46–7. The setting (so to speak) of *The Sun Rising through Vapour* is not an identifiable one, but a pencil sketch exists in the 'Spithead' sketchbook (see Butlin and Joll, cat. no. 95, pp. 68–9), although the painting's view towards the rising sun suggests an east-coast scene. Equally, the view of the ship from the shore recalls Turner's contemporary views of Sheerness, for example *Sheerness as seen from the Nore* (exh. 1808, oil on canvas, 105.4 x 149.8 cm, Loyd Collection: Butlin and Joll, cat. no. 76).

32 B. Venning, 'A macabre connoisseurship: Turner, Byron and the apprehension of shipwreck subjects in early nineteenth-century England', *Art History*, 8:3 (September 1985), 304–6.

33 The idea of the sanctity of the sea is implicit in the formation of the maritime character of the nation, but is more openly expressed during the wars with France, particularly in relation to apocalyptic imagery. See S. Cottrell, 'The Devil on two sticks:
franco-phobia in 1803', in Samuel (ed.), *Patriotism*, pp. 259–74. Important relevant contemporary texts are J. S. Clarke, *The Progress of Maritime Discovery, from the Earliest
Period to the Close of the Eighteenth Century*, I (no further vols published) (London,
1803); and, most revealingly in the contexts of loyalty and mutiny, *Naval Sermons
preached on board His Majesty's Ship 'The Impetueux', in the Western Squadron, during
its services off Brest* (London, 1798).

Border crossings: Cornwall and the English (imagi)nation

In 1859 the Prince Consort opened Brunel's graceful Royal Albert Bridge. Nearly half a mile long, it spanned the width of the Tamar river, so long the unbridgeable border between Cornwall and England. Just as a picture frame is supposed to mark the boundary between the 'real' and 'imagined' worlds but always merges with both, so the Prince Albert Bridge stands as a steel monument to the indeterminate nature of the Cornish–English border, dramatically illustrating the impossibility of imagining where England ends and Cornwall begins. That is not to say that there had ever been a time when that boundary had been clearly legible, for Cornwall had always existed on the margins of Englishness, both a county of England and a foreign country. It is this ambivalent position of Cornwall in the English imagination, and of England in the Cornish imagination – of the Cornish as English, but not English – that interests me here.[1]

Cornwall's place on the margins of England and Englishness perhaps helps explain its comparative neglect in historical analyses of 'Englishness' and of the formation of British national identity.[2] Despite the determined efforts of a new generation of Cornish nationalist historians to map the construction of Cornwall as a nation, Cornish history remains deeply unsettling to the national imaginary.[3] I want to suggest that an examination of the relationship between Cornwall and the English imagination radically destabilises the categories and narratives of both English and Cornish national identity, not least by blurring the understanding of the nation as founded upon an opposition between 'the real' and 'the imaginary'. Since the publication of Benedict Anderson's *Imagined Communities*, histories of national identity have tended to reinforce such essentialist distinctions, the emphasis on the nation as 'imagined community' simply inverting previous accounts of national essences and origins.[4] I want to problematise this dichotomy by historicising its construction in debates about the nature of Cornish national identity during the nineteenth and twentieth centuries.

The notion of a 'real' or 'authentic' Cornish nation, rooted in the language and culture of its labouring men, emerged during the nineteenth century as a product of the English imagination of Cornwall as a primitive 'Celtic' land of myth and romance against which the forward march of English Anglo-Saxon civility could be plotted. Ironically, the only way in which the Cornish sub-altern could speak itself as a nation was by appropriating this English romance with the Cornish labouring poor.[5] In attempting to secure the labouring poor as the referent of Cornish national identity, Cornish nationalists drew directly upon the narratives and tropes of the English imperial imaginary. However, they did so in ways which enabled them to provide a critique of English moder-nity and to deny that Cornwall merely inscribed the prehistory of English civil-isation. By the late nineteenth century, this critique of English modernity struck a chord with many in England itself who saw in Cornwall a chance to recapture a pre-industrial, rural and manly Old England that they feared had been lost. This continual traffic in the tropes and narratives of the Cornish and English national imaginaries perpetually undercut the attempt to map Cornwall and England as discrete nations.

This account of the cultural exchange between Cornwall and England, of the symbolic traffic over Brunel's Royal Albert Bridge with which I started, begins in the mid-nineteenth century. Many antiquarians had then feared that their chances of discovering the essence of Cornwall had per-ished in 1777 with the death of Dolly Pentreath, supposedly the last native speaker of the Cornish language.[6] Others, however, like the metropolitan lawyer and Fellow of the Society of Antiquaries William Sandys (alias Uncle Jan Treenoodle), whose *Specimens of the Cornish Provincial Dialect* (1846) pointedly began with a frontispiece of Dolly Pentreath, believed that remnants of Cornish were still to be found in the phonology and vocabu-lary of contemporary Cornish dialect. This attempt to use dialect as an emblem of difference, a foundation upon which to build a sense of Cornish identity, helps in part to explain the explosion of interest in it on both sides of the Tamar from the 1840s. Yet, although the metropolitan antiquarian impulse remained important, the mid-nineteenth-century boom in dialect publications owed more to its popular uses by writers such as J. T. Tregellas, W. B. Forfar and H. J. Daniel.[7] Generally respectable and wealthy men, they wrote mainly comic tales about the lives, loves and labours of the Cornish labouring poor, and found receptive audiences in both Cornwall and London.

In their work Cornishness was no longer located in a vanishing language or dialect. Instead, the subject of their tales – the stoic and simple, but manly and humorous Cornishman, 'with all his rough sense of honour, his kind heart, his self-reliance, his naivite [sic], his ingenuity, and his keen quiet powers of wit and observation' – inadvertently became the object, the source of Cornish national identity.[8] As Mrs Miles said in the introduction to a collection of *Original Cornish Ballads* in 1846, it was not 'the ludicrous rusticity' of their dialect, but the peasantry itself who were the nation's referent:

> [They] constitute one of the most decided features of its nationality, and retain the broad stamp of those characteristic qualities, which distinguish one people from another . . . . In the peasantry of a country, the poet and the philosopher seek the most picturesque, and the most moral aspects of human nature; nor do they seek them in vain.[9]

This reification of the peasantry as a pastoral and deeply moral people, whose very primitivism ensured their proximity to the original essence of Cornishness, became central to the imagination of both Cornish and English national identity. Even by the 1870s and 1880s, when it was common for dialect writers to lament the death of Cornish dialect at the hands of the 'English' railways, newspapers and national education, they remained insistent that the 'primitive' purity of the Cornish labouring poor had not yet been entirely lost.[10] It is too easy to dismiss such sentiments as merely the product of the bucolic imagination of the upper classes.[11] Often, as in the most popular genre of dialect tales, in which a bemused Cornishman visits London, the simple, naive but honest virtues of the Cornish folk were favourably compared to the sophistication, artificiality and duplicity of the aristocracy and metropolitan modernity.[12]

Much of the appeal of dialect tales lay in their claim to represent Cornwall-as-it-really-was. Dialect writers were fond of portraying themselves as ventriloquist's dummies, giving voice to the 'real' Cornish folk. Their authorial presence was for the most part erased, appearing only briefly in a preface to reassure readers of the Cornishness of the author and the authenticity of the tales. Typically, it was said of Tregellas that, being 'a thorough Cornishman by birth and association, and by all his predilections, and beloved accordingly by all good Cornishmen, he felt a complete sympathy with those whose characteristics he delighted to study and reproduce'.[13] Indeed, the authenticity of Tregellas's tales rested on the claim that the folk were not just the subjects of his tales, but their original source, collected by him from 'the midst of their places of labour and of carousal; when and where, unfettered and at ease, they express themselves naturally and unreservedly'.[14] The authority of this conception of the 'real' Cornwall as rooted in its 'primitive' folk was to shape many subsequent representations of Cornishness and its relationship to Englishness.

This shift in interest from language and dialect to the folk themselves as the referents of Cornish national identity gave new urgency to the study of folklore from the mid-nineteenth century onwards. And yet it is important not to characterise the discovery of the Cornish (or any other) folk as stemming simply from an anti-rationalist romance of a pre-industrial golden age;[15] it also drew directly upon the authority of science and the discourse of the 'real'. Since the early nineteenth century Cornwall's scientific community – centred upon such institutions as the Royal Geological Society of Cornwall (1814), the Royal Institution of Cornwall (1818), the Royal Cornwall Polytechnic Society (1833) and the Penzance Natural History and Antiquarian Society (1839) – had intensely scrutinised and mapped the natural, physical and cultural geographies of Cornwall. Just as species of fish and strata of rock were categorised so were the customs, legends and dialects of its inhabitants.

This work culminated in the publication of two collections of Cornish folklore: Robert Hunt's *Popular Romances of the West of England: or Drolls, Traditions and Superstitions of Old Cornwall* (1865) and William Bottrell's three-volume *Traditions and Hearthside Stories of West Cornwall* (1870–80). Hunt's work, in particular, won him a reputation as the founding father of Cornish folklore, earning him a prized place among the portraits of Walter Scott, Thomas Wright, Hans Christian Andersen and the brothers Grimm at the International Folklore Congress of 1891.[16] Despite this later acclamation and his rigorous appeals to the authority of science, Hunt – a fellow of both the Statistical and Royal Societies – remained so embarrassed by his interest in myths and legends that he waited forty years before publishing *The Popular Romances*, until the discipline of folklore had acquired a voguish intellectual credibility as the scientific record of 'primitive' cultures vanishing in the face of the forward march of civilisation and reason.

Central to recent work in the history of ethnographic ideas has been the recognition that the growth of interest in the cultures of so-called 'primitive' peoples, which spread across philology, natural history, archaeology, history and folklore from the 1830s, was motivated less by a humanitarian desire to understand the alterity of other 'races' or 'cultures' in far-flung corners of the Empire than by a desire to better regulate the savages within England itself – be they women and children, the peasantry, the urban poor or the ethnic other.[17] It was an ambivalent discourse in which the romantic rhetoric of a world that had been lost was offset by the realisation that loss was an essential element of modernity, that progress unfolded itself in lineal stages as *humankind* learnt to exercise their reason and control nature. Like the colonial 'primitive', 'the savage within' was a prisoner of nature and irrationality, a remnant from an earlier stage of civilisation against which the 'civilised' could measure their own modernity. The study of folklore became a means of writing the prehistory of civilisation, of tracing the antiquity of English institutions, customs and languages in order to emphasise their progressive development and their distance from those of other races and peoples. Within this framework the Cornish were commonly assumed to occupy a lower point on the evolutionary scale, being part of a 'Celtic' people who were driven back to the peripheries of Britain by the racially superior Anglo-Saxons.[18] Comparisons of 'the Celt' with the 'African Negro' were frequently made by figures such as John Beddoes, whose *The Races of Britain* (1885) confidently asserted that Cornwall, along with the west of Ireland and Scotland, contained the highest proportion of 'nigrescence' within Britain (figure 18). As the Cornish were 'decidedly the darkest people in England proper' the concern was that, with greater mobility, they might 'swamp the blond Teutons of England' and destroy the whole edifice of English civility and modernity.[19]

Increasingly, Cornish antiquarians and folklorists challenged this narrative of modernity and cultural difference with its linear models of development and civilisation. For Hunt and Bottrell, Cornish folklore flatly refused to be incorporated within such a sequential conception of time and modernity. Hunt traced how Cornwall's most ancient 'celtic superstitions [had] lingered on' despite the successive invasions of the 'Roman and Saxon, Danish and Norman civilisations',[20] while both he and Bottrell fretted about the indeterminate racial genealogies of folk-tales and customs that were continually changing form as they were used and performed in different ways.[21] Nonetheless, both Hunt and Bottrell were at pains to locate Cornishness in a 'primitive', dark and wild 'Celtic' culture, and in doing so inevitably invited comparisons with modern England as the apparent source of civility. Thus, for Hunt,

> Those wild dreams which swayed with irresistible force the skin-clad Briton of the Cornish hills, have not yet entirely lost their power where even the National and British Schools are busy with the people, and Mechanics' Institutions are diffusing the truth of science. In the infancy of the race, terror was the moving power: in the maturity of the people, the dark shadow still sometimes rises, like a spectre, partially eclipsing the mild radiance of that Christian truth which shines upon the land.[22]

It is Hunt's equal ambivalence about the superstitions of 'Old Cornwall' as about the rationality and Christianity of English modernity which is most striking. If 'Old Cornwall' remained unenlightened by the shining truths of science, education and Christianity, it supplied ample evidence of the 'rude traditions of a race who appear to have possessed much native intelligence, minds wildly poetical, and great fertility of imagination'.[23] Indeed, Hunt's fear was that English modernity – with its newspapers, railways, educational system and Anglican church – would erase 'the spectres of romance which were [once] the ruling spirits of the place'.[24] Instead he invited his readers to reflect upon the world the English had already lost under what he called the 'constantly repressing influences of Christian teaching, and of the advances of civilisation'.[25]

For Hunt it was Cornwall's geographical isolation, the fact that 'England, with many persons, appeared to terminate on the shores of the river Tamar',

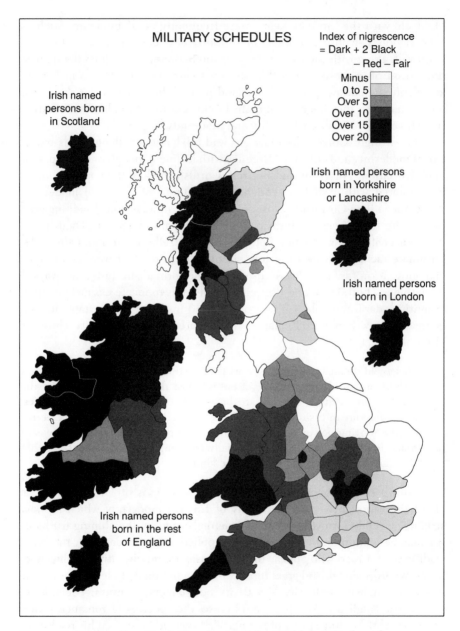

Figure 18 'Cornwall as Dark Continent': John Beddoes's 'Index of Nigrescence' from J. Beddoes, *The Races of Britain* (London, 1885)

that had preserved Cornwall's racial and cultural purity.[26] Thirty years later, in 1893, the same reasoning led the Ethnographic Survey of the British Isles to subject the language, folklore and physiology of the Cornish 'race' to extensive study in an unrivalled thirty-five locations.[27] Informed both by the long-standing ethnographic concern with racial mixing and hybridity and by contemporary social anxieties about urban and national degeneration, the Ethnographic Survey saw in Cornwall a positive reservoir of, admittedly 'Celtic', racial purity.[28] Requesting its volunteers to provide information on physical type, current traditions and beliefs, peculiarities of dialect, monuments and other remains of ancient culture, it emphasised the continuity and purity of ancient racial characteristics and the search for their origins. Cornwall's geographical position was thought to have provided a unique opportunity to study a remarkably uncorrupted race of 'primitive' people. Indeed the more 'primitive' they seemed, the purer their credentials; hence the Survey's reliance on small, secluded villages where the 'native' population had 'continued for generations without any influx of new blood'.[29]

Much of the 1893 report on Cornwall was concerned with the possibility of the dilution of racial purity either from the 'intermixture of Spanish blood from the Armada' or from English tourists.[30] Significantly, greater store was set by a crude but voguish pseudo-scientific physical anthropology than by attention to 'original traditions and beliefs'; bodies and physical remains were now more scientifically reliable than myths and legends. The two approaches were, however, never entirely incompatible, as the very serious scientific pursuit of the physical remains of giants illustrated; the discovery of very large coffins at Wendron church was held up as evidence of 'the former existence of a race of large men once living in the locality'.[31] Ultimately, for all the talk of physical types and scientific process, the Survey's concluding psychological profile of the Cornish character owed a great deal to an admittedly unsympathetic reading of dialect tales.

> The people are very warm and kindly, quick-witted, and keen. Their faults are characteristically Celtic: they are not very 'straight', and are exceedingly suspicious; they fall out easily among themselves, but do not make up again easily; feuds go on from year to year, and last out lifetimes. They have a very curious habit of giving, by preference, any reason for their action except the one that has really determined it . . . . The Cornish Celt is prolific and exceedingly prone to sexual irregularity.[32]

It was a portrait which reaffirmed the impression of many in England of a simple and 'primitive' 'Celtic' people still awaiting the civilising influence of their 'Teutonic' modernity.

The imperial dimension to these English encounters with what appeared a dark, uncharted and uncivilised land conveniently close to home, came into even sharper relief with the settlement of an English artists' 'colony' at Newlyn from the 1880s.[33] Recalling the foundation of this 'colony' in 1900, its figure-head, Alexander Stanhope Forbes, echoed the language of English colonial administrators and expatriates throughout the British Empire.

> These settlers, these artistic outlanders journeyed down to this Rand district of the West, where the treasure they sought was to be found in such profusion. And they met with a kindly reception at the hands of the natives, fortunately provoking no resentment and creating no ill-feeling . . . . Thus . . . they increased and multiplied and became almost as closely identified with the county as its famous pilchards, or that celebrated rock at St. Michael hard by, where they had elected to dwell.[34]

The imperial narrative of discovery became one of possession; Cornwall became the land of the artist as coloniser.

Significantly, the imperial imaginary of the artist colony at Newlyn was enunciated through what Stanhope Forbes described as an 'unflinching realism' which abandoned what were perceived to be the artificial light and subjects of the studio and classical traditions in order to paint 'real' subjects in their 'natural' environment. This deeply romantic version of 'the real' and of 'nature' depended upon the now familiar portrayal of the Cornish as a race distinguished by their 'primitive' and intricate relationship to nature. Once again the Cornish native plays nature to the Englishmen's nurture in Stanhope Forbes's description of how in Newlyn

> the people seemed to fall naturally into their places, and to harmonise with their surroundings . . . [with fishermen] obliged to don their quaint sou-westers and duck-frocks and all the rest of the picturesque attire which one is always struck with in strolling through a fishing village . . . not only the dress, but its wearers were alike weather-stained, and tanned into harmony by the sun and the salt wind, so that the whole scene was in keeping and of one piece. Nature has . . . built up a race of people well knit and comely, fit habitants of such a region.[35]

Stanhope Forbes then found the 'real' Cornwall in a picturesque paradise where the landscape and people remained untainted by what he called the 'inappropriate ornamentation' of the feminised forces of modern fashion and architecture – of villadom, fringes and crinolettes which 'were appalling with these surroundings of sea, boats, fish, etc.'[36] For Stanhope Forbes and his colleagues at Newlyn, Cornwall was deeply masculine. Their work focused repeatedly on men (especially fishermen) at work (figure 19); on their heroic strength and courage in battling against the elements; or their absent presence, as in Walter Langley's *But Men Must Work and Women Must Weep* (figure 20), where the heroic and fatal struggle of men is written on the distraught and hopeless faces of their wives and mothers.

There is much else that could be said about this artistic representation of

Figure 19 Alexander Stanhope Forbes,
Fish Sale on Newlyn Beach

Figure 20 Walter Langley, *But Men
Must Work and Women Must Weep*

the Cornish, not least about its reception by its models and subjects – the inhabitants of Newlyn – which appears to have been considerably less rapturous than Stanhope Forbes cared to recall.[37] Much, too, could be made of the very marked persistence of these tropes in the very different 'modernism' of the St Ives 'school', especially in the fascination with nature and the uniquely abstract and surreal forms suggested by Cornwall's landscape, sea and light, now uncritically celebrated in the St Ives Tate Gallery.[38] The continuities between the two schools were perhaps most evident in the discovery of 'primitivism' in the shape of peasant painter Alfred Wallis.[39] It was the apparently 'naive' nature of Wallis's work that proved so appealing to modernists like Ben Nicholson and Christopher Wood intent on stripping art of the dead hand of Renaissance traditions and returning it to its 'primitive' state. Not only did Wallis repeatedly paint the ordinary everyday subjects of his life; he did so with 'childlike' simplicity and 'intuition' in materials (like cardboard and boat-paint) available to all. The celebration of 'primitivism' owed much to the idealisation of Wallis as an other-worldly, uneducated, peasant painter whose impoverished life had finely attuned him to the 'natural' rhythms of his unspoilt environment. As Penny Florence has recently suggested, English artists and critics since Nicholson have tended to subsume Wallis's Cornish alterity and difference within some form of transcendental 'primitive' consciousness or 'nature' over which they claim a superior knowledge.[40] Here again, Cornwall was imagined in terms of a universal myth of origin, its 'primitive' natural essence providing a benchmark from which the cultured English could assess the progress and discontents of their own modernity. Cornish difference was only exalted in order to be subsequently denied by the all-knowing, imperial gaze of the English artist.

English antiquarians, folklorists and artists were joined in Cornwall by tourists keen to experience this picturesque and uncorrupted Arcadia. While many travellers during the eighteenth and early nineteenth centuries had been drawn to the most distant and 'exotic' parts of the Empire, others were no less struck by the difference of places closer to home. Whereas much of the eighteenth-century discourse of travel was enunciated and authorised through the scientific tropes of discovery, observation and classification, by the early nineteenth century the emphasis was increasingly on travel as a romantic quest in which the experience of the beauty and sublimity of other landscapes and cultures became a means of aesthetic and spiritual fulfilment.[41] Although this shift from the 'scientific' to the 'sentimental' has been somewhat overplayed, it remains a useful point of departure for discussing the Englishman's walking tour of Cornwall in the mid-nineteenth century.

As Wallace has argued, a number of developments in the early nineteenth century removed the traditional associations of vagrancy and poverty from walking, and elevated it to a cultural activity capable of rehabilitating the individual and society by restoring the bond with nature that industrialisation and urbanisation had threatened.[42] While Peter Smith Baker's account of his walking tour through Cornwall in 1840 was a prelapsarian narrative, a discovery of an uncharted landscape and a lost Eden, a return to the innocence of childhood,[43] for the popular novelist Wilkie Collins such adventures offered a means of metamorphosis, a reinvention of the self. Revelling in the facelessness of being a stranger in a strange land, he recalled how he and his companion walked 'through the country comfortably as mappers, trodgers, tradesmen, guinea-pig-mongers, and poor back burdened vagabond lads, altogether, or one at a time, just as the peasantry pleased'.[44] Although much has been written on the bourgeois male pleasures of the urban *flâneur* – exploring the city as spectator, navigating its labyrinthine streets and surveying its dark strangers, while maintaining a suitable distance and containing his own visceral excitement[45] – few have acknowledged that the countryside was also full of hidden pleasures and dangers for the wandering *flâneur*. Touring Cornwall on foot offered not just the discovery and exploration of the 'Other', but of the 'Self' as well.

Although the arrival of the railway with the construction of the Royal Albert Bridge in 1859 made Cornwall accessible to a larger number of English tourists (Thomas Cook operated his first package tour to Land's End in 1860), it also became more distant and remote. Rail travel not only allowed the rural *flâneur* to consume Cornwall at ever greater speeds, it engendered a totalising panoramic vision of the Cornish landscape – absorbed effortlessly from the safety and distance of carriage windows as the train climbed moors and crossed valleys and viaducts.[46] This vision, in which the tourist was positioned as the master of all they surveyed, was replicated in the proliferation of guide-books produced for the new rail-travelling public.[47] This genre – which, almost without exception, offered remarkably detailed 'scientific' introductions to Cornish history, geology, climate, language and the principal industries of mining, fishing and agriculture – represented a timeless and unchanging Cornish landscape and racial character, in order to help readers better to appreciate and negotiate the strange land they travelled. In providing detailed itineraries, the guide-books insisted that 'to get a correct idea of so singular and remote a county as Cornwall it is indispensable that it should be seen *thoroughly*',[48] although the routes and 'sights' they mapped were anything but exhaustive.

It was perhaps the Great Western Railway's marketing of 'The Cornish Riviera' in the early twentieth century that provided the most totalising representation of Cornwall for the English tourist.[49] Drawing upon late Victorian and Edwardian fears about urban degeneracy and the ailing health of the English body politic, the Great Western Railway invoked the authority of science to construct Cornwall as a health resort whose climate favourably compared to 'the

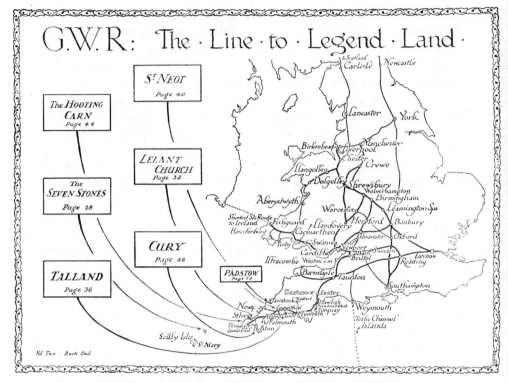

Figure 21 'Mapping Legend Land', from Great Western Railway, *Legend Land*, vol. I (London, 1922)

far-off and much less accessible shores of Southern France or Northern Africa, or the still more distant island of Madeira'.[50] The railway offered its travellers a brave new world of speed, science and modernity, equipping its 'Express' trains with special glass designed to admit 'health-giving ultra violet rays' so that 'passengers . . . will literally commence their sunlight treatment en route to the holiday destination'.[51] However, central to this image was the representation of Cornwall as a 'primitive' land of magic and romance (figure 21). In a series of booklets entitled *Legend Land*, Cornish and Welsh folk-tales were conflated together as variously 'Celtic' or 'Western', and presented as 'the simplest romances of a very simple people' who had 'more time to remember the tales of other days than [those] in busier, more prosaic, districts'.[52]

From the 1920s this ambivalence towards a 'primitive' culture untainted by modernity increasingly marked Great Western publicity. Cornish alterity was gradually subsumed by the representation of Cornwall as an earlier incarnation of Englishness, a place more English than an England ravaged by modernity. As S. P. B. Mais put it in the best-selling *The Cornish Riviera*:

Old England is everywhere crumbling about our ears, and it is a sorry business trying to find any traces of her nowadays in the Home Counties, but in the Duchy medievalism still exists, the candle lit by the early saints still burns, the age of chivalry is emphatically not dead, and our most remote ancestors still haunt the ancient places.[53]

Cornwall became a repository of all that England had once been before its fall into a corrosive and effeminate modernity. 'To know this part of England is to learn the purity of atmosphere never breathed in populous places. To taste the air, meat and drink of the open Cornish moors is to go back hundreds of years, when man was strong and free.'[54]

Such refrains for a pre-modern pastoral Eden have often marked English culture,[55] but they had especial resonance in an early twentieth century shaken to the core by the trauma of the First World War and obsessed with the spectre of national degeneracy. For many during the inter-war years the countryside provided a means of physical and mental rehabilitation, a flight from the mechanised monotony and dehumanising rigours of modern life.[56] And Cornwall offered the best escape of all, close to nature and 'mother earth in her primeval vesture', and far from 'the fret and fume of a money-grubbing world'.[57] Indeed, Cornwall was portrayed as so removed from English modernity, so utterly Other, that the following remarkable passage, published in C. E. Vulliamy's *Unknown Cornwall* in 1925 was, at the time, quite unremarkable:

In Cornwall you find what, in these days of enlightenment and sophistication, you do not find everywhere – a real peasantry. The Cornish peasant has a bluntness and a restful depth of ignorance which make him an appropriate and interesting figure in his own strange surroundings. In some respects he has a Mid-African simplicity. His presence helps you realize that you have travelled into a far and unfamiliar land. He shows an agreeable blend of those physical and mental characters which people of refinement expect to find in 'natives'. . . in the little stone cottages on the moors you will find the untainted aboriginal.[58]

Both pseudo-scientific and sentimental tropes merge here to evoke Cornwall as a foreign land – still rooted in the natural essence of its uncorrupted, aboriginal peasantry – through which English tourists could view themselves with a mixture of self-satisfaction and anxious regret.

Ironically, this representation of Cornwall was a victim of its own success, for Cornwall's increasing popularity among English tourists threatened to despoil the very romance and mystique it relied upon. By the 1920s, guidebooks were encouraging a quest for the 'unconquered', 'unknown' Cornwall off the beaten track, a Cornwall now opened up by the motor car. The car and motor coach brought with them a rash of new guide-books, with different itineraries, mapping Cornwall in still more convenient ways for those whose search for the panoramic gaze was restricted to the rear-view mirror. They also accentuated the anxiety that English modernity had begun to pollute Cornwall. In the 1930 survey of Cornwall conducted on behalf of the Cornwall Branch of the Council for the Preservation of Rural England (CPRE), the car joined the speculative builder, the electric pylon, and the gasworks as the main evils disfiguring the 'natural scenery' of the Cornish landscape.[59] Yet the careful cataloguing of 'inappropriate petrol filling stations and enamel advertisements' paled into insignificance beside the concerns voiced about the violation of the Cornish coast by 'the flimsy type of ill-designed bungalow and suburban villa', whose architectural character 'is in many cases as foreign to the landscape as their occupants are strangers to the ancient building traditions and customs of the Cornish people'.[60] Although this CPRE survey looked forward to and in many respects anticipated post-war developments, it had its origins in *The Cornish Magazine*'s debate about Cornwall's development as a tourist resort during the 1890s.[61] Indeed, Arthur Quiller-Couch, who as editor of that magazine had then warned that tourism would lead to a 'deterioration in [Cornish] manliness and independence', wrote a similarly gloomy preface to the CPRE 1930 survey, lamenting the 'in rush of motors and [the] descent of the ready made bungalow builder, the hotel investor, the holiday maker who thinks no cove complete without a minstrel (negro) and a gramophone, the *pater familias* who brings his youngster to Tintagel with spade and bucket'.[62]

Ironically, the Cornwall encountered by English antiquarians, artists and tourists had many similarities with the nation imagined by the nationalist 'Cornish Revival'. This 'Revival' can be more accurately described as an attempt to invent a distinctly 'Celtic' Cornish culture, a process which culminated in the formation of organisations like the Celtic-Cornish Society (1901), the Old Cornwall Society (1920) and the Cornish Gorseth (1928).[63] Despite their different emphases, these organisations believed that the essence of Cornishness lay in its 'Celtic' origins, origins clearly evident in the customs, folklore, place-names, dialect and, above all, the language of 'Old Cornwall'. By 'reviving' Cornwall's 'Celtic' traditions, especially its language, they sought to protect the 'Cornishness of Cornwall' from the corrosive influence of the 'cheap materialism' of England's modern mass culture.[64]

The 'Celtic' Cornwall that the Revivalists evoked was largely a pre-industrial one, a mystical land of legend and tradition, an age before the railways, education, newspapers, the cinema and even the spectre of Bolshevism had threatened the very Cornishness of Cornwall.[65] This was no simple nostalgic yearning for a mythical pre-industrial golden age, but rather a vision based on an ambivalent assessment of what English modernity lacked, especially a concern for the spiritual vacuum which Revivalists felt marked its materialism. So, despite Hamilton Jenkin's often moving account of the poverty of Cornwall's nineteenth-century labouring poor, the sense of loss and regret remained central.

> Their life, indeed, was hard and laborious, but it provided that variety of occupation for hand and brain which is so singularly lacking in our own age. Though none would wish to return, perhaps, to those long dark evenings of the past, lit only by the feeble rushlight or the miner's tallow dip, yet more and more is the realization growing that the old people found something therein which gave them both character and a philosophy of life – gifts which, perhaps, were more than compensatory for the absence of the gramophone, the cinema, the cheap newspaper, and even the wireless.[66]

This idea that material poverty created spiritual wealth was profoundly romantic, but its reification of Old Cornwall as a spiritual resource struck a chord with those like Morton Nance and Henry Jenner who, with Hamilton Jenkin, had founded the Old Cornwall Society and the Cornish Gorseth in order to search for a different type of Cornish modernity – one based upon an imagined 'Celtic' past.

Naturally the Revivalists set themselves up as the guardians of this 'Celtic' spirit and tradition; it was they who policed the Cornishness of Cornwall, they who distinguished between the fake and the authentic, visitor-lore and folklore, 'the real' and 'the imagined' Cornwall. This involved frequent denunciations of the effects of tourism and its materialist exploitation of Cornwall's 'Celtic' spiritual resources. As early as 1898, there were complaints that at Tintagel, the very heart of Arthurian Cornwall, 'facing Arthur's Castle – grinning down as it were, in derision at the ruins of its old state – there is being erected a modern hotel – "built in imitation of Arthur's Castle", as one is told! Bad taste cannot possibly go further.'[67] Fifty years later, Hamilton Jenkin was similarly disapproving of the way Helston's 'Furry-Day' was being exploited by the

> townspeople . . . [who] . . . have allowed it to become something . . . of a 'spectacle' . . . the crowds who now throng the pleasant old-world streets of Helston on Furry-day are for the most part alien-crowds, brought there in motor coaches from neighbouring 'resorts', and come only to gaze in wonder or amusement at a 'quaint' old ceremony of whose significance they know little and probably care less.[68]

The Revivalists' attempt to protect the spirit of 'Celtic' Cornwall had been corrupted by the very 'crude materialism' that they felt had threatened the Cornishness of Cornwall in the first place. It was not just that people were making money out of the ancient 'Celtic' Cornwall they had invented, but that the only people interested were those in Cornwall who were reaping good profits and those 'alien' visitors who came to discover another world of legend and romance.

On closer inspection this was not unsurprising as the 'Cornish Revival' had always been a peculiarly English affair; many of its leading figures were either English or exiled in England or further afield. The Cornish diaspora had produced Cornish Associations not just around Britain but across the globe, from South Africa to South America and New Zealand, and many of them invested much in the art of remaining Cornish – raising monies for the distressed at home, taking Cornish papers, organising Cornish festivities complete with pasties and saffron cake.[69] In contrast, many who lived in Cornwall felt alienated by the high cultural tone of a nationalist 'Revival' that seemed to deny the Cornishness of those who failed to meet its exacting standards. The initially sympathetic writer Jack Clemo quickly became disillusioned, complaining that 'I never gained a real mastery of the language. The jargon about tenses, genders and conjunctions was Greek to me. I had learnt only the rudiments of grammar at school, and wrote by instinct with a minimum of technical knowledge . . . . Cornish was a foreign language to me, as it is to all modern Cornish people.'[70] Similar sentiments were echoed by Herbert Thomas, the Managing Director of the Cornish Group of Newspapers in the 1920s:

> I know nothing of the original Cornish language; very little about the history of the tribes, or clans which drifted across the Tamar in prehistoric days; my mind is a blank about the various types of ecclesiastical architecture in the County; and I can still lose my way among the elder-hedges and fishing-net garden-plots between Mousehole and Lamorna, or in trying to tramp in a fog from Zennor to Penzance via Ding Dong, while some parts of my native county are as much a part of 'Unknown Cornwall' as they are to the Yorkshire or Midland tripper.

For Thomas, Cornwall was a hybrid and indeterminate nation:

> I know that we are of all shapes, sizes and colours, except jet black. I meet people with high cheek-bones, raven hair and sallow skins, who, in Chinese clothes would pass for sons of the Flowery Land. I encounter maidens of the Spanish types of beauty and physique; red-haired youths and flaxen haired men and maidens; giants and pygmies, merchant princes, missionaries, labourers, cranks and dullards . . . and there has been such an influx of 'foreigners' into Cornwall during the last century or so, that I think it takes quite a clever man (or woman) to picture us, analyze us and label us like exhibits in a museum.[71]

I have quoted this passage at length because it neatly encapsulates the limitations of both the English imperial and Cornish nationalist imaginaries; neither was ever entirely successful at constructing a stable, essential and discrete self-identity, for 'the Other' always returned to haunt and inhabit those very biological, historical and cultural foundations of 'the Self' from which it was excluded. Perhaps, then, we can reread the attempts to represent Cornwall and England as discrete, centred, stable and homogeneous nations as symptoms of their very insecurity and instability. Such a reading has

implications for the ways in which historians consider the nature and historical formation of British national identity. It suggests that it may be more productive to examine the internal relationships of the inherently unstable
'British Self', than to assume that 'the Other' is always overseas, somewhere
else.[72] And it also problematises the 'four-nations' model of British national
identity, one that tellingly ignores Cornwall or conflates its alterity within
Englishness, and ultimately rests upon its portrayal of a 'union' between four
discrete and bounded nations.[73] Crossing the border to Cornwall threatens to
unpick not just English history, but British history as well.

Notes

My thanks to Becky Conekin, Geoff Cubitt, Phil Eva, Peter Gatrell, Alison Light and Ros
Wyatt for comments on earlier drafts. Various versions of this essay have been presented at
Huddersfield and Manchester as well as the 'Imagining Nations' conference at York. The
research for this essay was generously supported by both the British Academy and the
University of Manchester.

1 H. K. Bhabha, 'Of mimicry and man: the ambivalence of colonial discourse', in his *The
   Location of Culture* (London, 1984), pp. 85–92.

2 On Britishness see T. Nairn, *The Break-Up of Britain* (London, 1981); R. Samuel (ed.),
   Patriotism: the Making and Unmaking of British National Identity, 3 vols (London, 1989);
   M. Crozier (ed.), *Varieties of Britishness* (Belfast, 1990); L. Colley, *Britons: Forging the
   Nation, 1707–1837* (London, 1992); A. Grant and K. Stringer (eds), *Uniting the Kingdom?
   The Making of British History* (London, 1995); P. Dodd, *The Battle Over Britain* (London,
   1995). On Englishness, see R. Colls and P. Dodd (eds), *Englishness: Politics and Culture
   1880–1920* (London, 1986); P. Gilroy, *There Ain't No Black in the Union Jack: the Cultural
   Politics of Race and Nation* (London, 1987); G. Newman, *The Rise of English
   Nationalism: a Cultural History 1740–1830* (London, 1987); A. Light, *Forever England:
   Femininity, Literature and Conservatism Between the Wars* (London, 1991).

3 See P. Payton, *The Making of Modern Cornwall: Historical Experience and the
   Persistence of Difference* (Redruth, 1992); P. Payton (ed.), *Cornwall since the War: the
   Contemporary History of a European Region* (Redruth, 1993); B. Deacon and P. Payton,
   'Re-inventing Cornwall: culture change on the European periphery', *Cornish Studies*,
   I, 2nd series (1993).

4 B. Anderson, *Imagined Communities: Reflections on the Origin and Spread of
   Nationalism* (London, 1983). See also E. Gellner, *Nations and Nationalism* (Oxford,
   1983); E. J. Hobsbawm, *Nations and Nationalism* (Cambridge, 1987); H. K. Bhabha
   (ed.), *Nation and Narration* (London, 1990).

5 G. Spivak, 'Can the subaltern speak? Speculations on widow sacrifice', in C. Nelson and
   L. Grossberg (eds), *Marxism and the Interpretation of Culture* (London, 1988), pp. 271–313;
   H. K. Bhabha, 'Signs taken for wonders', in his *The Location of Culture*, pp. 102–22.

6 For the protracted debate on the identity of the last native speaker of Cornish see
   P. Berresford Ellis, *The Cornish Language and its Literature* (London, 1974).

7 Even the classic late nineteenth-century antiquarian studies of Cornish dialect emphasised their debt to popular dialect writers. See F. W. P. Jago, *The Ancient Language and
   the Dialect of Cornwall with an Enlarged Glossary of Cornish Provincial Words* (Truro,
   1882); T. Quiller Couch and M. A. Courtney, *Glossary of Words in Use in Cornwall:
   Survey of English Dialect Society* (London, 1878–80).

8 I. T. Tregellas, *Peeps into the Homes and Haunts of the Rural Population of Cornwall* (Truro, 1868), p. vii.

9 M. Gervis, *Original Cornish Ballads: Chiefly Founded on Stories Humorously Told by Mr. Tregellas, in his Popular Lectures on 'Peculiarities'*. . . (Penryn, 1846), pp. 3–4.

10 'In this age of popular education, when the march of intellect is making such rapid strides, and "Board Schools" are teaching everybody everything . . . the higher classes of society would hardly believe that such primitive people . . . still exist. But so it is.' W. B. Forfar, *Cornish Poems and Selections from Pentowan* (Truro, 1885), p. i.

11 P. Joyce, *Visions of the People: Industrial England and the Question of Class, 1848–1914* (Cambridge, 1991), pp. 267–8.

12 For two good examples see Anon., 'Capt. Tom Teague's humourous and satirical remarks on Zebedee Jacka's real adventures at the Exhibition, in July, 1862', in *Four Tales in Verse and Prose in the Cornish Dialect* (Truro, n.d.); H. J. Daniel, *Mary Anne in London* (Devonport, n.d.).

13 Tregellas, *Peeps into the Homes and Haunts*, p. ix.

14 *Ibid.*, p. xi.

15 See P. Burke, *Popular Culture in Early Modern Europe* (London, 1978); Hobsbawm, *Nations and Nationalism*; W. A. Wilson, 'Herder, folklore and Romantic Nationalism', *Journal of Popular Culture*, 6 (1973), 819–35.

16 R. H. Dorson, *The British Folklorists: a History* (London, 1968), p. 320.

17 See N. Stepan, *The Idea of Race in Science: Great Britain 1800–1960* (London, 1982); G. Stocking, *Victorian Anthropology* (London, 1987); H. Kuklick, *The Savage Within: the Social History of British Anthropology, 1885–1945* (Cambridge, 1991); E. Barkan, *The Retreat of Scientific Racism: Changing Concepts of Race in Britain and the United States in between the Wars* (Cambridge, 1992); J. Urry, *Before Social Anthropology: Essays on the History of British Social Anthropology* (Reading, 1993); R. Young, *Colonial Desire: Hybridity in Theory, Culture and Race* (London, 1995).

18 For the centrality of race to nineteenth-century histories of England see J. Burrows, *A Liberal Descent: Victorian Historians and the English Past* (Cambridge, 1981); Young, *Colonial Desire*; J. Vernon, 'Narrating the Constitution: the discourse of "the real" and the fantasies of constitutional history', in J. Vernon (ed.), *Re-reading the Constitution: New Narratives in the Political History of England's Long Nineteenth Century* (Cambridge, 1996).

19 J. Beddoes, *The Races of Britain: a Contribution to the Anthropology of Western Europe* (London, 1885), pp. 285, 298. For an earlier example, see R. Knox, *The Races of Men: a Fragment* (London, 1850).

20 R. Hunt, *Popular Romances of the West of England: or Drolls, Traditions and Superstitions of Old Cornwall* (London, 1865), pp. 24–5.

21 Hunt, *Popular Romances*, p. 31; W. Bottrell, *Traditions and Hearthside Stories of the West of Cornwall*, 3 vols (Penzance, 1870–80), I: 46.

22 Hunt, *Popular Romances*, p. 25.

23 *Ibid.*, p. 22.

24 *Ibid.*, p. 25.

25 *Ibid.*, p. 25.

26 *Ibid.*, p. 25.

27 For the Ethnographic Survey's foundational role in the emergence of anthropology as a discipline, see Urry, *Before Social Anthropology*.

28 S. L. Gilman and J. E. Chamberlaine (eds), *Degeneration: the Dark Side of Progress* (London, 1985).

29 'Ethnographic Survey of the United Kingdom. First Report of the Committee', in *Report of the British Association for the Advancement of Science 1893* (London, 1894), p. 623.

30 *Ibid.*, p. 634.
31 *Ibid.*, p. 633.
32 *Ibid.*, p. 636.
33 See D. V. Baker, *Britain's Art Colony by the Sea* (London, 1959); C. Fox and F. Greenacre, *Painting in Newlyn 1880–1930* (London, 1985); T. Cross, *The Shining Sands: Artists in Newlyn and St. Ives 1880–1930* (Tiverton, 1994).
34 A. Stanhope Forbes, 'Cornwall from a painter's point of view', *Royal Cornwall Polytechnic Society. The Sixty Eighth Annual Report* (1900), pp. 51–2.
35 A. Stanhope Forbes, 'A Newlyn retrospect', *The Cornish Magazine* (1898), p. 83.
36 Quoted in C. Fox and F. Greenacre, *Artists of the Newlyn School* (Penzance, 1979).
37 See, for instance, *The Cornishman*, 5 October 1887.
38 See M. Tooby, *Tate St. Ives: an Illustrated Companion* (London, 1993) and Penny Florence's excellent critique 'Marketing the Tate Gallery at St. Ives', paper presented to 'The Romance of Place' conference at Exeter University, 16 April 1994.
39 See S. Berlin, 'Alfred Wallis', *Horizon*, 7:37 (1943); S. Berlin, *Alfred Wallis: Primitive* (Bristol, 1943; 2nd edn, 1992); E. Mullins, *Alfred Wallis: Cornish Primitive Painter* (London, 1967); G. Melly, *Alfred Wallis: Paintings from St. Ives* (Cambridge, 1993).
40 Florence, 'Marketing the Tate Gallery at St. Ives'.
41 See M. L. Pratt, *Imperial Eyes: Travel Writing and Transculturation* (London, 1992); J. Urry, *The Tourist Gaze: Leisure and Travel in Contemporary Societies* (London, 1990); J. Buzard, *The Beaten Track: European Tourism and the Ways to 'Culture' 1808–1918* (Oxford, 1994).
42 A. D. Wallace, *Walking, Literature, and English Culture: the Origins and Uses of Peripatetic in the Nineteenth Century* (Oxford, 1993).
43 P. Smith Baker, *Trip to the Far West* (London, 1840), p. 58.
44 W. W. Collins, *Rambles Beyond Railways; or, Notes in Cornwall Taken A-Foot* (London, 1861), p. 68.
45 See R. Sennett, *The Fall of Public Man* (Cambridge, 1973); P. Stallybrass and A. White, *The Politics and Poetics of Transgression* (Ithaca, NY, 1986); G. Pollock, 'Vicarious excitements: London: a Pilgrimage by Gustave Doré and Blanchard Jerrold, 1872', *New Formations*, 2 (1988), 25–50; S. Buck-Morss, 'The flâneur, the sandwichman and the whore: the politics of loitering', *New German Critique*, 13:39 (1986), 99–142; J. Walkowitz, *The City of Dreadful Delight: Narratives of Sexual Danger in Late-Victorian London* (London, 1993), ch. 1.
46 W. Schivelbusch, *The Railway Journey: the Industrialisation of Time and Space* (Leamington Spa, 1986).
47 See, for example, Anon., *The Stranger's Hand-Book to Cornwall, from Plymouth to Land's End. With Map and Illustrations* (Devonport, 1860); T. Hingston Harvey, *The Tourist's Guide Through Cornwall, by Road, by River and by Rail* (Truro, 1861); W. H. Tregellas, *Tourists' Guide to Cornwall and the Scilly Isles: Containing Succinct Information Concerning all the Principal Places and Objects of Interest in the County* (London, 1877).
48 Tregellas, *Tourist's Guide to Cornwall*, 4th edn (London, 1884), p. v (original emphasis). W. H. Tregellas was the son of dialect writer I. T. Tregellas.
49 See A. M. Broadley, *The Cornish Riviera* (London, 1903), the first edition of which sold a quarter of a million copies. It drew heavily upon Tregellas's *Tourists' Guide to Cornwall*, originally published in 1877, which went to seven editions by 1895. For a useful history of the Great Western Railway's innovative publicity, see R. Burdett Wilson, *Go Great Western: a History of GWR Publicity* (Newton Abbot, 1970).
50 Great Western Railway, *The Cornish Riviera. New and Enlarged 2nd edn* (London, 1905), pp. 5–6.
51 *Ibid.*, p. 17.

52 Lyonesse, *Legend Land*, III: 3 and I: i. For the full series see Lyonesse, *Legend Land. Being a collection of some of the OLD TALES told in those Western Parts of Britain served by the GREAT WESTERN RAILWAY, now retold by LYONESSE*, 4 vols (London, 1922–24).

53 S. P. B. Mais, *The Cornish Riviera* (London, 1928), p. 7.

54 Great Western Railway, *Sunny Cornwall. England's 'Mediterranean' Region. Pen and Pencil Sketches of the Cornish Riviera and Holiday Resorts* (London, n.d.), p. 14.

55 See M. Weiner, *English Culture and the Decline of the Industrial Spirit, 1850–1980* (Cambridge, 1981).

56 F. Trentmann, 'Civilization and its discontents: English Neo-Romanticism and the transformation of anti-modernism in twentieth-century Western culture', *Journal of Contemporary History*, 29 (1994), 583–625; A. Howkins, 'The discovery of rural England', in Colls and Dodd (eds.), *Englishness*, pp. 62–88; G. Boyes, *The Imagined Village: Culture, Ideology and the English Folk Revival* (Manchester, 1993); J. Taylor, *A Dream of England: Landscape, Photography and the Tourist's Imagination* (Manchester, 1994).

57 J. B. Cornish and J. A. D. Bridger (eds), *Penzance and the Lands End District*, 8th edn (Penzance, 1927). See also A. G. Folliot Stokes, *From Devon to St. Ives. The Cliffs, the Coves, the Moorland and some of the Birds and Flowers* (London, 1910), p. 17.

58 C. E. Vulliamy, *Unknown Cornwall. With Illustrations by Charles Simpson* (London, 1928), pp. 6–7. Both Vulliamy and Simpson had been students of Stanhope Forbes.

59 W. H. Thompson and C. Henderson (eds), *Cornwall: a Survey of its Coasts, Moors, and Valleys, with Suggestions for the Preservation of Amenities* (London, 1930).

60 Thompson and Henderson (eds), *Cornwall*, p. 4.

61 See, for example, the contributions of J. L. W. Page, A. H. Norway, J. H. Findlater and A. Quiller-Couch: *The Cornish Magazine*, I (Truro, 1898), pp. 159, 234–8.

62 A. Quiller-Couch, 'Preface', in Thompson and Henderson (eds.), *Cornwall*, p. x.

63 See Bernard Deacon's unpublished paper, 'The Cornish revival: an analysis' (Cornish Studies Library, Redruth, 1985).

64 R. M. Nance, 'What we stand for', *Old Cornwall*, 1 (April 1925), p. 3. The phrase 'cheap materialism' was Hamilton Jenkin's; see his *Cornwall and its People* (London, 1945), p. 315.

65 See, for example, Nance, 'What we stand for'; H. Jenner, *The Renaissance of Merry England* (St Ives, 1923).

66 Jenkin, *Cornwall and its People*, p. 326.

67 *The Cornish Magazine*, p. 236.

68 Jenkin, *Cornwall and its People*, p. 451.

69 See J. Klinsman, *The Cornish Handbook* (London, 1921); T. Roberts and C. Henderson (eds), *Tre, Pol and Pen. The Cornish Annual* (London, 1928); H. Miners, *The Story of the Bristol Cornish* (Bristol, 1975).

70 J. Clemo, *Confessions of a Rebel* (London, 1949), pp. 88–90.

71 H. Thomas, 'Ourselves', in Roberts and Henderson (eds), *Tre, Pol and Pen*, pp. 55–6.

72 Colley, *Britons*.

73 See R. Samuel, 'British dimensions: "Four Nations History"', *History Workshop Journal*, 40 (1995).

'What should they know of England who only England know?': Kipling on the boundaries of gender, art and empire

In 1891 *The Light that Failed*, the first novel-length work by the twenty-six-year-old Rudyard Kipling, was published in both book and magazine form. It played an important part in Kipling's pursuit of fulfilment, success and recognition as a writer, in which he had engaged vigorously since returning to England from India in October 1889. Literary analysts, while acknowledging the power and interest of the text, have rarely placed it in the canon of Kipling's most esteemed writing.[1] For those concerned with Kipling's life and work there is fertile ground for discussions of the novel's autobiographical aspects and of insights it may offer into the author.[2] My own purpose is to take *The Light that Failed* as a point of entry for an exploration of the cultural dynamics of British 'imaginings' of nation, empire and gender in the later nineteenth and early twentieth centuries. The novel's interest in this respect flows not just from its status as a youthful work by an author who became a widely read, discussed and quoted 'writer of empire', but from the particular opportunity it provides to examine the crucial – but still too often ignored or underestimated – *gendered* character of imaginings of Britain and its Empire at that time. This essay will suggest that gender issues lay close to the heart both of Kipling's own familiar and canonical imperialist *oeuvre* and of the broader patriotic and imperialist culture of which that *oeuvre* was an expression.

The last two decades of the nineteenth century can be seen as a distinctive 'moment' for histories of gender and empire as cultural and political themes in British lives and national self-imaging. Imperial themes appeared not only in celebrations of the Queen/Empress Victoria's Jubilees, of territorial expansion and of 'national' mission, achievement and destiny, but equally in contestations over Irish Home Rule, British interventions in Egypt and the Sudan (settings used in *The Light that Failed*), tariff policies, Anglo-Boer relations in South Africa, and colonial policy in India.[3] Gender themes were manifest in the emergence of campaigns on issues of work, education and civic status (both legal and political) for women, in responses to those campaigns, and in related fascination (both elite and popular) with the characteristics of femininity, masculinity and sexuality as expressed in science, popular journalism and artistic production.[4] From reactions to the so-called 'Ripper' murders, to women as workers in the mining industry or to their participation in public politics, to portrayals of imperial 'Britishness' in music-hall culture, in social or political debate, or in fiction for middle-class adult or adolescent readers, these themes were a feature of cultural as well as of political creation and consumption. Established conventions of imaginative representation of the 'exotic' attractions and fears stimulated by gender and ethnic difference combined with the conventions of rational, empirically based scientific knowledge and analysis in the formation and dissemination of concepts, images and beliefs which shaped and sustained concern with these issues. Whether we consider the impact of John Ruskin's imaginative conjuring of imperial mission on the young Cecil Rhodes alongside Ruskin's influential evocations of art and gender, or the emergence of feminist politics and thinking which linked women's claims to political and creative expression with their contribution to a British imperial mission, we can also focus on the interdependence of these themes.[5]

Such thematic interconnections were not, of course, fixed, stable or consistent. The power, popularity and persistent presence of Kipling's writings in English culture express not only the certainties but also the ambiguities, doubts and tensions involved in 'imperial mission' or in 'masculinity', which readers might share with the author. Kipling's 'troubled intimacy with empire' was expressed in writing which evoked his responses to his own experience as journalist, traveller and resident in British-ruled India. It also addressed the condition of others in Britain and its Empire, ranging from advocates, critics and reformers of empire to those engaged in the administrative, commercial, missionary or military networks of empire and the families and communities to which they were connected. To speak, as contemporaries did, of 'the Indian question', 'the woman question' or 'the Irish question' was to signal the controversial and contested character as well as the importance of imperial and gender issues. This essay will explore the cultural dimensions of controversy and contention which were entwined with formal and political manifestations of concern with such issues. Its emphasis will be on the range of ideas, images, desires and anxieties which were associated with gender and imperial relationships, and which connected them both in cultural production and consumption and in political argument and activity. The notion of 'relationships' is emphasised in order to focus on the personal, intimate and interactive elements in the activities and perceptions of the groups, families and communities who shaped and were shaped by British colonial or imperial environments.

Any understanding of these relationships must depend on a sense of the interconnections between cultural, material and political elements in the imperial or colonial setting. These interconnections may be explored from a number of starting points. Ordinary consumer goods (soap, sugar, tobacco) were used in the daily lives of households sustained by gender divisions (women washing and cooking, men smoking sociably) and by reliance on commercial and colonial networks which brought the products of global labour markets into those lives. These products were advertised by the representation of domestic and global roles (black women or children at washtubs, 'oriental' servants proffering coffee or cigarettes). Images of racial and cultural exoticism and hierarchy, of domestic labour and virtue, and of gender or other social differences played a key role in the creation and sharing of cultural assumptions, as they did in the making and maintenance of the markets on which production and commerce depended. The circulation of ideas and images also connected metropolis and empire through the development and transmission of social and moral norms, anxieties, debates and aspirations. Middle-class anxieties over the health and socialisation of lower-class children were linked to ideas of imperial mission through a concern with these children's future suitability as soldiers, mothers and employees. So too was intensified state intervention in schooling; schoolbooks offered stereotypes of colonial 'others' alongside prescriptive treatment of gender roles and the moral standards advocated for the lower classes by their 'betters'. Missionary writing and fund-raising material also conveyed such images, representing 'savage', 'depraved', 'heathen' people and practices to be transformed by missionary endeavours. This served not just to build confidence in the national Christian imperial project overseas, but also to forge solidarities within networks linked to church and chapel, which shaped moral and social norms within Britain. In a similar way, representations of 'alien' immodesty or polygamy or 'oriental luxury' were interwoven with scientific, Christian or feminist constructions of gender identity, marriage and family, to shape both dominant and alternative conceptions of domesticity and sexuality.[6]

The popularity and intelligibility of Kipling (or of Rider Haggard, or of orientalist art) must thus be understood in the context of socially broad and diverse cultural attachments. Constructions and representations of African polygamy, or of 'oriental' sexuality, or of masculine or military imperial mission and its moral or domestic feminine counterparts interacted with views of 'national identity' and contributed to a common fabric not of homogeneous stereotypes but of complex and ambivalent assumptions and visions. Kipling's writing may be related to this wider domain. *The Light that Failed* appeared in *Lippincott's Magazine* in a period when that journal also published Arthur Conan Doyle's *The Sign of Four* and Oscar Wilde's *The Picture of Dorian Gray*.[7] It shares with Conan Doyle's text the depiction of danger, darkness, crime and corruption in a great metropolis (London), and with Wilde's the presentation of autobiographical concerns and of debates on art and artists, as well as the tropes of orientalism and sexual speculations and anxieties. The purpose of this

observation is not to homogenise distinctive texts and authors into a single category, but rather to suggest that *The Light that Failed* offers the opportunity for
a detailed exploration of a cultural environment and moment which Kipling
shared with other cultural producers and their audiences.

The novel was produced in the period that followed Kipling's arrival in
London, in pursuit of what he called his 'Scheme' for achievement and
recognition as a writer, building on the impact made by the publication of his
'Indian' stories and other verse and journalism between 1888 and 1890. More
was involved in this self-conscious new departure than mere artistic or professional ambition. In pursuit of fulfilment and fame Kipling chose, for the first
time in his adult life, to reside separately from relatives or friends, taking on
the challenge of existence as an autonomous (male) adult as well as an aspiring writer. His refusal to accept money, his creation of a self-consciously eclec-
tic, eccentric, quasi-'bohemian' environment, and his experimentation with
London pubs, streets and music halls, as well as with the literary and journalistic coteries to which he gained access, have a number of significations.
At a time when the passage from boyhood to male adulthood was beginning
to be envisioned as a life stage in its own right ('youth') by reformers, writers
and moralists, Kipling was to work narratives of this transition into his first
novel and into his later writing (including the autobiographical *Something of
Myself*). Another crucial element in *The Light that Failed* is the narrative of the
struggles and vicissitudes of a young man as an aspiring artist-hero. This trope
was familiar in Kipling's time in both fictional and biographical writing, and
from the practice of nineteenth-century artists like the Pre-Raphaelite group,
which included Kipling's uncle Edward Burne-Jones. Kipling's use of the
theme of artistic development linked to a boy's emergence into manhood thus
had more than autobiographical resonance; as well as drawing on the established conventions of the *Bildungsroman*, his treatment of his central figure
Dick Heldar's 'success' and 'failure' as man and artist addressed specific contemporary concerns.[8]

The novel also reflects Kipling's rapid recognition of, and response to, the
presence within English culture of questions and anxieties about empire and
gender. His engagement with imperial themes stemmed from his own experience in India, from the largely 'Indian' subject matter of his earlier writing,
and from his consequent characterisation by others as an 'Indian' writer. It
also connected with the cultural dynamics of the increasing concern and controversy over imperial politics in the 1880s which were described earlier. These
dynamics elaborated and popularised existing discourses of race, ethnicity and
imperial mission in more explicit and varied forms. Depictions of British (or
English or Anglo-Saxon) virtue and global destiny were juxtaposed with depictions of those 'others' who could benefit from the civilising or at least restrain-
ing effects of British imperial power and superior culture. From political

addresses to a growing electorate to the choreography of royal or imperial public events, from Seeley's impassioned intellectual advocacy to jingoistic and ethnic motifs in music-hall entertainment, the cultural politics and political culture of race and empire grew louder and more accessible.

Kipling's contribution to these processes was sharply focused, though not without important ambivalences and contradictions. In his first months in England he produced polemical writings on imperial themes, such as 'India for the Indians', challenging Indian nationalism, and 'What it came to: an unequal tax', praising the healthy, socially unifying effects of war. His poem 'Cleared' indicted the links between the Liberal Party and Irish Nationalists, while the story 'The enlightenments of Pagett MP' attacked the Indian National Congress and its English supporters.[9] He revised and added to his 'Indian' stories and began to write the poems which eventually made up the *Barrack-Room Ballads*. His contribution to the culture of imperialism was made in a number of registers. His polemics staked out a place on the terrain of political opinion for an emotive, assertive, demagogic version of imperial mission, extending social boundaries and potential participation in its discourses. His poetry and fiction enriched the imaginative construction of India through British imperial eyes, powerfully fusing conventions of the orientalist imaginary (much though Kipling resented comparisons with Loti) with rationalist and empiricist conventions of ethnographic presentation of 'alien' cultures and knowing 'I've been there' reportage. It also established another 'imaginary' – the literary construction of the populist voice or experience of the low-ranking 'servants of empire', notably soldiers. Here imperial work and duty, previously more often associated with 'respectable' administrators, officers and missionaries, were reconfigured in the setting of the 'other ranks'. As well as engaging emotively with the party conflicts and imaginative worlds of the opinion-forming classes, Kipling supplied accessible imperialist views and images – and memorable and quotable verse ('What should they know of England who only England know?' in 1891, 'East is East and West is West' in 1889) – for the new politics of a widening electorate.

Equally striking, but less recognised, is Kipling's engagement with the so-called 'woman question' and other issues of gender. Some of his earliest comments on the London he found on returning from India focus, on the one hand, on the visibility of prostitution and, on the other, on encounters with women involved in various ways in the advocacy of rights and opportunities for women. Even in his highly selective and self-consciously 'autobiographical' *Something of Myself*, written over forty years later, Kipling drew attention to the presence of 'brotheldom' as a feature of his early experience of independence in London. The theme of prostitution plays a role in *The Light that Failed* and appears in other verse and prose written at that period ('One view of the question', *In Partibus*), and seems to have held a more general interest for him. While his cautious biographer Charles Carrington chose to comment on the supposedly shocking distinction between Kipling's reactions to London prostitutes and his experience of 'oriental' cities, the fact is that prostitution appears in an Indian setting in several of his tales of this period ('In the house of Sudhoo', 'On the city walls'), as well as forming a topic for his journalistic observations on Hong Kong and Burma, and featuring in his recollections of the controversies over the regulation of brothels, Indian army soldiers and venereal disease in India in the 1880s.[10]

Kipling was dealing here with an issue which by the later nineteenth century had become a matter of extended cultural and political concern. Prostitutes were a group who could be represented – whether in Henry Mayhew's reportage or in Pre-Raphaelite painting – simultaneously as victims and as manifestations of urban danger and immorality. The passing of the Contagious Diseases Acts during the 1860s provoked debates and campaigns in which a number of gender, national, class and imperial discourses were mobilised by moral reformers, medical experts, feminists and politicians. Specific concerns with 'male' and 'female' sexuality gave a sharpness to more general anxieties about gender roles and relations, and the impulse to regulate and police the sale of sexual services formed part of a larger aspiration to control or 'reform' the lives and behaviour of the urban lower classes. The visible and effective contribution of women to the campaigns against the Acts and against the sexual double standards they embodied marked a new stage in gender politics. The explicit focus of the provisions of the Acts on the issue of venereal disease in the armed forces, and the extension of the legal and political debate to India, served to interweave questions of sexuality with those concerning 'national' well-being and imperial mission, creating a gendered discourse on the 'health' (physical or symbolic) of nation, empire and the forces which sustained them.[11]

If prostitutes were one visible group of women whose presence in late nineteenth-century London challenged certain conventions of gender and 'femininity', while also sustaining them, so too were those critics of women's unequal and restricted position who were just beginning to be termed 'feminists'. Kipling's comments and correspondence from the early months of his sojourn in London and his later recollections record his responses to encounters both with convention and with its critics. Carrington retails Kipling's revealing account of a visit to his bachelor rooms by one of his aunt Burne-Jones's servant-girls: social hierarchy and cultural boundaries are both registered and subverted, as sexual innuendo, class relations and 'typical' gender roles are combined in a single knowing paragraph about his giving her tea, her mending his shirts and her references to marriage.[12] While this account forms a humorously patronising and self-congratulatory anecdote composed at the time, another episode which also focused on the accessibility of a single man's residence to single women was sufficiently significant to Kipling to be included in *Something of Myself* forty years later. Having met the traveller and writer Mary Kingsley at a tea party and pursued enjoyable conversation with her while walking towards his rooms, 'the world forgetting, I said: "Come up to my rooms and we'll talk it out." She agreed as a man would, then suddenly remembering said: "Oh, I forgot I was a woman. 'Fraid I mustn't." So I realised that my world was all to explore again.'[13] This brief account succinctly conveys the class and gender conventions which Kipling and Kingsley simultaneously accepted, 'forgot' and critiqued through a telling interplay of familiarity and strangeness, of spontaneity and constraint, of a 'world' that is both unfamiliar and 'his'. It also carries the flavour of an imperial or global context in which the confidence and involvement of the two protagonists in their respective experience of India and West Africa allowed them to disregard gender distinctions on a shared terrain of expertise and authority, as they were to do again in South Africa during the Boer War.

At another point on the spectrum of Kipling's engagement with women were his forceful and rhetorically violent reactions to encounters with women who concerned themselves with 'the woman question'. He 'knew' that one 'lathely' woman with whom he argued over women's rights was a *'pagal'* (lunatic or fool); he 'longed ardently' to kick Mrs Ashton Dilke, a London County Council member and suffrage writer, 'round the room forty times'; a discussion on divorce with Miss McCarthy, 'a virgin of emancipated lustre', 'made me want to send her to bed for a brazen little hussy'.[14] Thus, Kipling's awareness of gender politics played a significant role in his efforts to orient himself in the metropolitan world of the 1890s and gave a distinctive flavour to his self-assertion on the literary scene and self-promotion as an exponent of Indian and imperial themes. Whatever the 'autobiographical' slant one may choose to put upon this feature of Kipling's outlook and writing, the working-out of these themes of female identity, sexuality and emancipation in *The Light that Failed* connects any such personal concerns with those of the range of publics who engaged with these issues. The growing presence of female practitioners of painting or writing and of women's demands for education and political recognition stimulated gendered responses from medical experts, the artistic establishment, social commentators and popular humour, and Kipling's flawed treatment of these issues registers as a contribution to these responses.

The interaction of Kipling's own concerns with the cultural preoccupations of his audiences can be seen in the use of the trope of artistic creativity as the focus for his fable of failed dreams of masculine achievement in a global and imperial setting, *The Light that Failed*. The controversies which opposed aesthetic or art-for-art's-sake agendas for writing and visual art to purposive or representational or didactic agendas are enacted in the novel; they were also matters of public contention (the Ruskin versus Whistler case) and popular satire (Gilbert and Sullivan's *Patience*). Such debates intersected with the 'woman question' of the period at several levels. Medical and journalistic discussion of women's capacity for artistic achievement, or rather the configuration of such achievement as by definition 'masculine', overlapped with the characterisation of 'aesthetic' views or products as 'unmanly', 'effeminate' and hence morally dubious. Cartoon depictions of (unattractive) 'new women' or feminists associated them with weedy-looking aesthetes and opposed them to conventionally pleasing well-dressed women able to attract suitably 'manly' men.

Kipling utilised this dualistic juxtaposition of aesthetes with 'real' men, but also went beyond it. An 1889 poem, *In Partibus*, sent to his old Allahabad newspaper from London, projects his hostile reaction to the city by juxtaposing the 'moo and coo' of 'long-haired things' talking about 'the Aims of Art' ('with womenfolk'!), whose 'chief way of winning goals consists of standing still', to the 'army man', who 'owns himself' and stands for 'proper' masculinity. However, in *The Light that Failed*, the central character Dick Heldar is both hero (German *Held*) and artist. He is also located in the world of manly work and action by the attention given to the hard effort involved in the development of his artistic talent and career, by adventurous travel, work and hardship, and by his work as a war artist. Using this context and a conventional plot of the artist's struggle to be true to himself in the teeth of professional difficulties and commercial pressures, Kipling reworks the artist-as-hero paradigm familiar in nineteenth-century depictions of artistic creativity within a global and imperial set of references. Dick's initial success is gained with sketches and paintings of British imperial warfare in Egypt and the Sudan, while his professional development draws on experiences like the production of a major painting while on the lower deck of a ship 'loafing from Lima to Auckland'. The emotional attachment to ships and soldiers which is emphasised as a dominant feature of his character consolidates a rapprochement between the artist and the world of action in which men use skill and courage to deal with danger and assert dominance, rather than an opposition between them.

Kipling achieved this rapprochement by depicting the intimate connections of work, masculinity and fulfilment in artistic endeavour as much as in military life or imperial duty. He had already evoked these connections in his portrayal of the bonding between his 'soldiers three' (among the most popular creations in his early Indian tales). This bonding reappears among the writers and painters in *The Light that Failed* and among the imperial administrators and experts of the British *raj* in India depicted in his fiction and memoirs. In all these groups, solidarity, commitment to doing one's work well, and self-conscious pleasure in all-male company reinforce each other. This symbiosis of masculinity, work and intimacy is portrayed and celebrated in ways which challenge or disregard the cultural and ideological boundaries or oppositions between 'personal' and 'professional' life, between 'material', 'cultural' and political' elements in men's lives, and between supposedly 'feminine' characteristics like tenderness and 'masculine' ones like toughness. Kipling's depictions also, of course, reflected the actual homosociality of the worlds of imperial and military activity, as well as of art, journalism and literature.[15]

Such male intimacy and its representations were, however, both ambivalent and vulnerable, since they raised questions both about the basis of male exclusivity and about the sexual and erotic implications of homosociality. Male cultural networks, male friendships and all-male institutions like schools or the armed services attracted attention from opinion-formers and decision-makers increasingly concerned with distinctions between 'manly', 'healthy' male interactions in such settings and their 'unhealthy', 'unnatural' or 'immoral' possibilities. Comfortable, even assertive, masculine homosociality was coloured by the anxieties arising from this concern at a time when categories like 'homosexual' were emerging in the discourses of medicine, education, social policy and criminology. Kipling's portrayal of Dick Heldar's friendships with men in *The Light that Failed* expresses these ambivalences. The value, pleasure and importance of male bonding and closeness are celebrated and sharply contrasted with the failure of women to provide Dick with real support or understanding (exemplified by Maisie, the focus of his destructive passion), or indeed with their outright destructive untrustworthiness (exemplified by Bessie, who destroys his major painting). It is male friends and colleagues who offer Dick the closest and most reliable relationships, expressed both in robust critical concern for his artistic activity and in tender loving care in his illness and unhappiness. He dies in a man's arms. Forms of tenderness have, however, to be rather consciously distanced from any appearance of collusion with the 'dangerous' implications of male homosociality. The vigorous physical horseplay among the friends, references to rivalry over women, and the depiction of 'hearty' joking, singing and smoking seem to assert the differences between these manly heterosexual men and the effete 'long-haired things' who aroused criticism and anxiety. Juxtaposed as they are with representations of tenderness and affection between Dick and his closest friend Torpenhow, legitimised in the language of 'comradeship' and 'brotherhood', they signal Kipling's sensitivity to the ambiguities of male intimacy, rather than the crude polarities he had adopted in *In Partibus*.[16]

The other main challenge to male exclusivity came from the varied initiatives which sought to secure for women access to advanced education, political rights, professional employment and artistic opportunity and recognition. Often presented in terms of social and legal reform, this challenge can also be understood as a confrontation with the homosocial cultures of learning, politics and professional or artistic life. On the one hand, the confrontation involved the formation of female networks, institutions and campaigns to pursue and support women's rights and aspirations. On the other, this period saw the beginnings of a female presence and contribution in formerly all-male arenas, whether in party political institutions, in universities or in other prestigious cultural settings. Given the strength and sharpness of Kipling's reactions to his encounters with middle-class women activists, it is not surprising that the theme of women unsuccessfully pursuing artistic endeavours plays a major role in *The Light that Failed*. What is striking is the complexity and ambiguity with which the theme is developed.

The presentation of Maisie, the 'new woman' trying to make her way independently, as deficient in 'real' talent or application (her persistence is depicted as 'irrational' pride), lacking grasp of her own strengths and weaknesses, and concerned with public success rather than professional skill or artistic integrity, is negative in many ways. It is linked to the depiction of her inadequacy as a loving and understanding friend or lover, and of her 'unwomanly' unwillingness to support Dick as an artist or to stand by him when he goes blind. A range of commentators have found the combination of these negative depictions misogynistic.[17] Yet the portrayal of Maisie as artist – rather than as the object of Dick's passion – is more complex than this implies. Kipling evokes the isolation and difficulties of a woman in her situation sympathetically, even as he contrasts her limitations with Dick's talent and understanding, and he even allows her moments of self-knowledge on these issues. Whether or not one follows Seymour-Smith's insistent but contorted argument detecting Kipling's own autobiographical uncertainties (artistic and sexual) beneath this confusing presentation of Maisie,[18] it suggests that, for Kipling as for others, the arrival of independent women in the world of artistic activity was not a simple issue.

This suggestion gains force with consideration of the second depiction of a 'new woman' artist in the novel, that of the anonymous 'red-haired girl' who shares Maisie's house and works alongside her. Leaving speculation on her nameless state aside, it should be noted that derogatory comment on her appearance and behaviour, and Dick's dislike of her, sit beside references to her intelligence, artistic ability and personal integrity. She confronts Dick with an effective, 'truthful' sketch conveying his relationship to Maisie, and is left to finish her *Melancolia* painting, which Maisie cannot make a success. She is the source of powerful, perceptive and passionate comment on Maisie's duplicitous treatment of Dick, and of strong emotional response to Dick himself and the calamity of his blinding.[19] Even if this last element is seen as a romantic fantasy of female devotion, it still moves readers some way from mere caricature or denigration of female artists. Just as Kipling hovers on a boundary in his treatment of male intimacy – the boundary between acceptable and unacceptable male love – so he takes up an ambivalent and liminal position in relation to the uncomfortable challenge to men posed by women's aspiration to independent artistic careers, thus encapsulating the complexity of the *fin-de-siècle* 'crisis of masculinity'.

It may well be useful to see *The Light that Failed*, like other texts of its time, as expressing a set of dilemmas rather than a set of propositions. In the area of gender politics, it evokes the ambiguities of male bonding, the tensions between professional aspiration and emotional desire, the contradictions of dominance and need in male expectations of women, and the problematic nature of models of companionate marriage. Such issues had entered political and cultural debate during the later nineteenth century, and are usually discussed in relation to 'the woman question', to radical and liberal politics, or to histories of masculinity. I would argue that, for Kipling and others, these issues were also part of an ethnic, national, racial and imperial 'imaginary'. As has been pointed out, Kipling situated creative activity, whether in literature or in the visual arts, within masculinised spheres of work and action, but the geographical extent of these spheres was imperial and global. Dick and his associates are war artists and war correspondents, their skills explicitly entwined on the one hand with British military, diplomatic and colonial activity overseas (Egypt, the Balkans, the Sudan), and on the other, with cultural and market interests in their work in the imperial metropolis. Dick's pictures excite responses from soldiers seeing them displayed who 'recognise' his 'accurate' depictions of their work, from editors and publishers seeking to exploit a marketable product, from 'discriminating' colleagues, and from those who want a glamorous portrayal of war and empire.[20]

While Dick's relationships with the varied audiences for and interests in his work are there to drive the plot and to celebrate artists as hero-craftsmen, they also hint at broader dilemmas. On returning to England Kipling was sharply aware of tensions between public enthusiasm for (some) depictions of imperial experience, general ignorance of what he saw as the realities of that experience, and the passions mobilised in political debates on empire, whether among contending British politicians or between metropolitan and colonial interests.[21] The tensions which he experienced in his own career as an 'Indian' writer were a personal instance of a more widespread feature of imperial relationships – the tendency in one sense to encompass a significant cross-section of British people in a common context, and in another to divide and confuse metropolitan, settler and colonial agendas. Historians have frequently explored and explained such divisions in terms of conflict over policy; through Kipling's work the tensions can also be recognised as cultural. The imperial dimension of culture in Britain, and the cultural dimension of imperial experience, were compounded of imagination, involvement and ignorance – a compound manifest in missionary activity and writing, in popular fiction and poetry, and in visual forms. As analysts of 'orientalism' like Jullian, Said or Moore-Gilbert have suggested, it was the ambiguous and sometimes contradictory blending of imagined or fantastical presentations of empire and 'the Orient' with 'expert' or experiential depictions of these subjects that gave the compound cultural power.[22] Kipling expresses this in *The Light that Failed*, as elsewhere, by representing the combination of enthusiasm and misconception in public perceptions of the 'exotic' worlds depicted by Dick Heldar (and himself) in work which is shown as the product of both their 'knowledge' and their 'imagination'.

If Kipling sought to inspire and inform his metropolitan readers about the world of imperial endeavour and to express the cultural complexities of imperial relationships, these objectives were intimately associated with views of 'Englishness' and of its connection to empire. In *The Light that Failed*, English artistic achievement is linked not only (as has been seen) to imperial activity, but also to the specificity of English artistic tradition, practice and values, sharply contrasted with 'French' equivalents. The distinctive and superior character of English art is evoked through European comparisons and with acknowledgement of Dick's debt to French studio experience. Dick's acquisition of artistic skill, knowledge and maturity, using English confidence in exploiting such global resources, is constructed through the appropriation of such experience, and of global travel ranging from India to Australia and the South Seas, and of 'exotic' subject matter (Somali muleteers, Chinese sailors, and a 'Negro-Jewess-Cuban').[23] Unlike some other constructions of 'Englishness', Kipling's depictions are strongly flavoured with Anglo-Indian and gypsy elements, which constantly project it as a global presence. Managing Levantines, French and Egyptians in Port Said, taking what he wants from French art teachers, ordering servants about on a South Sea island, or poaching an Italian sea-captain's girlfriend, are all part and parcel of Dick's success as artist and Englishman – 'spoiling the Egyptians', as he puts it. To be English is both to engage with the exotic and to differentiate oneself from it at the same time: it involves leaving England and criticising it as well as identifying with it. In 'The English flag' (a poem published contemporaneously with *The Light that Failed*), Kipling called on the 'winds of the world' to answer the question 'what is the flag of England?' For, as he put it, 'what should they know of England who only England know?'[24]

For Kipling, then, the imagining of Englishness, and the true understanding of England's mission, involved an 'outsider' vision, best grounded in the 'colonial' experience and insight that he claimed for himself and attributed to Dick Heldar. Dick's would-be masterwork, *Melancolia*, is his outsider's view of the imperial metropolis, and his patriotism expresses itself in the yearning to see and paint the 'beautiful men' of the Guards regiment, imagined from his Sudanese experience. The war artists and correspondents who are his associates combine patriotic commitment to the military and imperial ventures of the British government with vigorous criticisms of its mistakes and shortcomings, based on their 'first-hand' knowledge. This evocation of a patriotism located on the imperial periphery is the positive variant of the anger with which Kipling (like some of his fictional characters) treats the incomprehension or sanitising and glamorising misrepresentation of the imperial experience by metropolitan commentators. At the extreme of the spectrum of anger, Kipling presented his antipathy to the metropolis and its misconceptions of empire through *Indian* characters, like the Muslim 'narrator' of 'One view of the question', written in the same period as *The Light that Failed*. Just as the 'English' virtues and values of manhood and creativity are tested and validated in imperial contexts, so the criticisms of an 'England' which falls short of these values and virtues are the responsibility of its imperial subjects as created by the knowing colonial Kipling.

Kipling's portrayal of English mastery of creativity and imperial power also involved other manipulations. The 'Negro-Jewess-Cuban' who acts as model for Dick Heldar's first great imaginative work has 'morals to match' her illiteracy, her sexual availability, her ethnically mixed origins and her social inferiority. Bessie Broke, who sits for his second picture, is called by Dick an 'immoral Jezebel', a 'drab of the streets', a 'little piece of dirt', the 'sort' who steals, and sells sexual services. The relationship between artist and model is used to articulate gender, class, racial and sexual hierarchies which are clearly presented as the normal expected constituents of sociocultural 'reality'; this is paralleled by Dick's hiring of Zanzibari dancing girls in Port Said, and opposed to his exploitation of the failed artist Binat as a model. Although experience of poverty is part of the portrayal of Dick as a committed artist and tough male, it is sharply distinguished from the social hierarchy which separates him and his peers from streetwalkers like Bessie, or from the grasping, ingratiating, dishonest landlord and his family. These characters – unlike the soldiers and sailors of similar 'class' – have not 'gone forth' as the winds of the world bid them to do to sustain the English flag in its global setting, and hence their 'Englishness' is made less visible than their 'street-bred' qualities and 'Board School' educational deficiencies.[25] The portrayal of the 'Negro-Jewess-Cuban' is perfunctory, that of the landlord's family clichéd, that of Bessie sufficiently complex to sustain the narrative and the well-worn convention which opposes her easy, mercenary, excessive sexuality to Maisie's asexual virginal coldness. At whatever level they are presented, however, they set off the masculine, artistic, 'English' qualities which are the centre of Kipling's interest.

Such qualities are less a matter of fixed 'types' or ideals than of complex negotiations and moving or permeable frontiers. Dick is often in danger of being childish (rather than manly), mercenary and meretricious (rather than creative and professional), and isolated and introverted (rather than part of the world of imperial action). He doesn't quite 'belong' at his public school or in the fraternity of correspondents. While this presentation flows partly from the romantic convention on which Kipling relied, it also conveys the unstable character of 'masculinity', 'creativity' and 'belonging', and the need for constant appropriate action by those seeking to sustain such attributes. Arguably Kipling is taking a biographical perspective here, but he also offers a more general insight into the operations of masculinity in late nineteenth-century English and imperial settings. Commenting on a dramatisation of *The Light that Failed*, Max Beerbohm teasingly wondered if the name Kipling veiled 'a female identity', and thought that the soldier-loving misogynist characterisation of Heldar and his friends might be 'fondly created out of the inner consciousness of a female novelist'.[26] It is as if Beerbohm responded to the ambivalence of a text in which, like Kipling himself with Mary Kingsley, Dick talks to his beloved Maisie on shared artistic concerns, as if she were a man. Beerbohm's response also acknowledges the unfixed character of gender roles and images more generally, furnishing an ironic comment on the 'man's world' which Kipling inhabited and celebrated in his writing.

'Knowing' and 'imagining' England and empire could be said to have involved displacement as well as certainty for Kipling and his contemporaries. The social movements which brought Kipling's parents from modest circumstances to socialise with Viceroys of India and kept Kipling himself moving between England and India were, of course, movements also experienced by many less well-known people. As a journalist and writer, Kipling sought both to celebrate his craft and mission in the same fashion as other professionals or men of action, and to assuage doubts about the 'manliness' of artistic activity, by forging connections between that activity and the world of action and populist discourse. On this basis he staked claims to present 'empire' to an English audience, and England to audiences in the Empire. These claims were only initiated in the 1890s but were congruent with the growing identification of imperial issues, relationships and activities as constituent components of 'national' life in that period, a process with an extended history already behind it. Like his contemporaries, Kipling also knew and imagined England and empire in terms of gender and other social hierarchies and power relationships. Feminists constructed distinctively feminised or womanly agendas and missions within the Empire, either upholding 'the race' and 'English' civilisation or uplifting native sisters, while male writers and experts claimed the role of interpreters and analysts of empire for English consumption. For Kipling, talking anthropology with Mary Kingsley led them both momentarily to 'forget' her position as a 'respectable woman', as though imperial interests overrode gender codes, yet at the crucial moment the latter prevailed.

Such observations serve to reinsert *The Light that Failed* in a cultural and historical setting which is part of its significance as a text. For all the individual and autobiographical qualities of Kipling's work, his articulation of some of the connections and inconsistencies between masculinity, art and empire linked him to shared imaginings of solidarity, identity and difference (men/women, art/action, England/the world) which were part of a common culture. For Kipling and for his contemporaries, the uncertainties and slippages of gender, of colonial–metropolitan relations, of culture and politics seemed as significant and telling as the supposed certainties of imperial and patriarchal power with its class and racialised characteristics. It is the simultaneous expression of certainty and uncertainty that gives Kipling's text, in its context, its richness, resonance and interest.

Notes

1 See, for example, M. Kinkead-Weekes, 'Vision in Kipling's novels', in A. Rutherford (ed.), *Kipling's Mind and Art* (Edinburgh, 1964); R. Jarrell, *Kipling, Auden and Co.* (Manchester, 1986); J. Lyon, 'Introduction' to R. Kipling, *The Light that Failed* (Penguin edn, London, 1988: all subsequent page references relate to this edition). More general comments on the flawed, uneven or contradictory character of Kipling's work are developed by Jarrell, by C. S. Lewis, 'Kipling's world', in E. L. Gilbert (ed.), *Kipling and his Critics* (London, 1966) and by J. Bayley, *The Uses of Division* (London, 1976).

2 See, for example, C. Carrington, *Rudyard Kipling: his Life and Work* (1955; Penguin edn, London, 1970), chs 6–7; A. Wilson, *The Strange Ride of Rudyard Kipling* (London, 1977), ch. 3, parts i-ii; M. Seymour-Smith, *Rudyard Kipling* (London, 1990), chs. 12–14. More general aspects of Kipling's 'imperialism' are discussed in P. Mason, *Kipling: the Glass, the Shadow and the Fire* (London, 1975); A. Sandison, *The Wheel of Empire* (London, 1967); J. McClure, *Kipling and Conrad: the Colonial Fiction* (Cambridge, Mass., 1981). A restricted discussion of imperialism in the context of themes which I take further here is P. Kaarsholm, 'Kipling and masculinity', in R. Samuel (ed.), *Patriotism: the Making and Unmaking of British National Identity* (London, 1989), vol. 3: *National Fictions*.

3 On Ireland, see J. Loughlin, *Gladstone, Home Rule and the Irish Question* (Dublin, 1986). On Egypt and the Sudan, see A. Schölch, *Egypt for the Egyptians* (London, 1981); A. G. Hopkins, 'The Victorians and Africa: a reconsideration of the occupation of Egypt', *Journal of African History*, 27 (1986); Daly, *Empire on the Nile* (Cambridge, 1986); G. Sanderson, *England, Europe and the Upper Nile* (Edinburgh, 1965). On South Africa, see A. N. Porter, *The Origins of the South African War 1877–95* (Manchester, 1980). On India, see S. Gopal, *British Policy in India 1858–1905* (Cambridge, 1965); R. J. Moore, *Liberalism and Indian Politics 1872–1922* (London, 1966). On imperialist ideas, see B. Semmel, *Imperialism and Social Reform* (London, 1960); H. Cunningham, 'Jingoism in 1877–8', *Victorian Studies*, 14 (1971); C. C. Eldridge, *England's Mission: the Imperial Idea in the Age of Gladstone and Disraeli* (Sevenoaks, 1978); H. Cunningham, 'The language of patriotism', *History Workshop Journal*, 12 (1981); D. Cannadine, 'The context, performance and meaning of ritual: the British monarchy and the invention of tradition', in E. J. Hobsbawm and T. Ranger (eds), *The Invention of Tradition* (Cambridge, 1983).

4 See P. Levine, *Victorian Feminism 1850–1900* (London, 1987); D. Rubinstein, *Before the Suffragettes: Women's Emancipation in the 1890s* (Brighton, 1986); M. Shanley, *Feminism, Marriage and the Law 1850–95* (Princeton, 1989); A. John, *By the Sweat of*

their Brow: Women Workers at Victorian Coal Mines (London, 1984); B. Caine, *Victorian Feminists* (Oxford, 1992); P. Hollis, *Women in Public 1850–1900* (London, 1979); P. Hollis, *Ladies Elect: Women in English Local Government 1865–1914* (Oxford, 1987); L. Bland, *Banishing the Beast: English Feminism and Sexual Morality* (London, 1995).

5   See J. de Groot, ' "Sex" and "race": the construction of language and image in the nineteenth century', in S. Mendus and J. Rendall (eds), *Sexuality and Subordination* (London, 1989); V. G. Kiernan, *The Lords of Human Kind* (London, 1969); N. Chaudhuri and M. Strobel (eds), *Western Women and Imperialism* (Bloomington, 1992); P. Brantlinger, *Rule of Darkness: British Literature and Imperialism* (Ithaca, NY and London, 1988); A. Davin, 'Imperialism and motherhood', *History Workshop Journal*, 5 (1978); S. Gilman, *Difference and Pathology: Stereotypes of Sexuality, Race and Madness* (Ithaca, NY, 1985); J. Ruskin, 'Of queens' gardens', in E. Cook and A. Wedderburn (eds.), *Complete Works of John Ruskin* (London, 1910–12), vol. 18.

6   See A. McClintock, *Imperial Leather: Race, Gender and Sexuality in the Colonial Context* (London, 1995), ch. 5; T. Richards, *The Commodity Culture of Victorian Britain: Advertising and Spectacle 1851–1914* (London, 1990); Davin, 'Imperialism and motherhood'; K. Jayawardena, *The White Woman's Other Burden* (London, 1995), part I; C. Hall, *White, Male and Middle Class* (London 1995), part III; B. Melman, *Women's Orients: English Women and the Middle East* (London, 1992); J. Richards (ed.), *Imperialism and Juvenile Literature* (Manchester, 1989); J. S. Bratton, *The Impact of Victorian Children's Fiction* (London, 1981); J. MacKenzie (ed.), *Imperialism and Popular Culture* (Manchester, 1986); J. MacKenzie, *Propaganda and Empire* (Manchester, 1984); K. Castle, *Britannia's Children* (London, 1996).

7   The *Lippincott's Monthly Magazine* version of *The Light that Failed* appeared in January 1891 and was reprinted five times. It was shorter than the book version published by Macmillan in March 1891, and had a 'happy' ending. *The Sign of Four* was published in *Lippincott's* in early 1890, *The Picture of Dorian Gray* later in the same year.

8   See J. Springhall, *Coming of Age: Adolescence in Britain 1860–1950* (London, 1986); J. Springhall, *Youth, Empire and Society: British Youth Movements 1883–1940* (London, 1977); C. Battersby, *Gender and Genius* (London, 1989), on ideas about gender and creativity; N. Clarke, 'Strenuous idleness: Thomas Carlyle and the man of letters as hero', in M. Roper and J. Tosh (eds), *Manful Assertions* (London, 1991); T. Broughton, 'The Froude–Carlyle embroilment: married life as a literary problem', *Victorian Studies*, 38 (1995).

9   The four items cited here were published respectively in *St. James's Gazette*, December 1889; *ibid.*, January 1990; *Scots Observer*, 8 March 1990; *Contemporary Review*, August 1990.

10 Carrington, *Rudyard Kipling*, p. 190; Wilson, *The Strange Ride*, p. 188; R. Kipling, *Something of Myself* (London, 1937), p. 56.

11 See J. Walkowitz, *Prostitution and Victorian Society* (London, 1980); J. Walkowitz, *City of Dreadful Delight* (London, 1992), chs 1–4, 7; Bland, *Banishing the Beast*, ch. 3; K. Ballhatchet, *Race, Sex and Class under the Raj* (London, 1980); P. Levine, 'Venereal disease, prostitution and the politics of empire', *Journal of the History of Sexuality*, 4 (1994); P. Levine, 'Re-reading the 1890s: venereal disease as "constitutional crisis" in Britain and British India', *Journal of Asian Studies*, 55 (1996).

12 Quoted in Carrington, *Rudyard Kipling*, p. 191.

13 Kipling, *Something of Myself*, pp. 77–8.

14 T. Pinney (ed.), *Letters of Rudyard Kipling*, 4 vols (London, 1990): letters to Caroline Taylor of 2 November 1889 (on the 'lathely woman' and Mrs Dilke) and to Edmonia Hill, covering his activities of 3–25 December (on Miss McCarthy).

15 On artistic aspects of these issues, see K. Bendiner, *An Introduction to Victorian Painting* (London 1985) on Holman Hunt and Whistler. J. Rothenstein, *A Pot of Paint: Artists of the 1890s* (London, 1929), with its reference to the Ruskin/Whistler case in the title, is a contemporary view. The Pre-Raphaelite Brotherhood is a good case of male bonding. See also S. Casteras, 'Excluding women: the cult of male genius', in L. Shires (ed.), *Re-writing the Victorians* (London, 1992); Battersby, *Gender and Genius*. On military aspects, see E. Spiers, *The Army and Society 1815–1914* (London, 1980); G. Harries-Jenkins, *The Army in British Society* (London, 1977); P. Mason, *A Matter of Honour* (London, 1974); J. MacKenzie, *Popular Imperialism and the Military* (Manchester, 1992). On administrators, see the elegiac P. Woodruff, *Men Who Ruled India* (London, 1987); C. Dewey, *Anglo-Indian Attitudes: the Mind of the Indian Civil Service* (London, 1993); Y. D. Gunderia, *In the Districts of the Raj* (London, 1992).

16 See E. Cohen, *Talk on the Wilde Side* (London, 1993), part I; F. Mort, *Dangerous Sexualities* (London, 1987); J. R. Honey, *Tom Brown's Universe* (London, 1977); N. Vance, *The Sinews of the Spirit: the Ideal of Christian Manliness in Victorian Literature and Religious Thought* (Cambridge, 1985); G. Mosse, *Nationalism and Sexuality* (Madison, 1985); A. Gilbert, 'Buggery and the British navy', *Journal of Social History*, 10 (1976); B. Haley, *The Healthy Body and Victorian Culture* (Cambridge, Mass., 1978); J. Weeks, *Sex, Politics and Society* (London, 1981). The telling passages on masculinity in *The Light that Failed* are on pp. 40–1, 47–9, 58–9, 64–7, 90–6, 100–8, 130–3, 136–49, 162–5, and 208 (the final page, on which Dick dies in Torpenhow's arms).

17 See, for example, Lyon, 'Introduction', pp. vii, xi–xii, xix–xxi; Mason, *Kipling*, pp. 91–2; Wilson, *The Strange Ride*, pp. 203, 210, 212–15; Seymour-Smith, *Rudyard Kipling*, pp. 159, 176, 178.

18 Seymour-Smith, *Rudyard Kipling*, ch. 14 lays out this argument; Kipling, *The Light that Failed*, pp. 54–5, 74–6, 83–4, 152–4, 159–61 show some of the complexities.

19 Kipling, *The Light that Failed*, pp. 58, 61, 63–4, 68, 72, 110–11, 113–14, 150–6, 171.

20 *Ibid.*, pp. 30, 32–7, 40–1, 53.

21 Carrington, *Rudyard Kipling*, pp. 178–80, 186, 192–4, 198–200; Wilson, *The Strange Ride*, pp. 193–7; Kipling, *Something of Myself*, pp. 77–93. The critic Edmund Gosse commented (in *The Century*, October 1891) that Kipling's 'vigorous rendering of unhackneyed experience' filled the void in 'Anglo-Saxon' (*sic*) fiction, which Gosse thought had become 'curiously feminized'. See also Seymour-Smith, *Rudyard Kipling*, pp. 122–6.

22 See P. Jullian, *The Orientalists* (Oxford, 1977), pp. 28, 38, 48–74; E. Said, *Orientalism* (London, 1978), chs 1 (parts ii–iii), 2 (parts i, iii–iv); B. Moore Gilbert, *Kipling and Orientalism* (London, 1986), chs 2, 4.

23 Kipling, *The Light that Failed*, pp. 20, 28–9, 39, 77–80, 97–9.

24 'The English flag' appeared in *St. James's Gazette*, 4 April 1891, and in the collection *Barrack-Room Ballads* later that year. Kipling recounts a version of its composition in *Something of Myself*, pp. 89–90.

25 Kipling, *The Light that Failed*, pp. 98, 115, 117, 122, 166–71, 187, 189–90.

26 *Ibid.*, pp. 38–43 illustrates these points, including language very similar to that of *In Partibus*. Beerbohm's comments (quoted in Carrington, *Rudyard Kipling*, pp. 216–17) were in the *Saturday Review*, 14 February 1903.

PART IV

THE INVENTORY OF NATIONHOOD

Science and nationhood: cultures of imagined communities

> It may be taken for granted that a flourishing state of science . . . is essential
> to the survival and prosperity of a modern nation and at the same time a sure
> index of that nation's cultural vitality.[1]

In 1862, the printmaker William Walker published 'A Great Historical
Engraving, in the Best Style of Stipple and Mezzotinto, representing by Fifty
most Authentic Portraits, the Distinguished Men of Science of Great Britain,
Living in A.D. 1807/8, Assembled in the Library of the Royal Institution' (figure
22).[2] The print and its title are significant in two ways. First, they are indicative of the widespread public interest and investment in the lives and portraits
of men of science that had developed in the course of the eighteenth and early
nineteenth centuries. Prominent men of science and medical practitioners
had become 'objects of imitation and emulation', as Thomas Pettigrew put it

Figure 22 **William Walker** *et al.*, *The Distinguished Men of Science of Great
Britain, Living in A.D. 1807/8*, 1862

in the preface to his *Medical Portrait Gallery*, a collection of sixty 'biographical memoirs' of celebrated physicians and surgeons with accompanying portrait engravings, published in 1840.[3] By the middle of the nineteenth century,
as works like Walker's print and Pettigrew's *Gallery* testify, biography and portraiture had become central genres not only for the construction of medical
and scientific identity, but also – in ways I shall explore – for the working-out
and management of relationships between nationhood and the practice of
science and medicine. [4]

Second, Walker's print is remarkable for its depiction of the scientists of
a particular country as a collectivity. The print, of course, embodies a strate-
gic fiction. It is not a genuine group portrait, but an invented scene based on
pre-existing individual portraits. The men portrayed never met as a group, and
it is possible that some of them never even set foot in the Royal Institution in
Albemarle Street, London. Yet the image makes strong claims to authenticity,
both in the likenesses themselves and in the scientists' signatures that appear
at the bottom of some versions. Through this invented scene the image evokes
the intellectual achievements of Great Britain half a century earlier. The
choice of setting is certainly significant. Despite the fact that over half of those
portrayed were Fellows of the Royal Society, the national collectivity being
evoked was clearly felt to be more aptly conveyed by a self-consciously
modern, reformist institution. While there had been persistent dissatisfaction
with the management of the Royal Society, which had been founded under
Charles II's patronage and was increasingly associated with establishment
amateurism, the Royal Institution, founded in 1799, was dedicated to scientific research, to the dissemination of scientific and medical knowledge and to
social improvement by rational means. Indeed, the signs of the Royal
Institution's modernity were visible in the library itself: its convex glass roof
was a noted feat of engineering, and its mirror had been at the time of its
presentation 'the largest convex mirror ever made in Great Britain'.[5]

The thinking that lay behind the print was explained in a book designed
to accompany it, *Memoirs of the Distinguished Men of Science of Great Britain
Living in the Years 1807–8*. According to the introduction, by Robert Hunt,
Keeper of the Mining Record:

> We have advanced to our present position in the scale of nations by the efforts
> of a few chosen minds. Every branch of human industry has been benefitted by
> the discoveries of science. The Discoverers are therefore deserving of that hero-
> worship which, sooner or later, they receive from all. . . . [The engraving] is ded-
> icated to those men whose names shine forth from the bead-roll of science,
> surrounded with the glory which belongs to the Priests of Nature and Truth. [6]

The emphasis on discoveries, the sense of general human benefit derived from
science, the constant balancing of particular national claims to scientific glory

with references to science as a means of universal advancement – all these are characteristic elements in ways of representing science and medicine that are explored in this essay. Hunt's introduction does not, however, explain the significance attached by the creators of the print to the particular historical moment 1807–8. By implication, this was a time of special flowering in British science, but the point is not spelt out. It has been suggested that one inspiration for 'Men of Science' was the appearance in 1845 of *Lives of Men of Letters and Science*, by Henry, Lord Brougham. Brougham and Walker certainly knew each other.[7] Brougham's controversial work, which also combined biography and portraiture, was not restricted to British figures, although they certainly predominated, or to men of science strictly defined, and his grouping of these figures by reference to a monarch's reign rather than to a moment in the life of a nation introduces a political ambiguity not present in Walker's print. Like the print and Hunt's remarks, however, the *Lives of Men of Letters and Science* defined an earlier era and celebrated its scientific achievements, with reference to some of the same figures – Watt, Cavendish, Davy and Banks – while conveying a sense of the immediate, continuing benefits and glories to be derived from these achievements.

In the preface Brougham explained his enterprise. He characterised the age as particularly distinguished in the natural and political sciences, mentioning chemistry, political economy and pure mathematics in particular. He also signalled the significance of the political changes of the age, of its democratising tendencies, its concern with 'the rights of the people'. Indeed, he suggested direct links between intellectual and political achievement:

> The diffusion of knowledge among the community at large is the work of our own age, and it has made all the conquests of science both in recent and in older times of incalculably greater value, of incomparably higher importance to the interests of mankind, than they were while scientific study was confined within the narrow circles of the wealthy and the learned.[8]

What could not be spoken of directly here was the French Revolution, and the connections so often drawn, in reaction to it, between the new knowledge of the Enlightenment on the one hand, and the political chaos and excesses of the 1790s on the other.[9] By using the reign of an English monarch as his organising principle, and by concentrating on British figures, Brougham was able to create a sense that learning and the diffusion of knowledge were benign, without entirely losing their political freighting. As a Paleyite natural theologian Brougham was no radical, but as an experienced statesman who believed in the value to a state of rational and useful knowledge, he was alive to the political resonances of science.[10]

Brougham saw biography and portraiture as genres with a special kind of potency: 'I conceived', he explained, 'that as portrait painting is the historical painting in one sense, so the lives of eminent men, freely written, are truly the history of their times.' Thus biography became a way of 'exhibiting [the] power [of men who have passed from the stage] to raise the genuine glory as well of individuals as of nations'.[11] The wording here is significant: however much scientific and medical practitioners might display their knowledge as universally valid and of general benefit to humanity, they were, by the early nineteenth century, embedded in and contributors to a value system that celebrated both individual and national achievement. When the tangible advantages of scientific and medical advance were celebrated in eighteenth- and nineteenth-century writings, the high-blown rhetoric of philanthropy, with its stress on humanitarianism and benefaction, went only so far. It was repeatedly balanced and qualified by the rhetoric of nationality. And this rhetoric was habitually used not just to specify the source from which scientific knowledge sprang (the nation as producer of scientific talent) and the beneficiaries of that knowledge (the citizens of the nation) but also to express the identification of practitioners with that kind of polity called a 'nation'.

In the rest of this essay, I explore further the ways in which science and nationhood became intertwined between the eighteenth and twentieth centuries. I shall argue that the concept of 'nation' came to serve in this period as a vehicle through which the political aspirations of scientific communities and science's claims to public usefulness could be articulated and realised. By examining the mental and rhetorical strategies that were involved with this process, we can shed light on the often complex and confusing ways in which science and nationhood are connected in our own day. In the course of the twentieth century, it has come to be so taken for granted that science is for and of the nation that we can imagine only with difficulty the lengthy process by which this connection was established. Simultaneously, however, the international character of modern science has been so often stressed that links between science and distinctive national characteristics are sometimes construed as aberrant. Contemporary cultures present the science/nation nexus in the languages of pride, achievement, competition, rewards, and also in vaguer languages of publicity and popularity. A degree of ambiguity in the handling of these issues is perfectly understandable, given the complexity of the phenomena involved. One way of seeking greater conceptual clarity is to examine the processes of identification by which science and the idea of the nation became historically connected.

Most accounts of the evolving conceptual relationship between science and the nation associate the awareness of science as a national activity with strong political claims that can be understood as national*ist*. The term 'nationalist' is itself a problematic one, sometimes referring to specific political movements, and sometimes, in more general usage, to any powerful or emotive assertions made on behalf of a nation.[12] In this looser sense, a nationalist mentality with regard to science clearly existed in the early nineteenth century, as Charles Babbage's *Reflections on the Decline of Science in England*, published in 1830, makes clear.[13] The emphasis of historians of science and medicine has, however, generally been on the very end of the nineteenth and twentieth centuries, when nationalists in the stricter sense became prominent. Among the founding assumptions of most accounts is the claim that modern science is in its essence an international rather than a national enterprise. In writing about 'Nationalism and internationalism' in modern science, for example, Schroeder-Gudehus argues that 'scientific theory and practice are by nature international', that '"universalism" and "commonality" have been established as norms of scientific activity' and that 'the history of science unfolds as a cooperative enterprise with a distinctively trans-national character'.[14] Convictions of this kind have led some historians to search for early examples of international co-operation, which are especially precious if they show scientists valiantly getting together despite poor political relations between their countries. The genuine internationalism of science, however, is seen as coming into being in the late nineteenth century with a spate of congresses and organisations and the setting of international standards, at the same time as links between the state and science were being strengthened.[15]

Thus the historical context for both nationalism and internationalism in science is seen as one in which nationalism and internationalism were dominant issues on the world stage, and it is located in a quite specific phase of European political, diplomatic, economic and imperial development. The use of science for what are taken to be nationalistic purposes is thereby associated with expansionism, with a particular kind of military build-up, and with the kind of aggressive foreign policy that produced the two world wars. By implication, then, any tensions between nationalism and internationalism in science are associated with the character of political regimes rather than with scientific and medical cultures themselves. Co-operation and competition are not mutually exclusive in the practice of scientific and medical research, yet somehow the former seems more 'natural' than the latter. Hence rivalries and antagonisms between nations demand explanation in a way that the sharing of results and insights does not. For many historians – and scientists – scientific nationalism, as a species of excessive political nationalism, is a kind of perversion. This, then, is a view of the science/nation nexus that deploys particular assumptions about chronology, about the nature and politics of science, and about the sense of nationhood envisaged as a form of nationalism.[16]

There is, however, a different story to be told, a story that places science in a different relationship to the sense of nationhood, and which can shed light on both these terms and their intricate history. In his book *Imagined Communities*, Benedict Anderson suggested that nationalism is only possible when people can imagine themselves to be part of a nation, and that this in turn only became possible, in the last two hundred years or so, as a result of a number of specific shifts, cultural, political and economic, which generated an abstract idea of the nation and made that idea attractive to large segments of the population. Nations are thus imagined communities, each nation imagining itself in a distinctive style. Members feel comradeship with people they will never meet, and they have both a collective memory and a capacity to imagine their nation's future. I suggest that scientific and medical communities have been constructed in a similar manner, and that their members, as participants in national communities, forge their identities simultaneously at both these levels.[17]

This revised version of the science/nation story has no clear beginning, but many of its key elements were present in the seventeenth century and refined over the eighteenth and nineteenth centuries. Those who produced knowledge of the physical and human worlds worked hard to associate themselves and their enterprise both with nationhood and with a universal humanity. The associations between medicine, science and nations are primarily cultural, rather than deriving from direct state intervention, from political confrontations between nations, or from powerful institutions.[18] These cultural associations between science, medicine and nationhood were forged by two related processes. First, practitioners of science and medicine actively built imagined communities for themselves, which were based, more or less, on national boundaries. They created a sense of kinship with peers they would never meet but with whom they shared fundamental values. For example, the scientific or medical periodical, which began to flourish in the second half of the eighteenth century, and contained articles, book reviews and news, functioned in precisely the way Anderson suggests newspapers did for nations.[19] Integral to these shared values were new forms of memory. Those committed to science, to its branches and to medicine generated a fresh historical sense of their enterprises, new kinds of memorials to their illustrious members, and a belief in the need to assure a future for their fields. We can discern these values in portraiture, biographies, medals, statues, histories, reformist tracts and activities, and in institutions from the second half of the eighteenth century onwards. An excellent example is John Hunter, hero of early nineteenth-century scientific medicine in Britain. Sir Joshua Reynolds's portrait of him hangs in the Royal College of Surgeons in London, where his museum, the Hunterian, also a memorial to him, is housed. There were many print versions of Reynolds's clever image, and by the middle of the nineteenth century it had also spawned a statue, in its turn reproduced in a woodcut in the *Illustrated London News*.[20] James Watt, a hero of Britain's industrial revolution, was also cast as the embodiment of values shared by his compatriots and admired by his scientific peers. He too was widely commemorated and eulogised, in texts, images and statues (figure 23).[21]

Second, practitioners identified both themselves as individuals and their communities as collectivities with a relevant nation. They did so by continually commenting on a person's nationality, by offering praise in terms that suggested a mutual reinforcement between national glory and scientific achievement, by anxious references to situations elsewhere that seemed more favourable to the scientific enterprise, by stressing their contributions to the nation's well-being, by invitations to governments to offer more support and by presenting themselves as managers of natural and human resources, that is, as governors, as proto-politicians, as experts with a stake in the administration of the nation.[22]

Together these two processes – creating mini-imagined communities and identifying both their members and their achievements with the nation – made a major contribution to the construction of scientific and medical legitimacy. This took place in most European countries and in the USA, admittedly at very different paces, in the later eighteenth century and over the first half of the nineteenth.[23] Indeed, the attainment of such legitimacy was the precondition for the developments towards the end of the nineteenth century with which historians usually begin.

Although my main concern here is with the ways in which science and nationhood became linked, these processes need to be placed in the context of the universalist claims made by scientific and medical communities, since these were an equally significant vehicle for the advancement of assertions of intellectual authority. In using the phrase 'universalist claims', I mean to

Figure 23 C. E. Wagstaff after
Sir William Beechey, *James
Watt*, 1845

suggest both that the general validity of scientific ideas and methods was insisted upon and that the fruits of such ideas and methods were presented as benefiting the entire human race. The identification of natural knowledge with universal truth had important consequences. It enabled scientists and medical practitioners to associate themselves with the needs of humanity as a whole, that is, with a fantasy of their own beneficence that was underwritten by nature and/or by God. This association was made to work with the science/nation nexus rather than being in self-evident contradiction to it. Unlike other comparable communities, the scientific and medical ones proved capable both of successfully insinuating themselves into national structures and consciousness and, simultaneously, of claiming to be constituted around highly technical values which only they could adjudicate. This distinctive combination of integration and independence was achieved less by the existence of specific interpretations of nature about which everyone agreed – science and medicine have always been characterised by heated controversy – than by a broad consensus on the ground rules for generating what would count as knowledge. Science, technology and medicine, then, came to occupy a special and privileged place in modern nations, a place that was supported by claims about their public value. They provide an excellent example of the ways in which knowledge-generating communities create and reproduce distinctive subcultures, while drawing upon and manipulating more general concerns. Forms of visual and verbal representation developed – portraiture and biography, for example – both to show what was particular to the subculture and to act as a bridge to the 'parent' culture. Specific concepts, such as 'progress' and 'the discovery', acquired a talismanic quality and acted as a kind of currency for the exchange of goods, literally and metaphorically, between the two cultural levels.[24]

It was in the course of the eighteenth century that the term 'nation' became prominent, both in political and philosophical writings and in histories, including histories of science and medicine. Its meanings were initially more fluid than they became in the nineteenth and twentieth centuries, although certain connotations – both political and cultural – became well established. The main role of the abstract idea of the 'nation' seems to have been to sum up, from a cultural perspective, any given polity, whatever its constitutional structure. The term 'nation', like 'culture' and 'style', referred to an amalgam of language, way of life, institutions, writings and history. It was, in other words, a unit of analysis with a holistic undertow.[25]

This concept of nation appealed to writers on medicine and science in three closely related ways. First, it enabled individuals to be labelled and culturally contextualised. Thus the frequent acclamation of Newton as a great Englishman – 'Britain's justest pride', the 'glory of the British Nation' – assigned him to a category that was at one level merely descriptive but at another a form of shorthand for a range of other claims, not always compatible, about religion, political traditions, freedom of thought, the nature of genius, and so on.[26] Second, the concept offered a way of relating achievement to environment, reflecting the well-developed eighteenth-century assumption that genius was, in some significant sense, *of* the place in which it occurred.[27] Third, the concept encouraged specific associations between science or medicine and other features of a given society, above all its style of government, customs and manners.[28] It appealed precisely because it opened up ways of imagining scientific style as profoundly linked with, indeed as a major aspect of, national style.

We are dealing, in short, with complex practices of identification.[29] On the one hand, scientific practitioners identified themselves with a sense of national achievement and well-being; on the other, the well-being and prowess of nations was associated – that is, identified – with the success of individual scientific or medical figures, and increasingly with the idea of collective achievement. The commemoration – through portraits, medals or statues – of figures from the fairly recent past was one major way in which practitioners and commentators concerned with the joint prestige of nations and of scientific and/or medical knowledge could fix their sense of pride in cultural products. The number of memorials to scientists and doctors in Westminster Abbey, for example, increased markedly towards the end of the eighteenth and the early nineteenth centuries.[30] It may help, in analysing these processes of identification, to distinguish three aspects of nationhood with which identification was possible: first, with a figure or institution standing as a direct source of patronage; second, with the apparatus of government or administration and with specific political or administrative agendas; and finally, with the conspicuous achievements of a given 'national' unit.

The first type of identification – with a source of patronage – may seem at first sight to be particularly characteristic of court support for science, and to have relatively little to do with identification with a nation. Yet it is important to remember the significant ambiguity that surrounded the notion 'royal' when applied to organisations. The term might suggest the active, personal involvement of the monarch, but it could also indicate the unit of jurisdiction which that monarch governed – a proto-nation. Thus, a 'royal' scientific institution might receive the active patronage of a monarch, but the epithet could equally well be a device for elevating the status of an organisation that aspired to be 'national'. Given the interest of absolutist rulers in developing structured organisations or bureaucracies that were effective across their realms, 'royal' already carried in the seventeenth century some of the connotations that 'national' took up in the eighteenth and nineteenth centuries.[31] While some scientific or medical institutions, such as the Royal College of Physicians in London, were called 'royal' but had clearly delimited geographical remits, others certainly were national. To be active in such an organisation offered opportunities for identifying with a national endeavour. An obvious example might appear to be the Royal Society, in which Charles II, its initial patron, took rather little interest and which made itself a locus of British scientific privilege. In fact the Royal Institution – 'England's first major scientific laboratory [and] the locus of a crucial reorientation in the public conception of science' – is a more pertinent case.[32] Created in a spirit of reform by a group of men interested in science, social improvement and philanthropy, and soon associated with such nineteenth-century scientific heroes as Humphry Davy and Michael Faraday, heroes whom it helped to create, it was readily identified with British science as a whole, as its founders certainly intended it to be.[33] Equipped with laboratories and a library, and dedicated to the idea that science should be applied to everyday life, it not only embodied innovation, reform and utility in its organisation and staff, but actively promoted these values in its public lectures and publications. The Royal Institution was consciously designed to promote science for the nation: royal patronage and national function neatly coincided.

The second type of identification – with the apparatus of government and political agendas – is clearly familiar from the twentieth century, when elaborate research projects require equally elaborate funding and administration, usually 'national' in character. Yet it is hardly a new phenomenon: it was a notable feature of Napoleonic France, for example.[34] The relationships between science and the practice of self-consciously rational administration are central to an investigation of how nationhood is constructed. Although historians have explored these relationships with reference to France since the time of Colbert, the theme has perhaps been associated, too narrowly, with absolutism and with other forms of overtly authoritarian rule. The trends since the middle of the seventeenth century towards gathering increasingly sophisticated statistics, and making ever more elaborate maps for administrative purposes, generated mechanisms in a wide variety of political contexts whereby those with expertise could identify with national political projects and through them with the nation itself.[35]

Obvious instances of this interaction with the state on the part of groups of experts, which generated a sense of kinship with the nation, were thrown up in eighteenth-century Britain by the heated controversies about the size and quality of the population and about life insurance. When a healthy and growing population was taken to be central to social, economic and political well-being, those who identified trends and proposed remedies for unnecessary loss of life yoked their expertise to the national interest in a particularly powerful manner; if they had something to offer on the emotive subject of infant mortality, the identification between expertise and the nation's vitality was further enhanced. Indeed, eighteenth-century medical practitioners, scientists and reformers mobilised profound anxieties about population decline, excessive infant mortality (especially in cities) and preventable death, creating discourses that slid effortlessly between the themes of individual action and of national well-being. Members of these groups presented themselves as the most effective mediators between individuals and nations, as the reformers who, by advising on individual actions, promoted the health and welfare of the nation. A good example of this is the medical practitioner hailed as a 'pioneer of demography', William Black – the author not only of works on epidemics and mortality patterns but also of a huge comparative history of medicine (1782) in which 'nation' was a key analytical term.[36]

The third kind of identification – with a nation's conspicuous achievements – looks at first sight the most straightforward as well as the easiest to trace historically. It rests, however, on specific cultural manoeuvres which now seem familiar but which need, from a historical point of view, to be made strange. Competitive nationalism, for that is the phenomenon in question, requires, so to speak, a unit of currency. It needs measurable comparisons. If practitioners are to associate themselves with national glory, and a nation's citizens are to find their country's reputation enhanced by the findings of science, medicine and technology, they require a sense of what sets their political unit, and its achievements, apart by comparison with other such units. The historical preconditions of international comparisons are a quantifying spirit, a clear sense of nations as units for accounting purposes, and something that can be measured. All these features were certainly present in Babbage's *Reflections on the Decline of Science in England*. Nonetheless, it is not immediately obvious what science and medicine had that made them apt for such competitive display in the second half of the eighteenth century. I want to suggest that the unit of currency was 'the discovery' – that the concept of *a* discovery, an isolated event which reifies the scientific process, developed alongside the ideas of 'nation' and of science as integral to the nation, and that the processes by means of which this concept was crystallised became much more prominent towards the end of the eighteenth century. Characteristically – and vitally – a discovery constituted a publicly acknowledged innovation. It was taken to be the product of an original outstanding mind, was associated with an individual or with a very limited number of individuals, and manifested clear intellectual, practical and/or humanitarian value. It also generated a symbol or a tag, so that by presenting a pared-down version of a discovery, other ideas or emotions could readily be evoked – pride, heroism, relief of suffering, and so on.[37]

The heroisation of individual scientists was thus integral to the particular kind of fetishisation of science we are dealing with. Since science and medicine were highly abstract, their values were most conveniently rooted through their practitioners, who came, quite literally, to embody these values. Hence the importance of portraiture, of the idea that the face was the index of the mind. The associations between one heroic man, one discovery, one nation and universal benefit became deeply pleasing to the modern mind.[38] Both scientists and non-scientists could identify with this associative chain. Indeed, a number of genres of literature developed that helped to disseminate the cult of 'discoveries' – and with it the values of science – to a wide public. Forms of biography, with their elaborate interplay with portraiture, are perhaps the most historically significant. The history of writing scientific and medical biography is a somewhat neglected area, but the chronological pattern I have been hinting at here, with the first significant forays occurring in the second half of the eighteenth century, and developing more fully over the nineteenth century, aided by the increasingly standardised format of the obituary, is clear.[39] Sir David Brewster's *The Life of Sir Isaac Newton* (1831) constitutes an important landmark. Brewster was a prolific journalist, a productive researcher, a tireless promoter of the benefits and importance of science and an instigator of the British Association for the Advancement of Science. Newton's place in a national pantheon had been secure since the time of his death. The *Life* is full of references to the adequacy of Newton's recognition by the nation, both in his lifetime and subsequently. Its subject was widely recognised as the single most outstanding British scientist, and a variety of editions, both condensed and expanded, appeared.[40]

I have presented the related interests in discoveries and in scientific heroes in terms of the ready opportunities they provided for conspicuous display and for identification. However, 'discovery' had another dimension, one that was already in currency in the seventeenth century. The idea of discovering new lands and that of finding new knowledge were often compared with one another, and this suggests a sense of 'discovery' not only as something achieved, but as an opening, as an invitation into the future.[41] Thus 'discovery' is culturally congruent with an important feature of Anderson's account of the nation – the fact that it invites those who identify with it to look forward, while drawing on the past as they do so. Such congruence is not surprising, since both concepts drew tremendous energy from beliefs in humanly produced progress. The desire for an improved future was a veritable obsession of scientists and medical practitioners of the late eighteenth and early nineteenth centuries, a period in which reform and the national interest were linked at many levels and during which histories of science and medicine chronicled the discoveries of the past, celebrated the achievements of the present and conjured up exciting visions of worlds to come.[42]

Reform – looking to and bringing about an improved future – was possibly the key issue for scientific and medical practitioners of this period, not only in Britain, and it had, as I have hinted, a utopian element.[43] Expert reformers had a vision of the future, which they were actively trying to bring about, indeed, which they felt they had a unique capacity to realise. The reform movements within science and medicine could be seen as coming from self-interested impulses directed at establishing orthodoxies of practice and thought – the elimination, in the medical case, of quackery, and in the scientific ones, of 'pseudosciences'. Such an interpretation, however, does not give sufficient weight either to the strong connections between philanthropy and reform or to the attempts to produce concrete improvements based on scientific and medical knowledge in areas such as agriculture.[44] The theme of reform relates to that of the nation because the nation was taken to be both the relevant political unit and the main beneficiary of reform. Nations were the most practical and realistic units for reformers to target, especially in a context where hope was invested in legislative changes. Imagining a better future for the nation, of which medical practitioners and men of science would be the harbingers, went hand in hand with memorialising past achievements and celebrating contemporary discoveries. The resulting cultural forms both brought specialised communities together and linked them to a wider public.

A notable twentieth-century exemplification of these themes is the *Britain in Pictures* series, published during the Second World War under the editorship of Walter James Turner.[45] Two volumes are particularly relevant: *British Medicine* by R. McNair Wilson and *British Scientists* by Sir Richard Gregory. They were made possible by and in turn epitomise the trends discussed in this essay. It is notable how they drew upon an earlier mindset of reform, discovery and scientific style. Wilson detected a distinctive clinical style in British medicine. 'The English, contrary to general belief, are the most scientifically minded of all peoples, and so careful and exact in their observation that medical progress owes more to them than to any other race of mankind.' He also detected special British lineages of discovery. 'So rich, indeed, have been the contributions of Englishmen to medicine that only the greatest of great discoveries made by them can be recorded in any short account.' Furthermore, British medicine was, in his view, distinctively philanthropic and reformist. 'The English claim is . . . the persistent presentation of a method which . . . has proved its worth and by which the store of human knowledge has been enriched and human suffering in consequence alleviated in all parts of the world.' For Wilson, British medicine has been philanthropic and reformist.[46] Lest we are tempted to dismiss this as merely simplistic popularisation, of no particular historical interest, we should remember the ample evidence that practitioners formed their individual and collective identities around just these sentiments.[47]

That the author of *British Scientists* was one of the foremost scientific writers of his time reinforces the point that these are texts to be taken seriously. Richard Gregory was active as a lecturer on science as well as a journalist; he edited *Nature* from 1919 until 1938, and was a prime mover in organising a new section of the British Association for the Advancement of Science devoted to science education. He was also the author of *Discovery or the Spirit and Service of Science* (1916). In *British Scientists*, Gregory affirmed the internationalism of science, but stressed that there was 'every reason to be proud of the contributions of British scientists'. The main themes of this short work are the importance of experiment, the role of scientific institutions and the cataloguing of great discoveries. He laid particular stress on the Royal Institution: 'from the beginning it has been a creative centre for the advancement of natural knowledge and extension of interest in it'. He continued by asserting its importance on the world stage and lauding Davy and Faraday, its heroes. The Royal Institution was for Gregory an excellent example of an important aspect of his subject – the close relationships between pure and applied science, relationships that he considered particularly fruitful in the British context. *British Scientists* linked social utility, progress and reform to discovery as a high-value currency – a currency acceptable all over the world but also distinctively British.[48]

It should come as no surprise that Gregory included in his book the print of 'Distinguished Men of Science' with which I began. At the heart of the print sits James Watt. References to Watt by writers such as François Arago, Henry Brougham and Lord Jeffrey neatly exemplify the themes I have addressed in this essay. Such writers were concerned with Watt's lack of recognition from his nation, and with what this indicated about British attitudes to science more generally. They lauded the contribution his work made, both to British well-being, especially in the war with France, and to mankind as a whole, and they dwelt in detail on the memorials to him, especially Chantrey's statues, not just as fitting tributes but as objects of aesthetic pleasure. They celebrated Watt in terms of all the future changes his inventions would bring; they imagined people speaking of an 'Age of Watt', and they stressed the notion of discovery. This was partly because of an interest in who first worked out – that is 'discovered' – the composition of water, but it also reflected a sense, which Arago attributed to Watt himself, that 'scientific discoveries were property of the highest order', which thus had to be correctly attributed. The words Brougham inscribed on Watt's Westminster Abbey statue sum up the prevailing view of him as a man who 'enlarged the resources of his country, increased the power of man, and rose to an eminent place among the illustrious followers of science, and the real benefactors of the world'.[49]

Far from being 'mere' rhetoric, this language is indicative of the complex impulses felt by those who practised science, as well as by those, like Brougham, who supported them. These impulses drew them both to a close association, actual and imaginative, with nations, their culture and political apparatus, and to a universalism with marked utopian dimensions. Watt died in 1819, Brougham was publishing on him in the 1830s and 1840s, Arago's *Eloge* was published at least twice in English in the 1850s. The Walker print appeared in the 1860s. Yet the processes that make sense of these publications and images had started decades earlier and still retained enough life to surface again in the *Britain in Pictures* series in the 1940s. The science/nation nexus cannot, then, be understood mainly as a phenomenon of the late nineteenth and twentieth centuries.

My strategy has been to suggest some of the ways in which a cultural historian of science and medicine might take up the invitations offered by Benedict Anderson's *Imagined Communities*. My aim in doing so has been to indicate by example what might be distinctive about a cultural approach to the topic. Two final points may be made. First, the histories of science and medicine afford exceptionally rich examples of the 'imagining nations' theme; they therefore have something to contribute to a general historical perspective on nationhood. Second, there is a need for a broad chronological and conceptual framework within which such work can be developed; I have offered hints as to what this might consist of. It should include a generous time-frame, a concern with the construction of identities, a focus on particular genres of writing and visual display, an analysis of the mechanisms that mediate between science and nationhood, and an attention to the construction of key terms and devices through which 'science' and 'nation' came to acquire a shared cultural history.

Notes

My warm thanks to all those who have helped with this paper, especially Geoff Cubitt and Luke Davidson, who read earlier drafts and offered constructive suggestions.

1 H. Guerlac, 'Science and French national strength', in E. M. Earle (ed.), *Modern France: Problems of the Third and Fourth Republics* (Princeton, 1951), p. 81.
2 A. Clow, 'A re-examination of William Walker's "Distinguished Men of Science"', *Annals of Science*, 11:3 (1956), 183–93, plates XI–XV. See also K. K. Yung, *National Portrait Gallery Complete Illustrated Catalogue 1856–1979* (London, 1981), pp. 648–9; W. D. Hackmann, *Apples to Atoms: Portraits of Scientists from Newton to Rutherford* (London, 1986), pp. 39–41.
3 T. Pettigrew, *Medical Portrait Gallery: Biographical Memoirs of the Most Celebrated Physicians, Surgeons, etc. etc. who have contributed to the Advancement of Medical Science*, 4 vols in 2 (London, 1840). While I am not underestimating the important differences between science and medicine in this period, they exhibit significant common features with respect to nationhood.
4 C. Paul, *Science and Immortality: The Eloges of the Paris Academy of Sciences (1699–1791)* (Berkeley, Los Angeles and London, 1980); D. Outram, 'The language of natural power: the "éloges" of Georges Cuvier and the public language of nineteenth century science', *History of Science*, 16 (1978), 153–78; M. Shortland and R. Yeo (eds), *Telling Lives: Essays on Scientific Biography* (Cambridge, 1996). See also the works cited in note 11.
5 Clow, 'A re-examination', p. 184. The information about the roof is contained in the label on the copy owned by the Wellcome Trust.

6 W. Walker, Jr (ed.), *Memoirs of the Distinguished Men of Science of Great Britain Living in the Years 1807–8* (London, 1862), pp. viii–ix.

7 Henry, Lord Brougham, *Lives of Men of Letters and Science, who flourished in the Times of George III*, 2 vols (London, 1845–46). For evidence of contact between Brougham and Walker, see Clow, 'A re-examination', p. 185 and Walker, *Memoirs*, p. xi. On Brougham, see C. New, *The Life of Henry Brougham to 1830* (Oxford, 1961) and J. Crowther, *Statesmen of Science* (London, 1965), pp. 9–73, for whom Brougham was 'carrying Science into the Heart of the Nation'.

8 Brougham, *Lives*, p. viii. That Brougham's biographies were controversial is made clear in the *Quarterly Review*, 77 (1845–46), 105–39, and 97 (1855), 473–513.

9 W. F. Church (ed.), *The Influence of the Enlightenment on the French Revolution: Creative, Disastrous or Non-Existent?* (Boston, 1964) reveals how persistently the Revolution was linked to materialism and science deemed a breeding-ground for materialism. Coleridge condemned 'French' science and materialism in his 'Theory of life', *The Collected Works of Samuel Taylor Coleridge: Shorter Works and Fragments I* (London and Princeton, 1995), 11:1, pp. 481–557. However, the association could be given a positive cast. Erasmus Darwin confessed to James Watt on 19 January 1790, 'I feel myself becoming all french both in chemistry and politics', D. King-Hele (ed.), *The Letters of Erasmus Darwin* (Cambridge, 1981), p. 200. See also D. Brewster, 'On the effects of the French Revolution upon science and philosophy', *Edinburgh Magazine*, 16 (1800), 287–8.

10 W. Paley, *Natural Theology: Or, the Evidence of the Existence and Attributes of the Deity with illustrative notes by Henry, Lord Brougham and Sir Charles Bell*, 4 vols (London, 1836–39). Crowther stresses Brougham's commitment to science and reform (see note 7); for evidence of his relations with the British Association for the Advancement of Science, founded in 1831, see J. Morrell and A. Thackray, *Gentlemen of Science: Early Years of the British Association for the Advancement of Science* (Oxford, 1981).

11 Brougham, *Lives*, pp. ix–x. On biography and portraiture as genres see T. Hankins, 'In defence of biography: the use of biography in the history of science', *History of Science*, 17 (1979), 1–16; P. Korshin, 'The development of intellectual biography in the eighteenth century', *Journal of English and Germanic Philology*, 73 (1974), 513–23; S. Shapin, 'Personal development and intellectual biography: the case of Robert Boyle', *British Journal for the History of Science*, 26 (1993), 335–46; Shortland and Yeo, *Telling Lives*; D. Stauffer, *The Art of Biography in Eighteenth-Century England* (Princeton, 1941); S. Tomaselli, 'Collecting women: the female in scientific biography', *Science as Culture*, 4 (1988), 95–106; M. Hutt, 'Medical biography and autobiography in Britain, c. 1780–1920', unpublished D.Phil. thesis (University of Oxford, 1995); R. Wendorf, '*Ut pictura biographia*: biography and portrait painting as sister arts', in R. Wendorf (ed.), *Articulate Images: The Sister Arts from Hogarth to Tennyson* (Minneapolis, 1983), pp. 98–124; R. Brilliant, *Portraiture* (London, 1991); M. Pointon, *Hanging the Head: Portraiture and Social Formation in Eighteenth-Century England* (New Haven and London, 1993); J. Woodall (ed.), *Portraiture: Facing the Subject* (Manchester, 1997). The close ties between biography and portraiture persist: according to Raymond Seitz, 'The DNB is a National Portrait Gallery in print', *The Times*, 27 June 1996.

12 R. Williams, 'Nationalist', in his *Keywords: A Vocabulary of Culture and Society*, rev. edn (London, 1983), pp. 213–14. See also H. Paul, *The Sorcerer's Apprentice: The French Scientist's Image of German Science 1840–1919* (Gainesville, 1972) and H. Paul, *From Knowledge to Power: The Rise of the Science Empire in France, 1860–1939* (Cambridge, 1985).

13 C. Babbage, *Reflections on the Decline of Science in England and on Some of its Causes*, ed. M. Campbell-Kelly (London, 1989). A nationalist mentality took many forms and did not necessarily entail the belief that British science was declining: Morrell and

Thackray, *Gentlemen of Science*, ch. 2, and G. Basalla, W. Coleman and R. Kargon (eds), *Victorian Science: A Self-Portrait from the Presidential Addresses to the British Association for the Advancement of Science* (New York, 1970). William Vernon Harcourt, in his address to the first meeting, set out the case for promoting national science while distancing himself from a declinist position. Indeed, he did so partly by celebrating recently deceased scientific and medical heroes (p. 30).

14 B. Schroeder-Gudehus, 'Nationalism and internationalism', in R. Olby *et al.* (eds), *Companion to the History of Modern Science* (London, 1990), p. 909. Cf. J.-J. Salomon, 'The *Internationale* of science', *Science Studies*, 1 (1971), 23–42: 'Even the idea of national scientific communities is contradictory; there can only be one scientific community, which must therefore be international' (p. 24).

15 C. Russell, *Science and Social Change 1700–1900* (Basingstoke and London, 1983), esp. ch. 13; Schroeder-Gudehus, 'Nationalism and internationalism'; Salomon, 'The *Internationale* of science', esp. p. 30.

16 In addition to works cited elsewhere, see on nation/alism E. Kedourie, *Nationalism* (Oxford, 1993); M. Thom, *Republics, Nations and Tribes* (London and New York, 1995); J. Breuilly, *Nationalism and the State* (Manchester, 1982); and on science, P. Forman, 'Scientific internationalism and the Weimar physicists: the ideology and its manipulation in Germany after World War I', *Isis*, 64 (1973), 151–80; B. Easlea, *Fathering the Unthinkable: Masculinity, Scientists and the Nuclear Arms Race* (London, 1983).

17 B. Anderson, *Imagined Communities: Reflections on the Origin and Spread of Nationalism*, rev. edn (London and New York, 1991). L. Jordanova, 'Science and national identity', in R. Chartier and P. Corsi (eds), *Sciences et langues en Europe* (Paris, 1996), pp. 221–31, sets out some of the ways in which Anderson's approach is relevant to the history of science.

18 Historians of science have been impressed by countries where state intervention in and provision for science was early and direct; hence, France has often been taken as a model, as it was by practitioners themselves by the early nineteenth century. See Russell, *Science and Social Change*; D. Knight, *The Age of Science: The Scientific World View in the Nineteenth Century* (Oxford, 1986), esp. chs 2, 4. Examples of work on France that display the close links between the state and science are: D. Outram, *Georges Cuvier: Science, Vocation and Authority in Post-revolutionary France* (Manchester, 1984), M. Crosland, *The Society of Arcueil: A View of French Science at The Time of Napoleon I* (London, 1967), R. Hahn, *The Anatomy of a Scientific Insitution: The Paris Academy of Sciences, 1666–1803* (Berkeley, 1971), D. Weiner, *The Citizen-Patient in Revolutionary and Imperial Paris* (Baltimore, 1993). As Morrell and Thackray show in *Gentlemen of Science*, 'Germany' was the immediate inspiration for the foundation of the British Association for the Advancement of Science (BAAS), but it was a Germany not yet united. Among English-speaking historians of science, French science has received more attention than German science, hence its paradigmatic status.

19 Anderson, *Imagined Communities*, pp. 32–6; W. Lefanu, *British Periodicals of Medicine 1640–1899*, rev. edn (Oxford, 1984); J. E. McClellan III, *Science Reorganized: Scientific Societies in the Eighteenth Century* (New York, 1985).

20 S. Jacyna, 'Images of John Hunter in the nineteenth century', *History of Science*, 21 (1983), 85–108; 'John Hunter', in *Dictionary of National Biography* (London, 1937–38), pp. 287–93; R. Burgess, *Portraits of Doctors and Scientists in the Wellcome Institute of the History of Medicine: A Catalogue* (London, 1973), pp. 179–80 lists many prints derived from the Reynolds portrait. The woodcut, from the *Illustrated London News*, 1864, is on p. 180, no. 1475.26. On the museum, see V. Negus, *History of the Trustees of the Hunterian Collection* (Edinburgh and London, 1966).

21 Burgess, *Portraits of Doctors and Scientists*, p. 384, lists thirteen images of James Watt; see also Hackmann, *Apples to Atoms*, pp. 33–4. Watt was greatly admired in his lifetime – 'have not you more mechanical invention, accuracy, and execution than any other person alive?', asked Erasmus Darwin in 1790 (King-Hele (ed.), *The Letters of Erasmus Darwin*, p. 200).

22 In addition to the items on 'éloges' in note 7, see W. Black, *An Historical Sketch of Medicine and Surgery, from their Origin to the Present Time* (London, 1782); A. D. Morison-Low and J. R. R. Christie (eds), *'Martyr of Science': Sir David Brewster 1781–1868* (Edinburgh, 1984), esp. pp. 25–9, 53–6.

23 In the USA, however, regional identities were also extremely important: J. H. Warner, 'The idea of Southern medical distinctiveness: medical knowledge and practice in the Old South', in R. L. Numbers and T. L. Savitt (eds), *Science and Medicine* (Baton Rouge and London, 1989), pp. 179–205.

24 R. Nisbet, *History of the Idea of Progress* (London, 1980), part II. See p. 203, where he quotes from the American Constitution: 'The Congress shall have Power . . . . To promote the *Progress* of Science and useful Arts, by securing for limited Times to Authors and Inventors the exclusive Right to their respective Writings and *Discoveries*' (my emphasis).

25 Williams, *Keywords*, pp. 87–93, 213–14; 'Style in science', a thematic issue of *Science in Context*, 4:2 (1991); Thom, *Republics, Nations and Tribes*; L. Fleck, *Genesis and Development of a Scientific Fact* (Chicago, 1979).

26 M. H. Nicolson, *Newton Demands the Muse: Newton's Opticks and the Eighteenth Century Poets* (Hamden, 1963), p. 11; R. S. Westfall, *Never at Rest: A Biography of Isaac Newton* (Cambridge, 1980), p. 873. See also D. Brewster, *The Life of Sir Isaac Newton* (London, 1831), esp. ch. 14, and M. McNeil, 'Newton as a national hero', in J. Fauvel *et al.* (eds), *Let Newton Be! A New Perspective on His Life and Works* (Oxford, 1988), pp. 223–40.

27 On genius and science, see R. Yeo, 'Genius, method, and morality: images of Newton in Britain, 1760–1860', *Science in Context*, 2 (1988), 257–84, and S. Schaffer, 'Genius in Romantic natural philosophy', in A. Cunningham and N. Jardine (eds), *Romanticism and the Sciences* (Cambridge, 1990), pp. 82–98. On environment, see F. Driver and G. Rose (eds), *Nature and Science: Essays in the History of Geographical Knowledge* (Bristol, 1992).

28 See note 25. Virtually all the eighteenth- and nineteenth-century writers I mention assumed that science shared key features with other aspects of a nation's culture and politics; see, for example, Brewster, cited in note 9.

29 'Identity' has become a 'keyword' of the 1980s and 1990s; see, for example, K. A. Appiah and H. L. Gates, Jr (eds), *Identities* (Chicago and London, 1995), and R. Handler, 'Is "identity" a useful cross-cultural concept?', in J. R. Gillis (ed.), *Commemorations: The Politics of National Identity* (Princeton, 1994), pp. 27–40. I use 'identification' to draw attention to the continuous, ongoing processes whereby individuals and groups create and sustain their psychic links with, in this case, abstract ideas and ideals such as 'nation', 'progress', 'reform', and so on: see J. Laplanche and J.-B. Pontalis, *The Language of Psychoanalysis* (London, 1988); 'identification' is discussed on pp. 205–8.

30 C. Wilson *et al.*, *The New Bell's Cathedral Guides: Westminster Abbey* (London, 1986), ch. 7; A. R. Hall, *The Abbey Scientists* (London, 1966); F. Haskell, 'The apotheosis of Newton in art', in his *Past and Present in Art and Taste* (New Haven and London, 1987), pp. 218–37; and D. Bindman and M. Baker, *Roubiliac and the Eighteenth-Century Monument: Sculpture as Theatre* (New Haven and London, 1995).

31 Hahn, *Anatomy of a Scientific Institution*; D. Lux, *Patronage and Royal Science in Seventeenth-Century France: The Académie de Physique in Caen* (Ithaca, NY and

London, 1989), esp. ch. 7; A. Trout, *Jean-Baptiste Colbert* (Boston, 1978), esp. chs. 6, 9; M. Berman, *Social Change and Scientific Organization: The Royal Institution 1799–1844* (London, 1978).

32 Morrell and Thackray, *Gentlemen of Science*, pp. 52–7; Berman, *Social Change and Scientific Organization*, p. xxii.

33 On Davy, see D. Knight, *Humphry Davy: Science and Power* (Oxford, 1992) and 'From science to wisdom: Humphry Davy's life', in Shortland and Yeo (eds), *Telling Lives*, pp. 103–14; S. Forgan (ed.), *Science and the Sons of Genius: Studies on Humphry Davy* (London, 1980). On Faraday, see J. Tyndall, *Faraday as a Discoverer* (London, 1868); G. Cantor, 'Public images of Michael Faraday', in Shortland and Yeo (eds), *Telling Lives*, pp. 171–93; P. Gissing, 'Mythologising Michael: the lives of Faraday 1791–1992', unpublished BA dissertation (School of Science and Technology Studies, University of New South Wales, Australia, 1992).

34 D. Outram, *Georges Cuvier*; L. Bergeron, *France Under Napoleon* (Princeton, 1981), esp. pp. 199–204; R. Fox and G. Weisz (eds), *The Organization of Science and Technology in France 1808–1914* (Cambridge, 1980).

35 Trout, *Jean-Baptiste Colbert*, pp. 190–3; R. Briggs, 'The Académie Royale des Sciences and the pursuit of utility', *Past and Present*, 131 (1991), 38–88; J.-C. Perrot and S. J. Woolf, *State and Statistics in France, 1789–1815* (New York, 1984); T. Porter, *The Rise of Statistical Thinking 1820–1900* (Princeton, 1986), chs 1–3; T. Frangsmyr et al. (eds), *The Quantifying Spirit in the Eighteenth Century* (Berkeley and Los Angeles, 1990), ch. 12; P. Fara, *Sympathetic Attractions: Magnetic Practices, Beliefs, and Symbolism in Eighteenth-Century England* (Princeton, 1996), ch. 4.

36 Black, *Historical Sketch of Medicine and Surgery*; D. V. Glass, *Numbering the People: The Eighteenth-Century Population Controversy and the Development of Census and Vital Statistics in Britain* (London and New York, 1978); W. Coleman, *Death is a Social Disease: Public Health and Political Economy in Early Industrial France* (Madison, 1982).

37 Responses to Watt illustrate precisely these points; see, for example, Walker, *Memoirs of the Distinguished Men of Science* (1st edn), pp. 210–15 (2nd edn, 1864), pp. 137–41; Brougham, *Lives of Men of Letters and Science* (3rd edn, 1855), pp. 25–56; King-Hele (ed.), *The Letters of Erasmus Darwin*; F. Arago, *Historical Eloge of James Watt* (London and Edinburgh, 1839); G. Williamson, *Memorials of the Lineage, Early Life, Education, and Development of the Genius of James Watt* (Edinburgh, 1856).

38 Representations of Edward Jenner are an excellent example, especially the leaflet for the Jenner Museum, Berkeley, Gloucestershire: 'Discover how he developed the smallpox vaccine and how smallpox is the only disease to have been eradicated from the world.'

39 See the items on scientific and medical biography cited in note 11.

40 Morison-Low and Christie (eds), *'Martyr of Science'*, pp. 107–37, lists all the editions and versions of Brewster's writings on Newton.

41 Perhaps the shared idea of an 'atlas' conveys the point most forcefully. Equally revealing is the frontispiece for Francis Bacon's *Novum Organum* (London, 1620), part of his projected *Instauratio Magna*, which shows a ship sailing through the Pillars of Hercules and a motto, which may be loosely translated as 'Many shall pass through and learning be advanced'.

42 J. Passmore, *The Perfectibility of Man* (London, 1972); F. and F. Manuel, *Utopian Thought in the Western World* (Oxford, 1979); C. Webster, 'The historiography of medicine', in P. Corsi and P. Weindling (eds), *Information Sources in the History of Science and Medicine* (London, 1983), pp. 29–43; J. Christie, 'The development of the historiography of science', in R. C. Olby et al. (eds), *Companion to the History of Modern Science* (London, 1990), pp. 5–22.

43 A. Desmond, *The Politics of Evolution. Morphology, Medicine, and Reform in Radical London* (Chicago and London, 1989); R. French and A. Wear (eds), *British Medicine in an Age of Reform* (London and New York, 1991); I. Loudon, 'Medical practitioners 1750–1850 and the period of medical reform in Britain', in A. Wear (ed.), *Medicine in Society: Historical Essays* (Cambridge, 1992), pp. 219–47.

44 Berman, *Social Change and Scientific Organisation*; S. Wilmot, 'The Business of Improvement': *Agriculture and Scientific Culture in Britain, c. 1700–c. 1870* (Bristol, 1990).

45 'Walter James Turner', *Dictionary of National Biography 1941–1950* (London, 1959), pp. 892–3.

46 R. McNair Wilson, *British Medicine* (London, 1941), pp. 7, 48, 4.

47 E.g. James Watson, *The Double Helix: a Personal Account of the Discovery of the Structure of DNA* (London, 1968); 'Studmuffins of science', a calendar for 1996 issued by the American Association for the Advancement of Science.

48 Sir R. Gregory, *British Scientists* (London, 1941), pp. 7, 16–17; 'Richard Gregory', *Dictionary of National Biography 1951–1960* (London, 1971), pp. 433–5.

49 F. Arago, *Life of James Watt*, 3rd edn (Edinburgh and London, 1839), pp. 170, 139; the works cited in note 37; C. Binfield, *Sir Francis Chantrey: Sculptor to an Age 1781–1841* (Sheffield, 1981), pp. 48–9, 73–5; S. Dunkerley, *Francis Chantrey, Sculptor, from Norton to Knighthood* (Sheffield, 1995), plates 20, 29, pp. 47, 64, 82, 103.

Imagining national economies:
national and international economic statistics,
1900–1950

Over the twentieth century the perceived 'failure' of the national economy has played a central role in British narratives of national crisis or decline.[1] The economy has, however, remained marginal to the recent flurry of historical interest in national identity. In part this neglect has no doubt been a side-effect of the struggle to liberate cultural history from the straitjacket of the conventional historiography which prioritised 'political', 'economic' and 'social' reality over the more 'ephemeral' sphere of culture. Nevertheless, the role played by economic affairs in the historical construction of national identity demands attention.

One approach to this problem is suggested by recent studies of the emergence of the professional social sciences and their relationship to the nation-state. Anthony Giddens's historical sociology has been important in highlighting the way in which, through their association with the nation-state, the social sciences have come to conceive of their central object, society itself, in national terms.[2] When we speak of 'society' we in fact mean French, German or British society – a social unit whose distinctive outlines are assumed to be congruent with the political boundaries of the nation. This assumption is deeply ingrained, for instance, in the habit of taking national units as the basis for comparative empirical testing of general sociological hypotheses.[3]

Of all the social sciences, economics was undoubtedly the most successful in forging an alliance with the nation-state. Historical discussions of the emergence of economics as a profession have, however, largely taken for granted the existence of 'the national economy' as a distinct entity to which both the nation-state and a specialised scientific discipline addressed themselves.[4] Only recently has the concept of 'the economy' itself been historicised.[5] The social theorist Susan Buck-Morss, in an important intervention, has turned to Adam Smith and Hegel in an effort to understand the formation of modern conceptions of 'the economy'.[6] Her aim is to better understand the political implications of the current globalisation of capital, in particular the disintegration of inherited conceptions of the national economy.[7] However, Buck-Morss fails to analyse the way in which the concept of 'the economy' has, for most of the nineteenth and twentieth centuries, been imbricated with that of 'the nation'. A more satisfactory account in this respect is to be found in the essay on the history of the concept of *die Wirtschaft* (German for 'the economy') included in the final volume of the *Geschichtliche Grundbegriffe*.[8] In German the concept of 'the economy' was, in fact, originally constituted in relation to the idea of 'the nation'.[9] In eighteenth-century German the concepts of *Ökonomie* or *Wirtschaft* originally referred only to the management of the individual household or business. In the early nineteenth century the meanings of these terms were widened to embrace a conception of the economic system as a whole by adding a prefix pointing to the nation. As a result, two new terms emerged: *Nationalökonomie* – the science of the national economic system – and *Volkswirtschaft* – the 'national economy' itself.[10] It was only later, when the broader concept of the economic system had become commonplace, that these prefixes were dropped, allowing reference to be made simply to *die Wirtschaft*.

If the concept of the nation helped to constitute the concept of the economy, the reverse was also true. Harold James's study of German nationalist thought has highlighted the powerful way in which concepts of economic progress were harnessed in the first half of the nineteenth century to the cause of nation building.[11] The extension of railways and commerce was seen as promoting the emergence of a united national consciousness. David Head's study of the label 'Made in Germany' widens the focus from the writings of nationalist intellectuals. He describes how what was originally intended as a discriminatory label, imposed on German manufacturers by the British parliament in 1887, was appropriated as a national badge of honour.[12] Clearly, then, at least in the German case, the concepts of the economy and of the nation were constituted in ways which bound them inextricably together.[13] The political boundaries of the nation provided a framework within which individual business activity could be conceived of as part of a wider 'economic system'. The coherence of this economic system provided in turn the basis on which to imagine the gradual emergence of a solid national community bound together through ties of common interest.

In making 'the national economy' part of a cultural history of national identity, we are not merely widening our analysis of 'national identity'. In fact, such an approach to the history of the 'national economy' destabilises the dichotomy in which the sphere of 'representations, symbols and culture' is counterposed to the 'material, non-discursive realm' of 'economic reality'. The point here is not to deny that 'real' goods are produced by 'real labour' and sold for 'real money', but rather to understand the artificiality of the concept of 'the economic system' within which we group together enormously diverse activities of production, consumption and exchange. 'The economy' is not pre-existing reality, an object which we simply observe and theorise about. Our understanding of 'the economy' as a distinct entity, a distinct social 'sphere' or social 'system', is the product of a dramatic process of imaginative abstraction and representational labour.

In this sense, the notion of 'the economy' is like other abstract concepts such as 'the nation' or 'class', no more and no less. It is a concept created to make sense of, to systematise and to analyse an otherwise unintelligible reality. If actors commonly orientate and co-ordinate their activities and perceptions around such a concept, it may assume a reality independent of the individual speaker or actor. And this process may be accelerated if an abstract concept such as 'the economy' can be related meaningfully to another similar entity such as 'the nation'. We come then to speak of 'the national economy' in anthropomorphic terms. We speak as though 'the British economy' does things, as though it were an entity to which interests and motives could be ascribed. Deconstructive analysis – of a similar kind to that which has recently been applied to the concept of 'society' – is then required to reveal the way in which an abstract idea has taken on this independent existence.

This essay analyses the role played by economic statistics in helping to construct and perpetuate a reified understanding of 'the national economy'. The conventional understanding of statistics is, of course, that they are ideal tools for registering economic events 'happening out there'. The premise of this essay is that treating statistics simply as a mirror of reality underestimates what is in fact involved in their production. Such a view of statistics fails to do justice to the conceptual imagination and labour that actually make possible the process of quantifying abstraction. The gathering of statistics is, in fact, part of the active process through which an abstract conception of the 'national economy' is turned into objective reality. In the developed economies of the west we live under a rolling barrage of statistical data. The publication of quarterly estimates for gross domestic product,[14] or figures for the monthly rate of inflation, balance of trade, industrial output, consumer sales, unemployment or wages, punctuate public life. The progress of the national economy recorded by statistics is a key part of the narrative of the nation that is consumed daily by the newspaper-reading public.[15] Masses of data are quoted by newscasters, politicians and corporate spokespeople on radio and television. Imposing graphs flash across television screens and computer monitors.

This flood of statistics carries a national message. Citizens are invited to relate their individual and local economic experience, whether as employees or employers, as consumers or taxpayers, to a wider narrative, that of the national economy. Of course, we should not leap to hasty conclusions about the audience response to this flood of statistical messages. However, there can be no doubt about the reaction amongst the political commentators and financial journalists, whose job consists in large part in processing the latest batch of statistical reports for public consumption. When the indicators point up, the electorate and the consuming nation are enjoined to 'feel good'. When the indicators point down, pay increases and personal spending decisions are judged harshly against the standard of national economic conditions. Many of the administrative and economic practices which affect individual lives are co-ordinated around national economic indicators. Pay and welfare benefits, for instance, not to mention the dreaded mortgage interest rate, are pegged to indicators of the national cost of living. Statistics thus constitute and co-ordinate the imaginary community of the national economy.

And statistics have also helped to constitute the domain of the international. As Benedict Anderson has said, the cultural artefacts of nationality are 'modular', 'copiable'.[16] A national system of official statistics has become one more module in the tool kit of twentieth-century 'official nationalism'. Like a flag, postage stamps or passports, an estimate of gross domestic product allows a nation-state to be placed within an international hierarchy. Since the Second World War practically every country in the world has been ranked in terms of its gross domestic product and the rate of growth in this aggregate. Positions in the 'growth league' have come to preoccupy generations of policy makers and advisers. The crude language of 'national competitiveness' and 'national economic performance' resonates powerfully with other discourses of national machismo and competition, be they in the area of sport or war.

Unfortunately, much more is known about the history of economics and economic theory than about the history of economic statistics. Even though the developments of statistical and of theoretical concepts of the national economy were clearly closely intertwined in the first half of the twentieth century, it is the grand theoretical breakthroughs that have hogged the lime-light. In particular, historians in the English-speaking world have concentrated on the transformation in our understanding of the national economy wrought by the so-called 'Keynesian Revolution' of the 1930s and 1940s.[17] The aim of this essay, drawing on material from the USA, France, Great Britain and Germany, is to spin a rather different tale, focusing on the development of the national and international institutions of economic statistics which have so powerfully shaped our understanding of the national economy in the twentieth century.

It is hard to imagine that 100 years ago the basic economic statistics we now take for granted were largely non-existent.[18] In the late nineteenth century there were no official estimates of national income, expenditure or production, and no official indices of the cost of living or data on earnings or wages. Apart from the information on monetary and financial conditions supplied by national banks of issue, most information on current economic conditions was gleaned as a by-product from the administrative records of the state bureaucracy. Customs returns provided little more than rudimentary information on trade in most countries. The returns of taxes on particular industries and higher income-earners produced unreliable and out-of-date information on a small fraction of national income. The giant censuses of occupation carried out in most countries roughly every decade provided basic information on the changes to the social structure wrought by industrialisation and urbanisation. However, they had little value as guides to current economic conditions. To provide more up-to-date information other administrative records were pressed into service, such as the statistics of bankruptcies and defaults and the reports of trade inspectorates. Rough estimates of agricultural production were prepared for most countries on an annual basis; exceptionally well-organised and publicity-friendly industrial associations might publish annual reports as well. However, the kind of up-to-date statistical information which we take for granted today was almost entirely non-existent.

In the last quarter of the nineteenth century, there were unmistakable signs of change across the industrialising world. The departments of government most closely involved in administering the emerging industrialised and urbanised society were increasingly aware of the utility of authoritative official statistics. The increasingly complex negotiation of trade tariffs stimulated improvements to the statistics of foreign trade, including refinement of the classification of commodities and more rapid publication of the returns. The repertoire of official statistics increased. So-called Department of Labour Statistics were particularly active.[19] In collaboration with trade union movements they compiled new statistics on the cost of living, unemployment and wage movements. In a number of countries the first decade of the twentieth century witnessed the first comprehensive surveys of industrial production. Official statisticians were assisted in their efforts by economists who almost everywhere were enthusiastically embracing the demand for empirical testing of economic theories and the virtues of historical research.[20]

The preoccupations which motivated statistical initiatives in the decades before the First World War are well illustrated by the history of national income statistics in Britain, the USA and Germany.[21] The first estimates of national income had been prepared for Britain and France as early as the late seventeenth century. A cottage industry in such statistics had continued throughout the eighteenth and nineteenth centuries. The end of the nineteenth century, however, saw a marked revival in international interest in national income estimation. This was motivated above all by two concerns.

One motivation was to tell the story of national economic progress in the context of intensifying imperialist rivalry. An estimate of national income or even national wealth was a cornerstone of such a narrative. Karl Helfferich, for example, first published his highly influential estimate of German national income as part of a commemorative volume celebrating twenty-five years of German national progress under the rule of Wilhelm II.[22] His study of the growth of national income and wealth was not based on a rigorous labour theory of value. However, the triumphs of German labour were his theme. His statistics confirmed the cliché that 'France is the country of rents. Germany is the land of labour.'[23] According to Helfferich, it was the intensity of German labour which had allowed Germany's per capita income to exceed that of France, despite the latter's greater endowment with wealth.

The second problematic was that of intensified class conflict. In this confrontation a concept of national income played a key regulating role. The nation's income was the precise measure of what there was to be divided between the competing social classes. It was an interest in the distribution of national income which motivated new estimates of US national income around the turn of the century.[24] In Britain this preoccupation can be traced back to the birth of the language of class in the early nineteenth century.[25] A century later the work of A. L. Bowley and Josiah Stamp set a new standard in terms both of the precision with which the difficult concept of national income was defined and of the range of data used. Their refinements of method were motivated above all by the desire to resolve public arguments about the distribution of income between the social classes.[26]

A critical issue was how to relate these two different ideas of national income – as the measure of national economic advance, and as a measure of the 'cake' over which national class struggles were fought. In his desire to celebrate national progress Helfferich downplayed distributional issues and appealed to national unity as the foundation of Germany's prosperity, against the siren calls of 'class war and class hatred'.[27] However, in Wilhelmine Germany the rumblings of class conflict could not be silenced so easily. Critics from the left insisted that the price which had been paid for national economic progress was the immiseration of the German working class. In response Helfferich added a postscript to the third edition of his book, seeking to demonstrate that, at least in Prussia, there was no statistical evidence for any increase in the percentage of the population at the bottom of the income distribution.[28] In Britain as well, the two problems of class conflict and national economic progress could not be uncoupled. Alfred Marshall, in his standard textbook *Principles of Economics*, famously applied marginalist analysis to the problem of the distribution of a given 'national dividend' (national income) between capital and labour.[29] However, he also related this static analysis of income distribution to a rather less well-known historico-biological account of economic growth.[30] Marshall conceded that hard bargaining by trade unions might produce short-run advantages for the working class. However, he warned that in the long run a reduction in profits would extinguish the dynamic incentive motivating economic expansion.

Thus, by the turn of the century there was in wide circulation a concept of national income that was given significance by its insertion into the double problematic of class conflict and national rivalry.[31] Contemporary economists did their best to give empirical reality to this concept. However, national income estimation was still very much the business of individuals brave enough to make the necessary leaps of statistical faith. The raw data available for national income estimates was limited everywhere to the incomplete records generated by embryonic systems of income tax. Not surprisingly, no European bureau of official statistics gave its sanction to a national income estimate in the pre-war period.

The First World War and its aftermath, however, gave an entirely new urgency to national economic research. Historians' preoccupation with the 'Keynesian Revolution', which has directed attention towards the 1930s and the Second World War, has caused the impact of the First World War to be too often neglected.[32] The war tore apart the dense fabric of the nineteenth-century international economy. Economic government was nationalised. Unprecedented measures of rationing had to be introduced to ensure the supply of essential raw materials to national industry and to prevent starvation in the urban centres. To manage the labour force 'national bargains' were struck between labour movements, capital and the state administrations. The bureaucracy of the combatant states was transformed by the needs of economic planning. Federal states, such as the USA and Wilhelmine Germany, went through a rapid process of centralisation.[33] National economic administrations were created from scratch. After the end of the war, newly democratised parliaments and nationalist dictators adopted policies of domestic inflation and national economic protection.

In the war's aftermath the problems of national economic government were compounded by the international dilemma of reparations.[34] The reparations negotiations highlighted both the strong hold exerted by conceptions of the national economy and their intellectual limits. The imposition of huge reparations on Germany was premised on the crude nationalist idea that this would benefit the victors. However, as critics, led by Keynes, pointed out, the level of the original demands was absurd and the international ramifications of transferring such a huge volume of resources had not been properly worked out. A temporary solution was finally devised in early 1924 by a committee of non-political experts chaired by the American businessman Charles G. Dawes.

Central to the Dawes settlement was a linkage between reparations and 'Germany's capacity to pay'.[35] The problem was how to put into practice this commonsensical idea. The concept of national income was still far from generally accepted as a measure of 'national economic capacity'. And even if agreement had been reached on a definition of Germany's capacity to pay, it was clear that the available economic statistics were not adequate. For lack of more up-to-date data, Helfferich's pre-war estimates of German national income were pressed into service by many post-war commentators on the reparations question.[36] However, the Dawes Committee clearly needed more current information. The index of Germany's capacity to pay had to be cobbled together from the statistics that were certain to be regularly available. The result was extremely bizarre.[37] Starting in 1929, Germany's annual payments were linked to an index calculated according to the following formula:

$$\text{Index} = (a/a'' + b/b' + c/c'' + d/d'' + e/e' + f/f') \times 100/6$$

For the purposes of this formula:

a = sum of German imports and exports (a'' = average of 1912–13 and 1926–29 values)

b = sum of revenues and expenditures of the Reich, Prussian, Saxon and Bavarian governments (b' = average of 1927–29 values)

c = weight of goods transported on German railways (c'' = average of 1912–13 and 1926–29 values)

d = total retail value of sugar, tobacco, beer and brandy consumed in Germany (d'' = average of 1912–13 and 1926–29 values)

e = total population of Germany (e' = average of 1927–29 values)

f = per capita consumption of coal (f' = average of 1927–29 values)

If the index exceeded 100 Germany's annual payments were to increase in exact proportion. Years in which the index values fell below the base value were to be offset against 'surplus years'. Since the onset of the Great Depression in 1929 destroyed the basis of the Dawes Plan, this formula never actually came into effect. However, the experience of the Dawes Committee starkly illustrated the disparity between the importance and complexity of economic problems facing national governments in the early 1920s and the governmental and statistical capacities that were actually available.

This disparity was nowhere more evident than in the Weimar Republic. In response to the desperate need for better economic information, the Republic's Ministry of Economic Affairs, which was itself a product of the First World War, sponsored an intensive research programme to map out the empirical coordinates of the German national economy.[38] An unprecedented range of economic investigations were instigated by the Reich's Statistical Office, the state-sponsored Institute for Business-Cycle Research and a giant National Committee of Enquiry into the Conditions of Production and Distribution of the German Economy. By 1929 the German government was able to answer the index of the Dawes Committee with what was internationally acknowledged as the most sophisticated official estimate of national income.

Weimar's research effort also had a new domestic agenda. The work of the Institute for Business-Cycle Research and the National Committee of Enquiry was premised on an optimistic corporatist vision of managed capitalism. The waste and inefficiency of unfettered capitalism were to be curbed by the sharing of up-to-date and comprehensive economic statistics between the state administration and the peak associations of business and labour. Analytical interests thus shifted away from the distribution of national income to the problem of achieving a steady expansion of the national economy over time. Above all, the aim was to stabilise the boom-to-bust cycles that Germany had experienced before and after the First World War. The national income statistics published by the Reich's Statistical Office were no longer an end in themselves. They were part of a comprehensive analysis of the business cycle.[39] Estimates of national income were complemented by figures for major expenditure items such as government outlays, industrial investment, an estimate of the balance of payments and figures for household savings. To complete statistical coverage of the circular flow of income, expenditure and production, Weimar's statisticians began planning a comprehensive census of industrial production.

The enormous German research effort was in part inspired by contemporary developments in the USA. In the 1920s the Harvard University Committee for Economic Research set the international standard in statistical time-series analysis.[40] The language of trends, cycles and seasonal adjustments that is still in use today is largely owed to the Committee, a university-based initiative that marketed its system of predictive economic barometers on a commercial basis. By contrast, the National Bureau of Economic Research (NBER), established in Washington in 1920, benefited from the patronage of Secretary of State for Commerce Herbert Hoover and the sponsorship of America's giant corporate foundations.[41] The Bureau was responsible for compiling the first annual estimates of US national income. As in Germany, these estimates were no longer simply interventions in the political struggle over the distribution of income. Compiled from figures both for income and expenditure, they were integrated into a comprehensive analysis of the business cycle. In Britain and France the war also produced calls for the creation of national statistical services.[42] However, these demands were in both countries resisted by conservative Treasury bureaucrats. In Britain this did not prevent independent statistical initiatives by the British Board of Trade and the Ministry of Agriculture.[43] Nor did it, of course, block innovative private work by British statisticians and economists in the field of business cycle research and national-income accounting. However, in both France and Britain it was to take the shock of a second world war to force the creation of central government offices dedicated to economic statistics.[44]

Thus, the First World War and its aftermath set in motion, at least in the USA and Germany and to a lesser extent in Britain, a new effort to find ways of making the national economy measurable. Yet it was clear that national problems of economic and social policy needed to be addressed in an international context. The Gold Standard, which had emerged as the cornerstone of economic government in the late nineteenth century, was based on intensive co-operation and co-ordination between national central banks.[45] The 1920s witnessed a vain struggle to achieve a similar harmony of economic policy and, as part of this effort, the League of Nations took steps to bring about a standardisation of national economic statistics. The League's aim was to foster the governmental capacities of nation-states through the international exchange of economic expertise. It gave unprecedented political clout to the International Statistical Institute, which had been established in 1885.[46] In 1928 a huge international congress on economic statistics resulted in a treaty requiring all major industrialised countries to maintain a common repertoire of basic economic statistics.[47] In addition, the economic advisers to the world's central banks, meeting under the auspices of the League, agreed to a free exchange of monetary statistics.[48] The League also sponsored conferences of the business-cycle economists to compare methods and data.[49]

The massive and unprecedented depression that hit the world economy between 1929 and 1932 destroyed any hope of a co-ordinated international approach to economic government. It also undermined faith in the predictive power of models based on the extrapolation of past cycles. To understand the dynamics of such a crisis one needed analytical equipment of sufficient generality to allow it to be applied to any historical case, however extreme. This was what was supplied by Keynes's path-breaking *General Theory*, published in 1936, and the innovative econometric modelling of Ragnar Frisch and Jan Tinbergen. Nevertheless, it was within the matrix of empirical economic knowledge assembled in the 1920s that the theoretical and technical breakthroughs of the 1930s were formulated. Frisch's and Tinbergen's equations may have been more rigorous, but the data they used were those first prepared by the business-cycle economists. And it is hard to imagine that Keynes could so easily have reformulated economic analysis in terms of aggregate demand if it had not been for a decade of statistical effort, which turned nebulous macroeconomic concepts into concrete realities measured by authoritative statistical series. Critics have pointed out that Keynes never explicitly justified his choice of the national economy and its aggregate components as the appropriate object for his theorising.[50] After all, the model of the circular flow of income, expenditure and production could be applied to an economic unit of any dimension. But this simply bears out the main argument of this essay. By the 1930s the basic building-blocks of Keynesian macroeconomics – national income, expenditure and production and their components, the monthly rate of unemployment, the national cost of living and the national average wage – were all reified objects which a theorist such as Keynes could take more or less for granted.

Taking into account the wider field of economic research developed during the 1920s also provides a framework for understanding the many innovative economists and statisticians of the inter-war years as something other than merely 'anticipators' or 'co-inventors' of Keynesian theory. When one considers the worldwide interest in problems of the business-cycle and national income estimation, it is hardly surprising that similar theories of effective demand were proposed by a string of economists other than Keynes throughout the 1930s. Rather than seeing this worldwide ferment simply as a prelude to the 'Keynesian Revolution', it seems more appropriate to view the Anglo-American narrative as a local variant on a more general theme, namely the emergence of a new theoretical and empirical vision of the national economy. Such an account of the inter-war years also suggests the need to reinterpret the experience of the Second World War. In the British narrative of the 'Keynesian Revolution' the war has a special place.[51] It finally brought Keynes himself into government in Britain. And in 1941 the war budget was the first to be based on an official estimate of British national income.[52] Unlike in the First World War, the mobilisation of the British economy for war was now dictated by a clear vision of what the national economy could sustain without experiencing disastrous inflation. Estimates of national income took on their now familiar shape as estimates of what nation-states could feasibly extract to fight wars. With the active assistance of German émigrés similar techniques were adopted for planning the war effort in the USA.[53]

In the triumphal narrative of economics as a policy–science it is less often noted that Hitler's regime matched the western allies in the use it made of statistics and economic research. The literature on the relationship between National Socialism and economic science has not surprisingly tended to focus on the exponents of specifically Nazi economics.[54] However, a greater degree of influence was probably exerted by the cadre of mainstream economic experts and statisticians which the Third Reich inherited from the Weimar Republic. It was with their assistance that the regime from 1934 onwards put in place an increasingly comprehensive system of economic controls, which itself generated a mass of administrative data. The official statisticians of the Reich added to this with a series of innovative censuses and surveys designed to provide a comprehensive database for economic planning. The publication of this mass of new economic data was restricted by increasingly paranoid security precautions. The Führer's speeches, however, which were littered with numbers documenting the regime's economic achievements, paid ample homage to the influence of German statisticians.[55] In Nazi Germany, as in the democratic west and the Soviet Union, statistics had become an indispensable element in political language.

During the war, economic experts and statisticians assumed an even more important role in Nazi Germany. At the heart of Speer's armaments ministry was a team of statisticians and economists recruited from the Institute for Business-Cycle Research which Weimar had established in 1925.[56] By 1944 they, like their British and American counterparts, had developed a national accounting scheme as well as numerous information systems to manage the bottlenecks in the Nazi war economy.[57] Unlike in Britain, however, the final years of the Second World War in Germany are properly viewed not as the beginning of a new technocratic era, but as the culmination of two decades of systematic effort by German economists, statisticians and government officials to make the national economy into a calculable and governable object.

At the same time as forging new and closer links between economic experts and the nation-state, the Second World War also propelled the process of internationalisation which had first gathered momentum in the inter-war years. Keynes's role in Anglo-American financial diplomacy is, of course, legendary. His personal shuttle diplomacy was backed up by an institutionalised system of co-operation between statisticians and economists from the USA, Britain and Canada who met regularly from 1944 onwards to standardise their statistical systems, particularly the centrepiece of wartime financial policy, the system of national accounts.[58] This would make their respective national economies directly comparable and allow a greater degree of co-ordination of economic and monetary policies. However, efforts at internationalisation were not confined to the western allies. Nazi control of Europe gave German statisticians the chance to impose their categories and statistical systems on the occupied territories. During 1941 a uniform system of labour statistics was installed throughout the Nazi Empire.[59] In the wake of Germany's armies the Institute for Business-Cycle Research swallowed up national Institutes of Economics in Vienna, Paris, Prague and Amsterdam. Beginning in 1943, economists from the Institute on secondment to Albert Speer's Planning Office set about creating an integrated information system to cover, not only labour, but also raw material supply and industrial production throughout the entire *Großraum*.

The victory of the anti-Nazi coalition secured the hegemony of the Anglo-American Keynesian consensus in the post-war western world. To avoid a repetition of the inter-war disaster, the western European nation-states were now harnessed to a much tighter framework of international political and economic co-operation. A system of standardised national accounts was one of the administrative underpinnings of this new international order. The system of national income, expenditure and production accounts developed by Canada, the USA and Britain during the Second World War was generalised across western Europe by the Organization for European Economic Cooperation (OEEC).[60] Disbursement of Marshall aid was made conditional on the ability of countries to make claims justified on the basis of standardised economic plans. The OEEC statistical unit was based in the Applied Economics Department of Cambridge University and, not surprisingly, the Standardized National Accounting scheme published by the OEEC in 1952 followed the Anglo-American model.

In addition, the wartime Anglo-American collaboration was globalised through the mediation of the United Nations (UN). The UN continued the work on standardised national income accounting begun by the League of Nations in 1939. With further refinements, this standard framework, again defined by the collaboration of US and British economists, became the UN standard in 1953.[61] And the UN encouraged its members to comply with this model by dispatching advisory teams to countries with underdeveloped statistical infrastructures and by making the calculation of membership fees conditional on national income estimates. In 1945 there were national income estimates for some 39 countries. By 1955 the ranking included 93 nations and by 1969 the total exceeded 130.[62]

The 1950s thus witnessed the institutionalisation of an international scheme of economic measurement which still shapes our dominant understanding of the economy half a century later. The global economy was divided into neat national segments. The national economies of the world could henceforth be ranked in terms of the per capita gross domestic product. It was on the basis of OEEC standards that the first of the highly influential league tables comparing the growth rates of the industrialised countries was published in 1954.[63] Projected backwards into the past by quantitative economic historians, the techniques of national income accounting were used to retell the story of the industrial revolution in terms of accelerating growth rates, investment shares and 'take-offs'. This history in turn became the approved narrative for the development of the underdeveloped world.

It is only over the last decades that the prevailing preoccupation with national aggregates has been challenged head-on, not only by the massive globalisation of capitalist business, but also by the rediscovery of the household, the local and the regional as significant dimensions of productive and reproductive activity. This has led historians, as well, to question the seductive appeal of national statistical aggregates.[64] This essay hopes to have contributed to this critical dialogue by sketching the processes through which, in the first half of this century, a specific model of the national economy acquired the status of fact.

Notes

Thanks to the Centre for History and Economics, King's College, Cambridge for the use of facilities during the completion of this essay, to Geoff Cubitt for his painstaking editorial work and to Becky E. Conekin (University of Michigan) for her love and advice.

1 See B. Supple, 'Fear of failing: economic history and the decline of Britain', *Economic History Review*, 47:3 (1994), 441–58.
2 A. Giddens, *The Nation-State and Violence* (Cambridge, 1985), pp. 179–81.

3 L. Raphael, 'Die Verwissenschaftlichung des Sozialen als methodische und konzeptionelle Herausforderung für eine Sozialgeschichte des 20. Jahrhunderts', *Geschichte und Gesellschaft*, 22 (1996), 165–93.

4 P. Mirowksi, 'What are the questions?', in R. E. Backhouse (ed.), *New Directions in Economic Methodology* (London, 1994), pp. 57–8.

5 T. Mitchell, 'Origins and limits of the modern idea of the economy', Advanced Study Center, International Institute, University of Michigan, Working Paper no. 12 (1995).

6 S. Buck-Morss, 'Envisioning capital: political economy on display', *Critical Inquiry*, 21:2 (1995), 434–67.

7 In 'Envisioning capital' Buck-Morss refers throughout simply to 'the economy', but she takes her diagnosis of the current situation from R. B. Reich, *The Work of Nations* (New York, 1991), who addresses the crisis not of 'the economy' as such but of 'the national economy'. Rather confusingly, given her reliance on Reich, Buck-Morss herself counterposes communities based on a liberal vision of commercial society to those based on ethnic nationalism, as though the ideas of 'the economy' and 'the nation' were contradictory rather than mutually reinforcing, as will be argued here.

8 J. Burckhardt, 'Wirtschaft', in O. Brunner, W. Conze and R. Koselleck (eds), *Geschichtliche Grundbegriffe: historisches Lexikon zur politisch-sozialen Sprache in Deutschland*, 7 (Stuttgart, 1992), pp. 511–94. For an English introduction to *Begriffsgeschichte* (the history of concepts), see M. Richter, 'Reconstructing the history of political languages: Pocock, Skinner, and the *Geschichtliche Grundbegriffe*', *History and Theory*, 29:1 (1990), 38–70.

9 Burckhardt, 'Wirtschaft', pp. 582–7.

10 Literally, *Volkswirtschaft* translates as 'people's economy', or 'the nation's economy'. The science of economics was also increasingly referred to as *Volkswirtschaftslehre*; see K. Tribe, *Governing Economy: The Reformation of German Economic Discourse 1750–1840* (Cambridge, 1988).

11 H. James, *A German Identity 1770–1990* (London, 1989).

12 D. Head, *Made in Germany: The Corporate Identity of a Nation* (London, 1992).

13 See also, on Italy, T. Mason, 'The Great Economic History Show', *History Workshop Journal*, 21 (1986), 3–35, and on Ireland, M. E. Daly, *Industrial Development and Irish National Identity, 1922–1939* (Syracuse, NY, 1992).

14 Gross domestic product (GDP) is defined as the total value of goods produced for final consumption within the national territory. Estimates of total national product are equivalent to, and are today more widely used than, estimates of national income.

15 B. Anderson, *Imagined Communities: Reflections on the Origin and Spread of Nationalism* (London, 1983), pp. 37–40.

16 *Ibid.*, pp. 78–128.

17 For a survey see P. A. Hall (ed.), *The Political Power of Economic Ideas: Keynesianism Across Nations* (Princeton, 1989).

18 This impressionistic survey is based on the fairly typical case of the German Empire. See G. Fürst, 'Wandlungen im Programm und in den Aufgaben der amtlichen Statistik in den letzten 100 Jahren', in *Statistisches Bundesamt, Bevölkerung und Wirtschaft 1872–1972* (Stuttgart, 1972), pp. 12–83 and W. Heimer, *Die Geschichte der deutschen Wirtschaftsstatistik von der Gründung des deutschen Reichs bis zur Gegenwart* (Frankfurt-on-Main, 1928).

19 For the British case see R. Davidson, *Whitehall and the Labour Problem in Late-Victorian and Edwardian Britain: A Study in Official Statistics and Social Control* (London, 1985). For an international review see Kaiserliches Statistisches Amt, 'Gebiete und Methoden der amtlichen Arbeiterstatistik in den wichtigsten Industriestaaten', in *Beiträge zur Arbeiterstatistik*, 12 (Berlin, 1913).

20 For Britain see G. M. Koot, *English Historical Economics, 1870–1926: the Rise of Economic History and Neomercantilism* (Cambridge, 1987).

21 For an international survey see P. Studenski, *The Income of Nations* (New York, 1958).

22 See the preface to K. Helfferich, *Deutschlands Volkswohlstand 1888–1913* (3rd edn, Berlin, 1914).

23 *Ibid.*, p. 100.

24 See J. Livingston, *Pragmatism and the Political Economy of Cultural Revolution, 1850–1940* (Chapel Hill, 1994), pp. 52–60.

25 See the discussion of Owenite economics in G. Stedman Jones, *Languages of Class* (Cambridge, 1983), pp. 118–19.

26 See the essays collected in A. L. Bowley and J. Stamp, *Three Studies on National Income* (London, 1938).

27 Helfferich, *Deutschlands Volkswohlstand*, p. 126.

28 See 'Die Verteilung des Volkseinkommens in Preussen 1896–1912', Appendix to Helfferich, *Deutschlands Volkswohlstand*.

29 A. Marshall, *Principles of Economics* (London, 1890).

30 D. Reisman, *Alfred Marshall: Progress and Politics* (London, 1987), pp. 67–117, 338–49.

31 This finding is at odds with the account of marginalism in Buck-Morss, 'Envisioning capital', pp. 460–3. Buck-Morss implies that Marshall evaded the issue of class conflict by taking flight into marginalist abstraction. In this judgement Buck-Morss is misled by her reliance on the ahistorical 'reconstruction' of the history of economic thought offered by M. Blaug, *Economic Theory in Retrospect* (Cambridge, 1985).

32 In P. Wagner's survey of the relationship between the state and social sciences, *Sozialwissenschaften und Staat: Frankreich, Italien, Deutschland 1870–1980* (Frankfurt-on-Main, 1990), for instance, there is hardly a mention of the First World War.

33 On the USA see S. Skowronek, *Building a New American State: The Expansion of National Administrative Capacities, 1877–1920* (Cambridge, 1982). On Germany see H. G. Ehlert, *Die Wirtschaftliche Zentralbehörde des Deutschen Reiches 1914 bis 1919: Das Problem der 'Gemeinwirtschaft' im Krieg und Frieden* (Wiesbaden, 1982).

34 See B. Kent, *The Spoils of War: The Politics, Economics, and Diplomacy of Reparations 1918–1932* (Oxford, 1989).

35 The idea was introduced into the discussion by German negotiators at the Spa Conference in 1920. See C. Bergmann, *The History of Reparations* (London, 1927), pp. 36–7.

36 See J. M. Keynes, *The Economic Consequences of the Peace* [1919], (London, 1971), pp. 128–30, and J. M. Keynes, *A Revision of the Treaty. Being a Sequel to the Economic Consequences of the Peace* [1922], (London, 1971), pp. 56–8.

37 For the rationale for the index, see 'Report of the First Committee of Experts to the Reparations Commission April 9 1924', Section VIII c., quoted in C. G. Dawes, *A Journal of Reparations* (London, 1939), pp. 308–10. Responsibility for the index is attributed to Josiah Stamp by both J. H. Jones, *Josiah Stamp: Public Servant* (London, 1964), p. 214, and Bergmann, *The History of Reparations*, pp. 236–8.

38 The following discussion of Weimar Germany is based on J. A. Tooze, 'Official statistics and economic governance in interwar Germany', unpublished Ph.D. thesis (University of London, 1996).

39 See F. Grünig, 'Die Anfänge der "Volkswirtschaftlichen Gesamtrechnung" in Deutschland', *Beiträge zur empirischen Konjunkturforschung: Festschrift zum 25jährigen Bestehen des DIW (IfK)* (Berlin, 1950), pp. 71–103.

40 For a discussion of the Harvard Committee's techniques see M. Morgan, *The History of Econometric Ideas* (Cambridge, 1990), pp. 56–63.

41 On the NBER see G. Alchon, *The Invisible Hand of Planning: Capitalism, Social Science, and the State in the 1920s* (Princeton, 1985).

42 On Great Britain see S. Howson and D. Winch, *The Economic Advisory Council 1930–1939: a Study in Economic Advice during Depression and Recovery* (Cambridge, 1977), p. 11; on France see A. Desrosières, 'Histoire des formes. Statistiques et sciences sociales avant 1940', *Revue Française de Sociologie*, 26:2 (1985), 277–310.

43 A. W. Coats, 'Britain: the rise of the specialists', in A. W. Coats (ed.), *Economists in Government: An International Comparative Study* (Durham, 1981), pp. 27–66, at 29–30.

44 On Great Britain see A. Cairncross and N. Watts, *The Economic Section 1939–1961: A Study in Economic Advising* (London, 1989), pp. 24–33. On France see R. F. Kuisel, *Capitalism and the State in Modern France: Renovation and Economic Management in the Twentieth Century* (Cambridge, 1981), pp. 133, 214–15.

45 See B. Eichengreen, *Golden Fetters: The Gold Standard and the Great Depression, 1919–1939* (Oxford, 1992).

46 J. Dupâquier and M. Dupâquier, *Histoire de la démographie* (Paris, 1985), pp. 317–20.

47 For a German report see H. Platzer, 'Die Internationale Konferenz über Wirtschaftsstatistiken in Genf 1928', *Allgemeines Statistisches Archiv*, 19:1 (1929), 66–75.

48 See Bundesarchiv Potsdam 25.01 Deutsche Reichsbank 6856 League of Nations C.S.B.E./I, '(a) Meeting of Statistical and Information Officers of Certain Banks of Issue. Collective Report', Paris, 17 April 1928.

49 See Bundesarchiv Potsdam 25.01 Deutsche Reichsbank 6855 Société des Nations. E./B.E./7, 'Minutes of Comité d'Experts Pour la Question des Barometres Économiques', Paris, 15 December 1926.

50 H. Radice, 'The national economy: a Keynesian myth?', *Capital and Class*, 22 (1984), 111–40.

51 For a summary of the literature see G. C. Peden, *Keynes, the Treasury and British Economic Policy* (London, 1988).

52 On the use of national income accounts in the 1941 budget see R. S. Sayers, '1941 – The first Keynesian budget', in *The Managed Economy: Essays in British Economic Policy and Performance since 1929* (Oxford, 1983), pp. 107–17.

53 C. S. Carson, 'The history of the United States national income and product accounts: the development of an analytical tool', *The Review of Income and Wealth*, 21:2 (1975), 153–81.

54 See A. Barkai, *Das Wirtschaftssystem des Nationalsozialismus: Ideologie, Theorie, Politik 1933–1945* (2nd edn, Frankfurt-on-Main, 1988) and C. Kruse, *Die Volkswirtschaftslehre im Nationalsozialismus* (Freiburg, 1988).

55 For contemporary comment see *The Economist*, 26 February 1938: 'Herr Hitler's figures'.

56 On the Institute's wartime work see J. A. Tooze, 'Thesen zur Geschichte des IfK/DIW 1925–1945', Deutsches Institut für Wirtschaftsforschung, Discussion Paper no. 82 (Berlin, 1993).

57 See Bundesarchiv Koblenz R3/156 no. 18, 'Arbeitsprogramm des DIW', July 1944.

58 E. F. Denison, 'Report on tripartite discussions of national income measurement', *Studies in Income and Wealth*, vol. 10 (New York, 1947).

59 See J. A. Tooze, 'The knowledge of occupation: reflections on the history of economic statistics in France and Germany, 1914–1950', in C. Didry, P. Wagner and B. Zimmermann (eds), *Institutions et conventions du travail en France et en Allemagne 1890–1990* (Paris, forthcoming).

60 From the German perspective see H. Bartels, 'Volkswirtschaftliche Gesamtrechnung und Sozialproduktberechnung in der Bundesrepublik', *Allgemeines Statistisches Archiv*, 36 (1952), 141–52.

61 United Nations, *A System of National Accounts and Supporting Tables* (New York, 1953).

62 J. W. Kendrick, 'The historical development of national-income accounts', *History of Political Economy*, 2:2 (1970), 284–315.

63 J. Tomlinson, 'Inventing decline: the falling behind of the British economy in the postwar years', *Economic History Review*, 49:4 (1996), 731–57 discusses the impact of these estimates in the British context.

64 For revisionist views of the British 'industrial revolution', see E. A. Wrigley, *Continuity, Chance and Change: The Character of the Industrial Revolution in England* (Cambridge, 1988) and M. Berg, *The Age of Manufactures 1700–1830: Industry, Innovation and Work in Britain* (London, 1994).

Money and nationalism

We in the west handle paper banknotes probably most days of our adult lives, yet only children and foreigners pause to inspect their imagery. The money that mediates between anonymous strangers is replete with visualised historical narratives and national portraits. Most European currencies are portrait galleries in little: a rich array of transcendent imagery that speaks of national achievement and a collective identity. In western culture – for all that our tender is scrutinised at the supermarket checkout – there remains something unseemly about examining too closely banknotes exchanged, as if such an action would mark a failure of trust, whether towards the individual or towards the Bank of England which 'promise[s] to pay the bearer . . .'. The reluctance to look closely at banknotes is, however, no measure of the significance of their design. Indeed, that very reluctance marks a confidence that all must be well and a vague sense of assurance that we know what is there, that it is familiar and predictable. This essay examines a species of imagery that reaches a wider audience and is more taken for granted than any other form of visual representation in the modern world. Its very failure to attract the view of those that handle it is, I suggest, a token of its power. Only when it is threatened, as for example by the monetary unification of Europe, do the familiar images surface, not to be analysed but to be thrust to the fore – a yardstick of integrity. It is easy to dismiss the *Daily Mail*'s superimposition of the head of the German Chancellor on to an English banknote as a xenophobic fantasy (figure 24). But in examining the imagery of banknotes we find that the aggressive visualisation of the nation-state through its individualistically perceived cultural history is so widespread as to be virtually universal.

If we take, for example, the Polish 10,000-zloty note (worth only one-thousandth of its face value since devaluation), we may observe that a banknote has a recto and a verso and it combines text and image, didactic and official information, and narrative that is part portrait (whether of person or place) and part overtly imaginary. The recto (figure 25), as is usual, bears the name of the bank and some kind of signature. This is a residual sign of the

Figure 24 The *Daily Mail*'s interpretation of what the single European
currency could look like, *Daily Mail*, 16 December 1995

receipts hand-signed by a banker for money deposited and, later, of the hand-
signed notes issued by public and private bankers as part of their function. It
may also bear a coat of arms or official national insignia of some kind. Like
coins, most contemporary European banknotes carry portrait heads on the
front – whether of the reigning sovereign or of some individual regarded as
being of national significance. Here are to be seen the Polish National Bank's

Figure 25, 26 **Polish
10,000 zloty recto
and verso 1995**

name, the denomination in figures and words, the eagle of the Piast dynasty (regarded as the authentic Polish racial group in a much-invaded country), and a bust of Stanislaw Wyspianski (1869–1907): painter, poet, theatre reformer and playwright. In keeping with his status as the leading figure in the so-called 'Young Poland' movement, part of the international Art Nouveau or *Jugendstil* based in Cracow,[1] the recto shows a background of floral decoration, and the verso (figure 26) a characteristic view of the Polish royal castle on Wawel Hill in Cracow. For Poles, the importance of Cracow as a cultural capital and the significance of Wawel Cathedral as the burial place of the Polish kings is intense.

Banknotes like this produce and reproduce national narratives in forms authorised by the state. Currency means not only 'the fact or quality of being current or passing from man to man as a medium of exchange' but also, more generally, that which flows, the fact or quality of being current, being prevalent.[2] The launching of a currency is akin to a declaration of peace, since currencies are notoriously dependent upon peace and stability. Though the international war of currencies ceases when actual war breaks out, different factions may issue rival currencies representing their separate claims to national identity. Moreover, the creation of a new state requires a new or reinvented currency. Thus on 30 May 1994, it was reported that the government of President Franjo Tudjman had decided to rename the Croatian currency after that used by the pro-Nazi puppet regime in Croatia during the Second World War. The Yugoslavian dinar was to be replaced by the kuna. The new kuna would be worth about seventeen cents and the notes would carry 'the portraits of Croatian heroes and martyrs, many from the Middle Ages'. The President defended this extremely contentious decision on the grounds that the choice of the kuna would be 'proof of Croatian sovereignty'.[3]

This episode highlights not just the political contentiousness but also the complex cultural significance of currency. The word 'kuna' means 'martenskin' in old Slavonic; Tudjman's choice links the contemporary Croatia to a pre-monetary era when furs were currency. The 'new' currency thus comes laden with non-monetary values and earlier associations; its naming is a self-conscious act of patriotic nostalgia, while the portraits carried on its banknotes establish precise links with a distant national past.

An examination of the imagery of paper currency offers a unique opportunity for assessing how the culture of finance (the absolute prerequisite for national sovereignty in the twentieth century) interacts with more readily recognisable cultural forms to produce and maintain distinct notions of national identity. Very soon after the foundation of the Bank of England in 1694, the government tried its first experiment in issuing printed cheques and printed paper money. There were already concerns about the debasement of coinage, but the printing of money and cheques (as opposed to the individual handwritten promissory note) caused concern to many, including John Locke, who strongly advocated the Gold Standard.[4] Until 1844, when the Bank Charter Act was passed, there were many small banks, often based in rural towns, which all issued their own notes. Some displayed topographical imagery or representations of allegorical females. Ringwood and Poole Bank in the 1820s, for example, had personifications of Britannia, Hibernia and Scotia on a £1 note, accompanied by putti representing the arts and sciences.[5] It was not until the 1960s that historical individuals began to appear on Bank of England notes, when the first full-time designer H. N. Eccleston invented a new and coherent series featuring Shakespeare, the Duke of Wellington, Florence Nightingale, Isaac Newton and on the £50 note, Christopher Wren.[6] Many European currencies feature the head of a monarch or president (thus Spanish notes have King Juan Carlos on the recto). In England we are accustomed to the Queen's head. This, however, is also a relative novelty. Apart from the government wartime issue which bore the head of King George V, the first time the reigning monarch appeared on a Bank of England note was in 1960.[7] Colour was used on notes issued in Scotland in 1777 and on notes of private banks in England in the early years of the nineteenth century, but when the Bank of England was offered colour in 1818–21 it refused it, only introducing colour and more artwork in 1925 on £1 and 10s notes. Treasury issues included colour in 1914, and a pictorial design in 1917.[8]

Historically coinage was exclusively a royal privilege (something echoed in words like 'crown' and 'sovereign' used to denote coins even after the foundation of the Bank of England) and the guarantee of money transactions meant an extension of the royal power into areas in which private and personal modes of exchange had previously existed. Roman gold and silver coins after the time of Augustus were minted exclusively in the name and at the command of the Emperor, and the Carolingian rulers strove to replace a barter economy by a monetary system. As Georg Simmel points out, self-sufficiency is encouraged in a barter economy, whereas power institutions (such as banks), in alliance with the state organisation, are a feature of monetary economies.[9] This is clearly evidenced in the abiding prominence of certain symbols. Central banks guard their credibility by ostensibly maintaining their independence; they are separate from national governments. Yet the Bank of England chose Britannia for its seal at its foundation in 1694 and it has since appeared on every note the Bank has issued.[10] Indeed, the new £50 note has revived the original representation of Britannia in front of a pile of money. It seems, therefore, that while a currency may serve to define an independent political entity, it also works explicitly and implicitly to define, establish and circulate the aspirations of a nation in the sense of an aggregation of persons claiming in an organised way to represent a racial, territorial or cultural bond of unity. The establishment of currency is thus a key stage in the process of transforming an 'imagined community', to use Benedict Anderson's words, into an actual body with executive powers.[11]

If nationalism and currency are a pair, so too are nationalism and portraiture. National boundaries are established by military conquest; images of military leaders may therefore represent an encapsulation of territorial claims. Language, on the other hand, is the element that most readily provides evidence of national difference in everyday experience. Since literature is usually understood to offer language in its best and most estimable form, it is no surprise that the portraits of authors can, like those of military figures, be used to sum up national identity. One thinks, for example, of the Temple of British Worthies at Stowe or Ludwig I's Valhalla near Regensburg containing the busts of more than a hundred German worthies. The bust format – which is also common in banknote portraits – is a means of claiming for a modern nation the position of heir to the Roman Imperium. It is also a form of abstraction: it offers full play to those aspects of the human form that were thought most susceptible to 'scientific' assessment (physiognomy and phrenology) and therefore most capable of encapsulating 'national character'. This connection between portraiture and national identity is parodied in a bitterly critical painting by the contemporary German artist Anselm Kiefer. This enormous painting, executed in 1976–77, is ironically entitled *Wege der Weltweisheit* (*Ways of Worldly Wisdom*) and incorporates the busts of German military leaders in a genealogical tree (figure 27).

The relationship between heroic human figures, nationalism, and national currencies was articulated most vividly by Carlyle in *On Heroes, Hero-Worship and the Heroic in History* (1840). Arguing that society is founded on hero-worship, Carlyle drew attention to the etymology of 'king' (*'Kon-ning, Kan-ning* – Man that *knows* or *cans*') and concluded that 'Society everywhere is some representation, not insupportably *in*accurate, of a graduated Worship of Heroes; – reverence and obedience done to men really great and wise. Not insupportably *in*accurate, I say! They are all as bank-notes, these social dignitaries, all representing gold: – and several of them, alas, always are forged notes.' Society could manage with some forged notes, but if most of them were forged there would be revolution. 'The notes being all false, and no gold to be had for *them*, people take to crying in their despair that there is no gold, that there never was any! – "Gold," Hero-worship, *is* nevertheless, as it was always and everywhere, and cannot cease till man himself ceases.'[12] Carlyle's rhetorical strategy here was to promote hero-worship not only as more reliable than paper money (which merely represents gold), but as more reliable and more permanent than gold itself. The very paper money that he, in common with many of his generation, held in such contempt would ironically offer the greatest possibility known for disseminating his heroes not only around the country but around the globe. Indeed, although his argument was founded on a

Figure 27 **Anselm Kiefer,** *Wege der Weltweisheit – die Hermannslacht,* **1978**

profound suspicion of paper money, his recognition that hero-worship is a currency offers one of the most remarkable insights ever made into how portraiture works.

Banknotes provide an image field for the play of representation of heroic subjects such as interested Carlyle and, as such, have clearly remained a staple medium for patriots ever since. But banknotes, as we have established, are not only imagery; they also represent monetary value. Coins, which were universally the unit of exchange in Europe until relatively recently, are also surfaces for inscription and have traditionally also borne portraits – heads of rulers. Of course, coins are today no longer intrinsically valuable and can, therefore, like paper money, be seen as mere symbols. Marc Shell, however, explains the important difference between coinage and paper currency: 'During its historical metamorphosis from commodity (a lump of gold) to coin (a commodity impressed with the stamp of the state) to paper money (a mere impression), solid metal undergoes and participates in culturally and philosophically subversive changes.'[13] Shell points out that coins are both symbols and commodities; this may precipitate some confusion between signs and things, but does not encourage their users to believe that symbol and commodity, or word and concept, are entirely separable. Paper money, on the other hand, does appear to be a symbol entirely disassociated from the commodity that it symbolises. It is for this reason that paper money is such a powerful image of the free-floating signifier or, as when Goethe's Mephistopheles produces paper money in *Faust*, the shadow of reality that replaces the substance.[14]

Money circulates, and is not only nationally but also internationally exchangeable. Therefore the imagery it carries must be readily comprehensible. Credit is an abstract form of money property and it eliminates the kind of individualistic culture that the creation, handling and circulation of paper money represents, while at the same time emphasising the cultural need for money as commodity *and* as symbol. In 1978 the European unit of account (the dollar) was transformed into the ecu, which floats against the dollar. The fact that this remains a money of account (it has no coinage – apart from the commemorative – and no paper notes)[15] may be at least in part due to the cultural need for the individualisation of national identity on a universally accessible image field at a time when European difference (at least in architecture, food and politics) is being rhetorically challenged and actually diminished.

Paper money is – perhaps apart from the television screen[16] – the most readily available and widely distributed medium for portraiture in the western world. Stamps, which might seem to have similar characteristics, offer by comparison very limited pictorial space; they are crude tokens of proof of purchase of a service (transporting objects). Paper money is the ultimate symbol, having itself no intrinsic worth, and it gives rise to ideas about worth, value, exchange, reciprocation, power, sin, justice, and so on. In his novel *Les Faux-Monnayeurs* (1925), André Gide writes of a novelist who, once he began writing metaphorically about money, found it took over: 'Ideas of exchange, depreciation, of inflation, etc. gradually invaded his book . . . and usurped the place of the characters.'[17] Paper money offers space for discursive and iconic acts of communication that are unique.[18]

Existing at a point of high conceptual tension, paper money functions in

ways that are contradictory (standing for the national, but of necessity internationally exchangeable). It presents the paradox of a nationalistic cultural
form which has a mass circulation but which is the commodity and the signifier of a system that divides nations into classes by economic provisions. All
European nations have currencies that are distinguished by name and by an
iconography which, almost without exception at the present time, involves
portraits of historic individuals. Portraiture would appear therefore to be a prerequisite for the articulation of national identity. But what of naming? At one
level, to read on a note 'cinq cents francs' simply informs us of the denomination. But naming is also richly associative, and every time it is used an authorised narrative of national history is set in train linking 'franc', 'free', 'Frank',
'Frankish' and 'France'. The word 'franc' as used in currency derives from
Francorum rex, which was inscribed on the most ancient coins of the kingdom.
Francus ('free') denoted the dominant group in Frankish Gaul. By the fourteenth century it was a gold coin equivalent to one livre (i.e. *la livre*, or one
pound weight of silver). It has been since 1789 the basic unit of French currency. It is not, however, the unique unit of national currency and other units
are similarly etymologically indicative of national aspirations. The écu
('shield') was originally a fourteenth-century coin bearing a royal shield on one
face; by the seventeenth century it was a silver coin equivalent to three livres
and by the eighteenth century a silver coin equivalent to five francs. The ecu,
as we know, is now the European currency of account. The louis, first equivalent to ten livres, was a gold coin bearing an image of King Louis XIII which,
in the nineteenth century, was reissued as a napoléon (note the metonymic
shift) and as such is still struck and traded today.

Paper money, then, has to compete as a cultural communicator with a class
of objects – coins – that not only have the advantage of apparently uniting form
and function, but also possess established cultural and historical identities
authorised by powerful linguistic associations. A further determinant is the
necessity of deterring counterfeiters. Forgery was a capital offence in England
until 1832 and nearly four hundred people were hanged for it between 1797 and
1829.[19] Italian and French notes specifically caution those tempted to commit
forgery, though it is hard to believe that anyone intending to counterfeit would
be deterred by these statements. The inscription has the status of a juridical
declaration rather than a piece of advice, and is commensurate with the banknote's functions as symbolic property. The gap between icon and practice is
amply illustrated by the embarassment of the Spanish with a paper currency
which, in 1995, was signed by a governor of the national bank who was in prison
for fraud and deception. The advent of colour photocopiers has exacerbated
the problem of forgery. It has been suggested that one reason for portraits on
banknotes is that the portrait of a known person can be a highly effective
weapon against forgery: 'This is apparent with portraits of reigning monarchs

whose faces are well known to the public', states Hewitt.[20] The same author suggests that another reason for portraits on banknotes is the 'need for modern, impersonal note-issuers to bring personality to their product'.[21]

As we never see the subjects on whom the portraits are based, nor even the original portraits on which the banknote designer has based the engraved portrait head, we are being invited here to recognise deviations from a standard representation rather than deviations from a unique original. There is little evidence to prove that viewers are adept at this; face recognition seems unlikely in this context to be more psychologically compelling than other forms of recognition.[22] It is hard to imagine that Austrians would notice if the hairs of Freud's beard (figure 28) were out of place or if Otto Wagner's ear was slightly differently constructed (figure 29), any more than they would notice whether the Josephinum Palace or the Post Office building on the reverse of the 50- and 500-schilling notes (figures 30 and 31) had an additional pilaster or window-pane. As for the notion of 'bringing personality' to the product, this would be to suggest a deliberate marketing strategy able to isolate something called 'personality'. What is not in doubt is that the need to deter counterfeiters results in the production of highly self-conscious structures involving naturalistic imagery, computer-produced abstraction, and technical anti-forgery devices. These visual strategies are rhetorical formations, however, and as such they also offer space both for counteracting the excremental associations of money (filthy lucre)[23] and for what Anderson calls 'thinking the nation'.[24] My concern here is to move beyond the recognition that the design of banknotes is 'dictated by the purpose of notes and how they are used' so that 'the issuing authority and amount of the note must be easily identifiable and the design must be as difficult as possible to forge',[25] and to ask how the imagery on banknotes might open up purposes that are undeclared, how it serves to articulate or to occlude philosophical values, how this category of imagery works dialectically in relation to national identity. Likewise, while I recognise that the design departments now in place in European national banks, and the committee structures established to monitor and implement new series, are an important part of the history of banking, they are not germane to my argument.[26] The detail of banknote imagery is attributable to individual designers working to briefs issued by committees that are themselves answerable to governors. But, of course, line management of this kind does not account either for the content of the imagery or for the way in which it is deployed. Banknotes are official art forms and, like university prospectuses and company annual reports, they work with rhetorical forms that are common to a culture; neither designer nor committee is responsible for the ideological character of this imagery.

If a single European currency has its problems, in other respects the currencies of Germany, France and England have drawn closer since around 1940.

Figure 28 **Austrian
50 schilling recto
1995**

Banknotes for the three countries now have different dimensions according
to their denomination, but they are all within the same size range.
Denominations are also congruent: the English £5 corresponds more or less
to the French 50F note, £10 to the 100F note, £20 to the 200F note, and so on.
France and Germany, however, still have notes for the smaller units (20F and
5 and 10 DM).[27] Every single banknote from the three series bears a portrait
on one side. The current series of Bank of England notes (series E) follows
the format established with the previous series (D), but now with portraits of
George Stephenson, Charles Dickens, Michael Faraday and Sir John
Houblon, first Governor of the Bank of England. It is worth pausing to
compare the old and new £50 notes, both still in circulation.[28] Wren in the
older series is presented as creator of the city of London; his portrait is a synthesis of images produced in the seventeenth century by J. B. Closterman
(figure 32) and Sir Godfrey Kneller (figure 33), themselves many times reproduced and copied.[29] The former provides the main source not only for the
head (figure 34), but also the hands and the juxtaposition of the head with St
Paul's. In place of the scroll, the compasses that appear in the Kneller are
placed in Wren's right hand, and the plan of St Paul's which appears in the
Kneller is made into a diagrammatic special feature in the left half of the
image space. There is a third famous image of Wren, the very flamboyant bust

Figure 29 **Austrian
500 schilling recto
1995**

Figure 30 **Austrian**
50 schilling verso
1995

by Pearce in the Ashmolean Museum. This seems to have been studiously
avoided. The background, with St Paul's from the river, is based on a mid-eigh-
teenth-century engraving. The denomination guilloche is derived from a
carving by Grinling Gibbons in St Paul's. Wren's interest in astronomy is
represented by the patterns in the sky and a section from Flamsteed's *Atlas
Coelestis* of 1729. The names of constellations are inserted into the patterning.
The new £50 note is, by comparison, intensely parochial, conservative and
even, one might say, revisionist. Britannia now occupies almost as much space
as the Queen's head (figures 35 and 36), and on the reverse, instead of an architect of international renown based on two original portraits, we have the first
Governor (figure 37), apparently based on a nineteenth-century copy after a
rare engraving after a lost portrait by Closterman and, inset in an oval on the
left, the totally unknown Bank of England Gatekeeper in front of Sir John
Houblon's House in Threadneedle Street, and the dates of the founding of the
Bank and the issuing of the note (1694–1994).[30]

In times of subsidiarity and euro-currency the Bank of England chooses
the largest denomination for an utterly self-referential image. Apart, however,
from Wren and Houblon, every other portrait on an English banknote represents an individual whose achievements fall within the nineteenth century
and who is understood in cultural terms as 'Victorian'. In each case the design

Figure 31 **Austrian**
500 schilling verso
1995

depends on an emblematic structure in which the portrait is accompanied by
a vignette narrative scene. This combination transforms the portrait from the
particular to the general – suggesting that this person is a type whose creative
intelligence and entrepreneurship are the key to the complex event represented alongside and, conversely, whose identity is summed up by the products imaged in the event. Thus on the verso of notes currently circulating,
Stephenson is accompanied by a design in which the *Rocket*'s chimney merges
into the supports of a viaduct across which a train pulling coal-wagons passes,

Figure 32 **J. B. Closterman, *Sir Christopher Wren***

led by a guard on horseback, and through which we catch a glimpse of a Coalbrookdale-like landscape with the smoking chimneys of an early industrial building (figure 38). Charles Dickens is accompanied by a representation of the cricket match from *Pickwick Papers* (figure 39), and Faraday delivers his lecture on the magneto-electric spark apparatus to the Royal Institution (figure 40). Stephenson started life as a cowherd, Dickens was the son of a clerk imprisoned for debt, Faraday the son of a blacksmith: it is hard to imagine a more apt summary of the values of self-help and entrepreneurship

Figure 33 **Sir Godfrey Kneller, *Sir Christopher Wren***

Figure 34, 35
**English £50 verso
and recto 1995
(series D)**

promulgated as national attributes throughout the Thatcher years. Moreover, in looking at the Pickwick cricket match, we might remind ourselves both of the populist definitions of national culture that emanated from the Tory-created Ministry of National Heritage (with its mixture of the arts, buildings and sport) and of the readiness of John Major and his colleagues to equate national identity with the game of cricket.[31]

French currency offers a display of imagery that produces a very different composite of national identity.[32] Whereas the English pound constructs a solidly nineteenth-century pantheon, the French franc identifies each denomination with a particular period and with a particular characteristic strand of what is readily interpretable as national greatness. Unlike the British (but like the German), the French notes offer complementary imagery on their two sides. This may be partly the result of not being obliged to include a royal image, but it is clearly more than that: the two sides of the note are conceived as continuous, only the number of the note providing any clear indication as to which might be the front and which the back. This forms a kind of narrative closure, producing an effect of concentration and single-mindedness. The largest denomination – the 500F note (1968) – represents the seventeenth century and philosophy in the person of Pascal in an identical portrait on both sides. He is

Figure 36, 37
**English £50 recto
and verso 1995
(series E)**

Figure 38 **English £5
verso 1995**

shown recto (figure 41) in raised head and shoulders between, on the left, the church of St Jacques de la Boucherie (a reconstruction, since nothing remains today but the Tour St Jacques), where he conducted one of his first important experiments, and, on the right, the cathedral of Clermont-Ferrand, also as it was in the seventeenth century. Verso (figure 42) are the colombier and the abbey of Port-Royal. These are depicted in naturalistic style subverted only on the back, where a framing device supported by pilasters between which are written warnings against counterfeiting gives the illusion of looking at a mural painting.

Figure 39 **English**
£10 verso 1995

Figure 40 **English**
£20 verso 1995

The 200F note (1981) is designed according to very different pictorial conventions. It is high baroque in its combination of Roman portrait bust, allegorical figure, heraldic devices and a patterned background made up of symbolic motifs. Montesquieu (born in 1689) is represented recto (figure 43) as a Roman senator (philosophers in Roman art are generally bearded), accompanied by his family coat of arms. On the left is a personification of France as a dignified and specifically unrevolutionary Marianne, on to which are superimposed the scales of justice in a cartouche which also refers to Montesquieu's *De l'esprit des lois*, published in 1748, a work which constitutes a profoundly liberal enquiry into the nature of the laws desirable in a good society. The background is made up of lyres, fasces, palms for the Académie Française and helmets of Minerva for the Académie des Sciences Morales et Politiques. The verso (figure 44) offers a slightly different but still Roman portrait of Montesquieu, this time accompanied by a specifically senatorial figure (referring to Montesquieu's *Dialogue de Sylla et d'Eucrate*), and a view of Château Montesquieu at La Brède in the Gironde with a floral background and figure intended to allude to the *Lettres persanes*. The note is a veritable biographical dictionary entry in visual form, unequivocally celebrating republican values of Justice and Virtue. The references to Rome not only remind us that

Figure 41, 42 French
500 francs recto and
verso 1995

Figure 43, 44 French
200 francs recto and
verso 1995

Figure 45, 46 **French
100 francs recto and
verso 1995**

Montesquieu was the author of *Considérations sur les causes de la grandeur des
Romains et de leur décadence* (1734), but also that he contributed crucially to
a modern state that is presented as heir to the best of the Roman republic.[33]

The artist Eugène Delacroix is portrayed on the 100F note with his paint-
brushes and the figures of Liberté and a boy *sans culottes* from his 1830 *Liberty
Leading the People* on the recto (figure 45) and, as diarist and correspondent,
with a quill and a view of his studio in the rue Furstenberg on the verso (figure
46). If Delacroix represents the visual arts of the nineteenth century in France,
Debussy, on the 20F (1992) small-format note, represents musical achievement. The boy prodigy is shown – in the now familiar French convention –
recto (figure 47) head and shoulders before the sea (indicating his most internationally celebrated composition, *La Mer*) and verso (figure 48) with a view
of St Germain-en-Laye, where he was born in 1862.

The most recently issued denomination is the 50F note (figures 49 and 50),
which marks an important departure. While it completes the series, adding a
twentieth-century hero to the pantheon, it is smaller in format, the portrait is
based on a photograph rather than an oil painting, it carries a portrait on one
side only and it gives great prominence to a fictional figure. Debussy is shown
mastering the seas through his art while Antoine de Saint-Exupéry, author of
Le Petit Prince (a work whose hero has a place in French culture easily as
significant as that of Pickwick in English culture), masters the skies. He

Figure 47, 48 **French 20 francs recto and verso 1995**

represents the achievement of France in transport and communications. The heterogeneous design, with its fragmentary images of Europe and Africa, aeroplanes and compasses, is closer in principle to the design of the English currency and is assertively internationalist. Unlike Pascal, Montesquieu and Delacroix, Antoine de Saint-Exupéry is one of France's major exports. In the year (1993) in which *Le Petit Prince* came out of copyright and at a time when the legacy of France's colonial past is proving highly threatening and problematic, the design of the 50F note serves to proclaim the nation's achievement as the producer of innocent fantasy and modern transportation systems. Saint-Exupéry was the founder-pilot of Air Postale and died in an air crash over the Sahara. His history legitimises an image which invokes other more recent achievements such as the TGV (high-speed passenger train) and the Channel Tunnel, while inscribing its nostalgic motifs across a map that acts as an oblique reminder of France's territorial conquests.

At the time of writing, Germany still has in circulation notes of small denominations (5 and 10 DM) that have been replaced by coins in the other two currencies.[34] There are also banknotes for very large denominations (500 and 1,000 DM, equivalent to roughly £205 and £350). The notes most commonly in circulation and which correspond most closely to the franc and pound denominations analysed here are the 20, 50 and 100 DM notes. What

Figure 49, 50 **French
50 francs recto and
verso 1995**

is significant in this is that modern Germany has eschewed the contemporary
and the recent past and, for the most part, has gone back to a pre-Bismarckian
period of German history. Moreover, two of the notes carry portraits of
women,[35] and, compared to the pound and franc notes, they are relatively
simple in design. Annette von Droste-Hülshoff (1797–1848) was a
Westphalian novelist and poet who wrote realist fictions of bourgeois life and
manners; she is represented with a laurel branch alongside a schematised
view of buildings at Meersburg on Lake Constance (figure 51). The verso
(figure 52) carries the symbol of the national bank and a writer's quill superimposed upon a naturalistic representation of a beech tree (an allusion to the
author's *Judenbuche*) inscribed in a circle against a background of computer-
produced patterning. An open book is superimposed over the watermark,
which is a repeat of the portrait. The colour ranges from mauve through pink
to green. The 50DM note is by contrast a mixture of browns, yellows and
greens and presents on the front Balthasar Neumann (1687–1753), court
architect to the Prince Bishop of Würzburg and one of the great figures of

Figure 51, 52
German 20 deutsche mark recto and verso 1995

German baroque architecture (figure 53). There is a close similarity here to the £50 note with its image of Wren; Neumann is represented in a full-frontal bust with his professional insignia – a proportional compass which he invented – against a view of Würzburg. On the verso (figure 54) is a synthetic view incorporating the *Treppenhaus* at the Würzburg Palace and the Benedictine Abbey of Neresheim with, superimposed over the watermark portrait, a ground plan of the Holy Cross Chapel at Kitzingen. A choice of ground plans and perspective views which appear to be derived from mathematically produced calculations is common on European banknotes. It may serve to suggest the collective and public to which the individual human subject and his or her attainment relate, but it also suggests controlled productivity and confidence in peacetime expansion. The 100DM note in shades of blue and green also has buildings and a portrait. It features Clara Schumann (1819–96) (figure 55). Born Clara Wieck, she was a composer, but much more famous as a pianist and interpreter of her husband Robert's work. She is portrayed alongside a view of the Leipzig Gewandhaus. On the verso (figure 56) is a grand piano, ready to be played, against a view of the Hoch'sche Konservatorium in Frankfurt, while superimposed on the watermark portrait is a tuning-fork vibrating into a fan form, subtly integrating motifs of femininity and music.

The simultaneous circulation of different notes is less like a Valhalla or a temple of worthies than an orchestra in which different individuals playing

Figure 53, 54
**German 50 deutsche
mark recto and
verso 1995**

different instruments work in concert to produce a particular effect. Whereas the English notes taken together assert a national confidence in inventive entrepreneurship and stalwart domestic values, and the French notes systematically and diachronically build up a picture of the modern state, the deutschmark notes occlude altogether the modern state and, by focusing on artists and architects from over a hundred years earlier, and on the achievements of women, invoke a national identity that is soft, non-agressive, non-adventurist, and imbued with secular values of social polite-ness. Yet the baroque which appears on the £50 and on the 50DM note in its explicit architectural form is, more generally, present on almost all these banknotes. So, too, are the methods of academic portraiture (concentration on heads, high relief effects, formal postures). These are the traditional mechanisms for the apotheosis of princes and the telling of national histo-ries. The deutschmark notes are nationalistic, in spite of their very rectitude on the subject of national identity. While the Bundesbank appears to be liberal in its decision to search out female national subjects to portray, it is clear that this is part of a less than liberal agenda (note, for example, the Brandenburg Gate on the recto of the 5DM note). The historical woman subject is here appropriated for the nation in ways that are by now wholly familiar from the work of scholars like Marina Warner.[36] While women as allegorical or emblematic subjects appear on some notes (and the English Queen falls into this category), so-called feminine values (rather than female

Figure 55, 56
**German 100
deutsche mark recto
and verso 1995**

achievements) are circulated in Germany by the representation of historical
individuals. While the English during the period 1975–92 had Florence
Nightingale on an English note, the associations of nursing, caring and self-
less dedication were readily absorbed into the dominant rhetoric and the
Bank of England has not, significantly, seen fit to find other candidates, least
of all to represent, say, a Mary Wollstonecraft or an Emmeline Pankhurst.
None of the currencies has even the least suggestion of an ethnic minority
represented in its imagery.

It is evident that in order to be regarded seriously as nations, peoples have
not only to have a history but have to be able to visually display that history. It
has been argued that the Hegelian distinction between 'historic' and 'unhistoric' nations was given a new meaning by Bauer in 1907 when he proposed
that being classed as 'unhistoric' did not imply an absence of history, but rather
that the nation lacked the class that could be bearers of its national culture.[37]
Thus, for example, the historic nations in the Austro-Hungarian Empire were
the Germans, Italians and Poles, all three of which had an aristocracy and the
first two of which possessed a bourgeoisie. It is evident from the visual
material presented in this essay that while motifs drawn from natural history
are not uncommon, in the three currencies examined portraits of people (and
secondarily of buildings) prevail. Many are produced with a density of design
and colour which (while it may be calculated to deter forgery) also appeals to
the childlike pleasure in handling colourful pieces of paper. Who does not

recall with some nostalgia the paper money of Monopoly or the miniature children's shop? Double-sided objects invite speculation and the pleasure of memory and association – we need to recall one side while looking at the other. Constructing national identity in a post-colonial era means creating something ostensibly novel, but in order to convey reliability banknote imagery always needs to offer what is already familiar. How, I wondered, when researching this topic, could difference be contained and articulated within the framework of the familiar? How could novelty be reconciled with continuity? The evolution and proliferation of banknote imagery in Europe is a modern phenomenon; commencing in the era of colonial expansion, through post-colonialism and into an era of neo-nationalism, it offers an index of cultural aspiration as statutory – as licensed and officially inscribed within and between nations. Paper money is of virtually no significance in the international financial markets of the late twentieth century, yet it shows no signs of diminishing as a major bearer of cultural values. For the British to 'be allowed to keep a miniature Queen's head on its version of the common Euro notes' remains a major issue.[38] Banknotes, it would appear, possess precisely the physical characteristics that lend themselves to regulatory discourses. Banknotes must be uniform within their own terms and no citizen can be without daily contact with them. That contact is of a particular and regulatory kind and the holder of the banknote is inevitably imbricated in the state. Banknotes serve as guarantor between two people. At the same time these notes we handle anonymously possess through their imagery a transcendent referent: national genius. Banknotes thus constitute a vehicle for the construction of national identity that far outweighs other comparable visual means available in the twentieth century. Perpetually present but never questioned, paper currency permits the classical ideal of the national pantheon to survive and flourish, maintaining in the public domain the constant reminder of the historical portrait as cypher for national identity.

Postscript

Depicting bridges between nations and gateways to the future, Europe's new euro banknotes were unveiled 'at the dawning of a new common Europe'. But what is this new common Europe? According to the map on the notes, parts of Finland are missing; Russia is there, but Turkey is not. Britain is clearly part of Europe, but looks somewhat misshapen. The Shetland Islands are missing and Wales will be unhappy with its bulge. There are no people in this future Europe; the designs show monuments and bridges, but no Europeans. 'The difficulty with people', said Alexander Lamfalussy, President of the European Central Bank, 'is that people usually belong to a country.'[39]

Notes

Many people have given generously of their knowledge and their time to respond to my questions about money. I am particularly indebted to David Bellos, Alan Cruse, François Duchêne, Vivien Hart, John Murdoch, David Robey, Sigrid Schade, Andrew Ward, Silke Wenk and Joanna Woodall. I would particularly like to thank Virginia Hewitt for generously giving time to discuss this research and also for reading a first draft of this paper, and Geoff Cubitt for his helpful editing.

1 I have relied for information concerning Polish history on J. Topolski, *An Outline History of Poland* (Warsaw: Interpress Publishers, 1986).

2 *Oxford English Dictionary* (2nd edn, 1989).

3 *International Herald Tribune*, 30 May 1994. I am grateful to Dr Vivien Hart for drawing my attention to this report.

4 The standard history remains R. D. Richards, *The Early History of Banking in England* (London: A. M. Kelley, 1929; repr. New York, 1965). An interesting essay drawing parallels between currency and notions of writing and authorship in this period is J. S. Peters, 'The bank, the press, and the "return of Nature" on currency, credit, and literary property in the 1690s', in J. Brewer and S. Staves (eds), *Early Modern Conceptions of Property* (London and New York, 1995).

5 Reproduced in V. Hewitt, *Beauty and the Banknote: Images of Women on Paper Money* (London: British Museum Press, 1994), p. 19.

6 V. H. Hewitt and J. M. Keyworth, *As Good as Gold: 300 Years of British Bank Note Design* (London: British Museum Press, 1987), p. 137.

7 *Ibid.*, p. 126.

8 *Ibid.*, p. 117.

9 G. Simmel, *The Philosophy of Money*, ed. D. Frisby, trans. T. Bottomore and D. Frisby (2nd edn 1907, enlarged 1978; London: Routledge, 1990).

10 See Hewitt and Keyworth, *As Good as Gold*, pp. 22, 25, and Hewitt, *Beauty and the Banknote*, p. 18. Hewitt offers a fascinating account of the transmutations of the image of Britannia.

11 B. Anderson, *Imagined Communities: Reflections on the Origin and Spread of Nationalism* (London and New York: Verso, 1991).

12 T. Carlyle, *On Heroes, Hero-Worship, and the Heroic in History*, ed. E. Rhys (London: Everyman Library, 1908), p. 249.

13 M. Shell, *Money, Language and Thought: Literary and Philosophical Economies from the Medieval to the Modern Era* (Berkeley and Los Angeles: University of California Press, 1982), p. 105. Virginia Hewitt has pointed out to me that in fact this is not a straight development, since coins and paper currencies coexist.

14 *Ibid.* I am much indebted to this fascinating literary and philosophical account.

15 It is used for public transactions within the business of the EU; for private institutions putting out bonds; and for writing cheques. Its circulation remains small by comparison with the deutschmark, yen or dollar. I am grateful to François Duchêne for patiently explaining to me these distinctions.

16 I owe this insight to John Murdoch.

17 A. Gide, *Les Faux-Monnayeurs* (1925), published in English as *The Coiners*, trans. D. Bussy (London: Cassell, 1950), p. 211.

18 For a discussion of the relationship between art and money, including a consideration of banknotes as art, see M. C. Taylor, *Disfiguring: Art, Architecture, Religion* (Chicago and London: University of Chicago Press, 1992), ch. 5, and M. Jones (ed.), *Fake: The Art of Deception* (London, 1990), pp. 56–7.

19 Figures from Bank of England Museum, London.

20 Hewitt, *Beauty and the Banknote*, p. 46.

21 *Ibid.*

22 I am, of course, aware that there is a literature of psychology on this topic. See, for example, V. Bruce, *Recognising Faces* (Hove, London and Hillsdale: Lawrence Erlbaum Associates, 1988).

23 The relationship of money to excrement can be found, for example, in Charles Dickens's *Our Mutual Friend* (London: Chapman and Hall, 1864–65).

24 Anderson, *Imagined Communities*, p. 22.

25 Hewitt and Keyworth, *As Good as Gold*, p. 7.

26 Some national banks put designs out to competition and involve external consultants. The Bank of England had a Design Committee for series D but decisions thereafter, for series E, were taken internally owing to the unwieldiness of the procedures and the long lead time involved. The Bank is currently considering the management and monitoring of design matters (personal communication from the Senior Designer at the Bank of England, for whose help I am most grateful). In France, decisions are taken by the Conseil Générale de la Banque de France. In Austria, proposals are submitted by the Printing Works (which employs artists) to the Bank's Board of Directors, which makes the final decision. In Spain, the Cash and Issue Department suggests to the Bank's Executive Board what themes might be appropriate and, once approved, the designs are selected after an open contest. I am grateful to the Bank of England and the national banks of France, Germany, Austria and Spain for responding helpfully to my enquiries.

27 Scotland has a £100 note and there are notes of higher values in Germany. The situation is, of course, constantly changing and this essay offers an account only of what was in circulation in spring 1995.

28 This is firstly because any new series is staggered (the £50 note was the last to be issued), and secondly because a period of overlap is allowed as old notes are gradually phased out.

29 Sir G. Kneller, National Portrait Gallery, no. 113; John Closterman, The Royal Society.

30 Engraved by R. Graves 'from a rare print by Williams after Closterman', published 1 August 1820 by T. H. Rodd, 17 Little Newport Street. For a discussion of this note, see D. Byatt, *Promises to Pay: The First Three Hundred Years of Bank of England Notes* (London, 1994), pp. 226–8.

31 For an analysis of cricketing imagery and nationalism, see M. Pointon, '"A latter-day Siegfried": Ian Botham at the National Portrait Gallery in 1986', *New Formations* (winter 1993), 22.

32 The Banque de France has recorded its intention with its new series to introduce a new modern style and to break with 'l'ancienne gamme de billets français ("hommes à perruques")' (Banque de France publicity material, Paris, 1996). Since writing this paper a new 500F note has been issued bearing portraits of Marie and Pierre Curie.

33 The best iconographical source book for French banknotes is J. de Larosière, *Trois siècles de billets français* (Paris, 1989).

34 I am informed (January 1995) that they are being phased out.

35 The 500DM note carries a portrait of Maria Sybilla Merian (1647–1717), traveller, artist and entomologist, and author of a history of insects published in French in 1730. I am grateful to Professor Dr Knut Borchardt and Professor Dr Michael Hutter for clarification of the iconography of the German notes.

36 M. Warner, *Monuments and Maidens: The Allegory of the Female Form* (London, 1985).

37 See J. Coakley, *The Social Origins of Nationalist Movements* (London: Sage, 1992), p. 5. The reference is to O. Bauer, *Die Nationalitätenfrage und die Sozialdemokratie* (Vienna: Volkbuschhandlung Ignaz Brand, 1907).

38 Kenneth Clark, Chancellor of the Exchequer, reported in the *Guardian*, 10 April 1995.

39 *The Independent*, 14 December 1996, front page, report by Sarah Helm of the European summit in Dublin.

INDEX